GW00319727

DUSTY SPRINGFIELD

Dusty Springfield

A LIFE IN MUSIC

EDWARD LEESON

 Robson Books

First published in Great Britain in 2001 by
Robson Books
10 Blenheim Court, Brewery Road, London N7 9NT

A member of the Chrysalis Group plc

British Library Cataloguing in Publication Data
A catalogue record for this title is available from the British Library

ISBN 1 86105 343 6

Designed and typeset by
EDWARD LEESON

Printed in Great Britain by
Creative Print & Design (Wales),
Ebbw Vale

For Hilary Kingsley

Contents

List of Illustrations

Picture credits appear beside photographs. The author and publishers have made every reasonable effort to contact all copyright-holders. Any errors that may have occurred are inadvertent, and anyone who for any reason has not been contacted is invited to write to the publishers so that a full acknowledgement may be made in subsequent editions of this work.

Preface

IN 1987, DUSTY SPRINGFIELD emerged reluctantly from retirement in California and returned to London to make a record with the Pet Shop Boys. When she arrived at the studio and asked them what they wanted from her, Neil Tennant said simply: 'The sound of your voice.' Always fiercely critical of her own performances, and genuinely bemused by the fact that people seemed to like her voice so much, this reply took her by surprise; she found it hard to understand why Neil Tennant and Chris Lowe had been so eager for her to cross the Atlantic merely to add a few bars to one of their records. She must have been even more surprised when the record itself, 'What Have I Done To Deserve This', became an enormous international success and restored her, almost overnight, to the mainstream of popular music.

A long, unsuccessful and at times humiliating struggle to revive her career had drained her of what little self-confidence she possessed and, no longer certain that she even wanted to begin all over again, she had become content merely to stay at home with her cats. But now, suddenly, everything seemed possible once more. She could put behind her more than a decade of pain – years in which her career had foundered, her life had degenerated in a haze of drugs and alcohol, and there had even been times when she had to fight to hold on to her very sanity – and recapture some of the glory of the golden years. Her fans had remained faithful and were waiting there when she returned; and her association with the Pet Shop Boys brought her to a new generation for whom the 1960s were not even a memory.

Dusty's recovery was remarkable. Success followed success, and she enjoyed a level of popularity that she had not known since the peak of her career in the sixties. But, in one final twist of fate, this revival in her fortunes would prove all too brief. Dusty's new career was cut short by breast cancer, which eventually claimed her life.

Ian Dury, who lost his own battle against cancer a year later, once remarked ruefully that 'There are few personalities in pop music. They're mostly drab, soppy little bank clerks who've had a result.' Dusty Springfield was undoubtedly a personality; and, for good or ill, she was seldom out of the headlines. Naturally shy and lacking in self-confidence, every day had been a battle as she fought to reconcile the private person with the confident, exuberant public image she was obliged to maintain, and the strain of this inner battle could give rise to the kind of behaviour that was certain to attract unwelcome attention. We all like to think we understand other people's lives better than they do themselves, and throughout her troubled career Dusty provided a tempting target for journalists and other amateur psychologists. Unfortunately, the picture that emerged was rarely flattering and was all too often little more than a grotesque caricature. This little book endeavours to present a serious and compassionate portrait of a deeply complex and uniquely gifted woman, and offers the first detailed consideration of her musical career; for at the heart of the story is a voice – and it is that voice, always remarkable and often almost miraculous, that the book attempts to celebrate.

I wish to thank Vicki Wickham for her encouragement and my publishers Jeremy Robson and Lorna Russell for their patience during the slow agony of the book's struggle for life; Cheryl Merritt for managing to trace photographs from my vague clues; Paul Howes of the *Dusty Springfield Bulletin*, to whose researches everyone who wishes to write seriously about Dusty must be indebted; and Hilary

PREFACE

Kingsley, whose gentle bullying kept me writing at those times when my confidence and my stamina flagged, and to whom the book is dedicated.

As with all who are naturally shy and introspective, Dusty was engaged in a continuing reassessment of her life; and, as it follows her down the years, the book makes generous use of Dusty's own attempts, in interviews, to understand herself and find some purpose and structure in what was at times a chaotic existence. I have tried to provide a precise source wherever possible, and to halt the tide of unattributed facts and quotations that have so often been allowed to pass for biography where Dusty is concerned.

I would also like to acknowledge a general indebtedness to Colin Larkin's mighty eight-volume *Encyclopedia of Popular Music*, which frequently came to the rescue of an ageing memory.

Any errors that may remain in the text are, of course, all my own work.

January 1 2001   EDWARD LEESON

'. . . if you set out to create a Dusty Springfield, then you ask for problems.'

DUSTY SPRINGFIELD

I

'Sing Up, Mary!'

THE GIRL WHO would become Dusty Springfield was born in the London suburb of West Hampstead on 16 April 1939, the second child of Catherine and Gerard Anthony O'Brien, and was christened Mary Isobel Catherine Bernadette. A son, Dion, had been born four years earlier.

Within a few months of the new baby's arrival, the family left London for High Wycombe in Buckinghamshire. The world was sliding towards war for the second time in a quarter of a century; and, although the family managed to avoid the full rigours of wartime life in the capital, Mary's earliest recollections were typical of a child of her generation. She remembered the drone of the returning bombers overhead, the street-party to celebrate victory when it finally came, and that landmark in so many lives at the time: the arrival of the first postwar consignment of bananas in 1946. (There had even been a wartime song with the plaintive title 'When Can I Have A Banana Again'.) She recalled that her first ambition had been to become a land-girl – though her dream of joining that cheery band of wartime farm labourers evaporated when she discovered how early in the morning they had to get up.[1]

Young Mary developed a talent for having silly accidents: she once fell from her pram on to the pavement, and on another occasion fell off a table on to a stone floor and hit her head. She would carry this talent with her into later life.

The O'Briens never managed to settle into their new home – they had not even bothered to unpack fully, and the neighbours complained because they never mowed the lawn – and when the war was over the family moved back to London, settling this time in Kent Gardens in the respectable suburb of Ealing. This was classic commuter territory, with the District Line carrying hundreds of workers to their offices every morning. Gerard, who was an income tax consultant with an office in Paddington, joined their number. The children were enrolled at good schools – Mary went to St Anne's Convent, while Dion attended nearby St Benedict's – and the family took their holidays in Bognor. Outwardly, the O'Briens presented a picture of comfortable suburban middle-class Catholic respectability.

But, in the words of their daughter, 'neither of my parents were very routine people'. Catherine ('Kay') was 31 years old when she married Gerard ('OB'), who was five years younger. 'A free spirit who had been trapped', Kay had married 'not because she wanted to, but because she thought she should' and 'resented it for the rest of her life'. Kay had theatrical ambitions that were never realised, and she resented the bonds of marriage, motherhood and suburban domesticity. 'She would make a trifle and then get bored with the whole idea so she'd hit it with an enormous spoon, saying "You're going to get it quicker this way." ' This 'slapstick' attitude to life was taken up by the rest of the family; tensions would be relieved by throwing food: 'things developed – out of an innocent slice of Spam being lobbed across the room – into an absolute mêlée'. Her parents were 'incurably irresponsible' and raised their children on a 'live-for-the-day rule'.

But there were darker forces at work. Increasingly resentful of what she saw as her domestic imprisonment, Kay came to dislike her husband and criticised him constantly. Rows were inevitable; for Gerard felt trapped, too. Born in India but sent to England to be educated at a public school in Derbyshire, he was shy and withdrawn – with disappointed ambitions of his own. He was a frustrated classical pianist, condemned to the daily drudgery of commuting and an accountant's office. His frustrations would often break out into violent rages. His daughter remembered 'an enraged man' with 'a maniacal streak in him', 'a lazy sod' with a 'real snap Irish temper'.[2]

Mary was embarrassed at having to go anywhere with her parents because the rows would continue outside the house, and she never invited friends home. Naturally shy and lacking in self-confidence, and denied any outward displays of affection – 'We are not a greatly sentimental family with hugs and kisses and all that' – she felt herself increasingly isolated in her own home.[3] On one occasion she went into the front room and held on to the hot-water pipes 'until they scalded me, until my palms turned bright red'. Unfortunately, no one noticed. This was probably no more than a childish attempt at attention-seeking. Mary was certainly alert to the possibilities: 'I used to imagine breaking my arm or falling ill. There's always a bit of drama – people always take notice, when you're ill.'[4]

This sense of isolation was intensified by her constant awareness of living in her brother's shadow. Dion had breezed through his school career, garnering an armful of academic honours. 'I was constantly comparing myself to him, and the feeling of inadequacy followed me through life.' Relations between brother and sister would always be difficult: 'We were never close'. Recalling her own schooldays, she described herself as 'A bit thick but extremely conscientious' – 'I've always wanted to get it right'. She liked History, Geography, French, and English Grammar. Her academic achievements were respectable but not exceptional. She eventually sat six O Levels and passed four, failing Maths and English Literature. She blamed the latter defeat on a disagreement with Jane Austen. At this time she preferred to read Budd Shulberg, Paul Gallico and 'books about kids in the theatre'. Lacking either the aptitude or the patience to follow a formal syllabus – 'I just wasn't that kind of bright' – she 'struggled through' to GCE and 'used to get very upset that I wasn't good enough'.[5] She was desperate for something in which she could excel.

At this time most homes in the country were still without the distraction of television, and the two dominant influences in young people's lives were radio and the cinema. Kay had sought escape from domestic drudgery in the cinema and had begun to take Mary with her. 'I used to love the pictures. I was brought up on the pictures.' In towns and cities cinemas were as numerous as sweetshops, and a fair range of films was available every week. This was also the golden age of the Hollywood musical, presenting an idealised view of small-town America as an endless romantic round of song and dance. Mary dreamed of 'dancing and singing my way through a wonderful world of music and Technicolor'. She also found relief from the tensions in the home: 'I used to retreat into a dream world of movies and songs'. She later claimed, rather fancifully, that she would save up her school lunch money – surviving on only broken biscuits ('9d. a pound') – and sneak up to the West End to see 'sexy foreign films'. This is hard to square with her recollection that she always wore school uniform when she went to the cinema because 'I didn't know how to dress up'.[6]

Radio was an equally potent force; and for Mary and Dion, as for most other young people in the mid-1950s, the greatest influence was *The Goon Show*. Indeed, the Goons must have seemed like a godsend in such an 'eccentric' household. Their influence would stay with Mary throughout her life, and Goonish inflections can be heard even in her last interviews.*

And the house was full of music. Although Gerard was a poor musician – playing slowly and deliberately as he followed the score – he gave his children a grounding in classical music.

> We would have quizzes when I was about nine. He'd play pieces of music; I'd have to guess the composer. He'd also tap out notations on the back of my hand. . . . I'd have to know what that was – the piece of music – by the timing of his fingers on the back of my hand.

Mary retained a lifelong appreciation of 'sparkling' Vivaldi and 'good old sobbing Tchaikovsky', while 'a good burst of Mozart can restore one's faith in the entire world'.[7]

---

* 'She called me Neddy Seagoon. I'd be Bluebottle, she'd do Eccles, and we'd go on for ever like this' (Mike Hurst interview, *A Girl Called Dusty*, BBC radio, 27 March 1999).

More significantly, her father also liked certain types of jazz and some jazz-influenced singers. 'I grew up listening to Ella Fitzgerald,' she recalled, but the greatest musical influence on her at this time was undoubtedly Peggy Lee. She had 'a fierce crush on Peggy Lee's voice. . . . I wanted to be Peggy Lee.' She knew that she could never sound like Peggy, but 'I *wanted* to! . . . It all sounds so effortless.' She even went so far as to declare that 'Peggy Lee, basically, is the reason I sing'.[8]

Peggy Lee would achieve broader popularity with the songs she wrote and sang for the Walt Disney cartoon *Lady and the Tramp* (1955) and with her enormous international success, 'Fever' (1958), but in the mid-1950s she made two classic LPs, *Black Coffee* (1953) and *Pete Kelly's Blues* (1955), which are among the finest recordings ever made by any female singer. *Pete Kelly's Blues* was taken from the soundtrack of a film, in which Peggy Lee also acted. For young Mary, Peggy Lee was everything she aspired to be: she was a great singer and a film star and she had blonde hair, which to Mary at the time was the very epitome of glamour. It is not difficult to imagine young Mary, in her bedroom, holding an imaginary microphone – or even a real one – and re-creating Peggy Lee performances such as 'Gee, Baby Ain't I Good To You' or 'You're My Thrill' or 'You Go To My Head'. She would later acknowledge her debt to Peggy by including a tribute to her in her cabaret act and in one of her television series.

Although she may not immediately have set her heart on a career in show business, Mary's discovery that she could sing was of immense importance; for with music, too, she was aware of being overshadowed by her brother. Dion had the natural aptitude for music that even his father lacked. He had learned to play the piano by ear at a very early age, he could sing, and had even begun to write his own songs. (His sister would later give one of his early efforts – a music-hall number entitled 'It Ain't All Honey' – its 'world première' on one of her television shows in 1967.) Mary 'furiously tried to keep up with him'. Initially, it was simply a little girl's emulation of an older brother: 'I often used to wonder whether if Dion had wanted to be a vet, I would have wanted to be one, too.' She learned to play the guitar and also began to sing. 'I started because he started, and I wanted to be better than him at something.' She realised that here was something that came naturally and effortlessly, and that at last she had found something she could do better than her brother.[9]

Mary and Dion began singing together – and here, too, their father's influence would prove crucial. As well as having a passion for music, Gerard was also a radio enthusiast. The family rarely ate dinner at the table because the table was usually covered in his radio equipment. Her father would set up a microphone, and Dion and Mary would 'broadcast' to family and neighbours in the next room, with Kay offering motherly advice: 'Sit up, Mary! Sing up, Mary!'

> That's the closest my parents ever got to being proud of us overtly. I'm sure they were seriously proud of my brother and I, but they thought it was bad form to talk about it.[10]

Gerard made tape-recordings, too; and so it was that Mary started to record almost as soon as she started to sing. 'I used to sing songs that had no connection with my age.'[11] She made her first recording at the age of 12: a spirited rendition of 'When The Midnight Choo Choo Leaves For Alabam'. This was not the piping performance of a child who would later develop a remarkable voice; the voice was already remarkable, recognisably an immature and unpolished version of the voice that would in a few years become one of the most famous in popular music.

And she took her talents beyond the home. She formed a group with two schoolfriends, singing 'bluesy' songs, but was disappointed that they did not appear to be as deeply committed to the act as she was. A school performance of 'St Louis Blues' – 'the first Catholic light show. It was purple' – outraged some of the staff. 'The nuns didn't complain – strangely. But the other teachers were horrified. It got me noticed for once, if nothing else. That pleased me.' She entered a talent contest at the Little Theatre in Ealing in May 1954, won her heat and was awarded a certificate of merit, 'but I decided not to go to the finals because I was also chosen for the school choir'.[12]

At what point in her amateur music-making Mary first began to dream of stardom is unknown, but when teachers asked her where her ambitions lay 'I always used to say the same thing: "I want to be a blues singer." God knows what that meant. But I had this smoky voice and I thought it would be appropriate.'[13] However, any early hopes of stardom she may have entertained were quickly dashed; for, no matter how irked Mary may have been at having to live constantly in her brother's shadow, far deeper anxieties were gnawing away at her.

At one time or another, every teenager has looked in a mirror and been appalled by the answering reflection. Somehow all the doubts and anxieties that assail us in adolescence become focused in our appearance. For most of us, such moments of panic soon pass; but, for Mary O'Brien, plump, shy and deeply unhappy, the image in the mirror spelled disaster. She was never able to express any affection for this 'awful, fat, ugly kid', 'the kind of child only a mother could love'. She was 'a very large child for a small child', 'hideous' and 'a blob' – 'just a disaster area'. Until her early teens she had waist-length red corkscrews – 'I could sit on them' – and, as if that was not enough, her acute shortsightedness condemned her to wearing round, wire-rimmed National Health glasses. With her school uniform of gym-slip and panama hat and her hockey stick, she was 'pure St Trinian's'.[14]

Mary spent much of her spare time in cinemas or poring over film magazines, so she knew what a star looked like – and it was nothing like the ghastly image gazing at her from the mirror. Stars were tall, blonde and glamorous. Mary O'Brien was short and plump with a red crop. Mary O'Brien was going nowhere.

Even at this age Mary was what a later writer would identify as 'a collision of contradictions'. Alongside her diffidence and her lack of self-confidence she possessed a stubborn singlemindedness and what she called 'a seething mass of ambition'. As she contemplated the wretched image before her, she reached the same conclusion as Mr

Polly, that 'There are no circumstances in the world that determined action cannot alter', and she decided to set about effecting a drastic transformation.[15] If Mary O'Brien stood no chance of realising her ambition, then Mary O'Brien would have to be changed. 'I just decided I wanted to be someone else. So I became someone else.' She even regarded such a discovery as a gift: 'it does take some talent to realise that person's a no-hoper; I mean, the next layer of talent is to get rid of her and try to become this other person'.[16]

Teenagers today enjoy freedom and affluence of which young people in the mid-1950s could only dream, and at this remove it may be hard to understand the acuteness of this crisis in Mary's life; but in the postwar years the situation was very different. Clothes-rationing placed severe constraints on everyone's wardrobe; and, in any case, parents exercised much tighter control over their children's appearance than they do today. In the mid-1950s a teenager's wardrobe was still restricted to school uniform, Sunday best, and that collection of oddments that were 'good enough for playing in'. Teenagers were left to dream of the day when they could leave school, earn their own living and buy their own clothes, finally able to make their own decisions about how they dressed. Unfortunately, at this time the youth revolution that would change things for ever still lay in the future, and young people usually effected the passage from adolescence to adulthood by becoming junior versions of their parents.

Mary was having none of this. She left school at the earliest opportunity, at the age of 15, and as soon as she began to earn some money embarked on the process of transformation which she had come to see as her only hope of happiness and fulfilment. In her bedroom she began to experiment with clothes and makeup. Former classmates who met Mary after she had left school were astonished by the change in her appearance.[17]

Her determination to transform a shy and frightened schoolgirl into an international star pushed all else aside; she sacrificed a healthy adolescence in pursuit of an ambition that she saw as her only hope. Mary had no 'silly youth', no teenage romances, she 'stopped growing emotionally' and never developed an ability to form relationships, because she was interested only in singing. 'I was always too busy practising songs and planning my career,' she reflected. 'My mother used to say: "Why can't you be like other girls?" '

Salvation had a price, and Mary would go on paying for the rest of her life.[18]

2

A Means to an End

AFTER LEAVING SCHOOL at the earliest opportunity, Mary was in no hurry to settle into comfortable regular employment. Indeed, there are no indications that she ever considered anything other than a career in show business.

She decided to become an actress. When we consider that she spent much of her spare time in cinemas and drew inspiration from her Hollywood screen heroines, this seems a natural choice; and, of course, acting is the perfect profession for the shy and insecure, offering a scripted life spent being someone else. Mary enrolled at the Jane Campbell acting school in Ealing – but lasted only two weeks. When later she came to reflect on her life for interviews, she was apt to tidy up past experience into little episodes from which a neat moral could be drawn, and she would blame this early setback on a lack of talent for mime: 'I couldn't open a window without the window being there.' A more likely explanation is that she was simply not prepared for a long slog through basic skills, and had expected to be playing leading roles from the moment she arrived. After all, when had she ever seen any of her Hollywood heroines mime the opening of a window or pretend to be a tree?* While Mary was not without ambition, she certainly lacked application; or perhaps it was simply

* Interviewed by Brian Matthew for BBC radio's *Saturday Club* in 1964, Dusty revealed that she still cherished dreams of an acting career, joking: 'I could take over where Margaret Rutherford left off.' In fact, at this time, Margaret Rutherford (1892–1972) had not actually 'left off'. As we shall see, Dusty's dream lingered for most of her life.

impatience. So she decided to concentrate on singing; that was something that seemed to come naturally to her. 'I had no idea singing would work, but I just did it.'[1]

Her life settled into a pattern of meaningless day jobs to earn a living while, in the evenings and at weekends, she made her first tentative steps towards a singing career. She worked in a laundry and in a record shop, and Bentalls in Ealing presented her with opportunities to sell dustbins, buttons, egg-whisks and toys. On one occasion, while demonstrating an electric train set for a small boy, she managed to blow the store's fuses.

Singing reunited her with her brother. For Dion, as for all young men at this time, National Service was a hurdle to be negotiated before he could give serious thought to a career. He joined the Royal Engineers but transferred to the Intelligence Corps where he was able to develop his natural flair for languages. On leaving the Army, he joined his father and the hundreds of other commuters every morning to take the District Line to the office. He became 'something in the City', although not with any enthusiasm: he, too, had set his heart on a career in music. He began to find work in his spare time singing at coming-out dances and Mayfair clubs, and sometimes he invited his sister to join him. 'They always wanted you to sing something they'd heard on their skiing hols,' she recalled. 'I used to sing in all these different languages. Didn't know what I was singing about but I was an incredible mimic.' Unfortunately, 'no one was listening', but 'it was good experience'. It could be tiring, too, with Mary and Dion catching the all-night bus from Oxford Street to Ealing Broadway and 'walking two miles home in thick fog'.[2]*

Mary also began to find work of her own. Sylvia Jones, owner of the Montrose Club in Belgravia, who gave Mary her first job, recalled: 'She was terribly young but extremely good. . . . She was 16,

---

* The experience seems to have left her with an aversion to restaurants offering live entertainment: 'I feel so bad for them that I have to listen. So I can't possibly eat. . . . But to me it's the height of rudeness to turn my back on someone who's sweating it out there in the corner. . . . It's awful. I mean, it's a rotten job, it really is a rotten job.'

self-possessed and had lovely auburn hair. I had to obtain her parents' permission to allow her to perform.' On St Patrick's Day the whole family came to the club, and Mary performed with brother Dion, 'singing songs from all over the world'.[3] Although her parents supported her, Mary's new career put considerable strain on her father:

> My father would come home in the rush hour and then get back on the Tube at Ealing and go to the bowels of Belgravia to dig me out of some drinking club. . . . It was really nice of him, but I gave him such a hard time.[4]

Like all aspiring entertainers, Mary read the *Stage* regularly, and one week she spotted an advertisement seeking a girl singer to join two others in a group. She attended an audition at a rehearsal room in Leicester Square, and was invited straight away to join Riss Chantelle and Lynne Abrams as the Lana Sisters. To Riss Chantelle, Mary came over as 'a well-educated girl, someone you could have a good conversation with'. Mary's voice was 'quite deep', and she would sing the bottom part of the trio, with Riss in the middle and Lynne at the top. 'When we sang together the sound blended perfectly.'[5]*

Her parents having left Ealing for Hove in the meantime, Mary – or 'Shan' as she had been renamed by Riss Chantelle – went to live at Lynne Abrams's home in Hertford.[6]

The Lana Sisters were a close-harmony group – they sang 'all fast and panic-stricken', according to Riss Chantelle – so there was no opportunity for any of them to develop an individual identity, but they worked hard and achieved a very polished sound. They secured a recording contract with Fontana, made television appearances on such shows as *6.5 Special* and *Drumbeat*, and toured with major artists of the day. Mary made her first professional stage appearance at the Savoy Theatre, Clacton: 'They told me not to whistle in the

---

* We can perhaps hear how Dusty's voice sounded in these early days by listening to her solos on the Springfields' 'Star Of Hope' and 'Far Away Places'.

dressing room so I did. Then somebody said "Go outside and turn round three times." I did and fell down a flight of stairs.[7] The girls wore silver lamé pants 'with pale blue tulle skirts with draw-strings which we would pull and whip back our skirts, like flashers, half-way through the act to reveal these little lamé numbers underneath' – and this was twenty years before Bucks Fizz discovered the joys of Velcro.[8]

The Lana Sisters' recording career was undistinguished. 'Chimes of Arcady', 'Buzzin'', 'Mr Dee-Jay', 'My Mother's Eyes', 'Tintarella Di Luna' were pleasant enough but enjoyed no success. There was little to distinguish the Lana Sisters from other girl groups around at the time. Even their recording of that infuriatingly catchy little song '(Seven Little Girls) Sitting On The Back Seat' sank without trace. Their last record, 'Down South', a sort of cowboy song released in 1960, was polished and professional but lacked any spark of life.

By the beginning of 1960, brother Dion had finally decided to renounce the world of finance for a full-time career in music. He had met another singer, Tim Feild, while playing at Hélène Cordet's fashionable nightclub in London. Tim was an Old Etonian who had served in the Royal Navy and then worked his way around the world. He, too, was set on a singing career, and he had even reached the semi-finals of a television talent show. The two young men decided to work together, and Dion asked his sister if she would like to join them.

And so Mary left the Lana Sisters. 'I hated it when they implied that I was letting them down, but I had to move on.'[9] Her eighteen months with the group had provided invaluable experience of re-cording studios and working with television cameras, and when she joined her brother and Tim she was the only one who had ever ap-peared on a stage.

The new group would be called the Springfields. The only expla-nation offered for the name was that they had chosen it after rehears-ing in a field on a beautiful spring day.[10] We are not obliged to believe this. Whatever the origins of the name, Dion and Mary obviously liked it, because they decided to take it as their own. Dion became

Tom Springfield, and Mary became Dusty Springfield. Dusty was a childhood nickname: 'You see, I was a bit of a tomboy, and my friends thought that Dusty was an appropriate nickname for a girl who liked to play football in the street with the boys.'[11] Tim Feild decided not to adopt the new name – even though he was halfway there already – so this change of identity was clearly a brother-and-sister thing.

Once they had put an act together they found work with remarkable ease. 'We started out and got booked sight unseen at Butlin's; we did 16 weeks running round the country in this very old Volkswagen bus.' It gave them the best-possible start. 'We got a chance to take off the rough edges.'[12]

Their good luck continued. No doubt using Dusty's link with Fontana through the Lana Sisters, they secured an audition with producer Johnny Franz and were promptly awarded a recording contract. Then they auditioned for the BBC and were approved unanimously – if rather patronisingly – by the five-strong Talent Selection Group: 'a good effort by present-day standards', 'a little square but refreshingly different from so much of the rubbish we hear today', 'a most marketable product'.[13]

At an electrical engineering factory in Wimbledon on 24 January 1961 the Springfields passed another important milestone in their career when they took time off from a tour with Charlie Drake to make the first of several appearances on *Workers' Playtime*. Top of the bill on this occasion was the vivacious singer Rosemary Squires. *Workers' Playtime* had begun life in May 1941 after Ernest Bevin had asked the BBC to create a cheerful variety programme to boost the war effort in Britain's factories. The show continued to tour the country long after the war, inflicting light entertainment on people who had really done nothing to deserve it. The Springfields now found themselves in a world that boasted such delights as Martin and David Lukins, a father-and-son accordion act, the rustic humour of Billy Burden ('It's a long walk to Dorset'), whistling Ronnie Ronalde and the usual gaggle of impressionists. (As it was radio, we were spared paper-tearers and jugglers.) Unfortunately, the chirpy Springfields fitted into this environment all too easily. Was this really what Dusty had had in mind when she sat in her bedroom and dreamed of stardom?*

Then came the offer of a television series. 'We didn't have a record or anything, but that was the BBC for you.'[14] And the Springfields did indeed suddenly breeze on to our television screens from out of nowhere.

How do we account for this astonishing success? There was certainly no shortage of singing groups at this time, so what made the Springfields so distinctive? Dusty recalled that at their BBC audition a producer had told them: 'You must make up your minds to be either a folk group or a pop group if you're going to be any success at all.' In fact, the Springfields probably owed their success in large measure to the fact that they were neither one thing nor the other. Dusty may have been the group's vocal driving force, but 'my brother was the ideas man'. From the very beginning Tom was the group's principal composer, and he had a remarkable talent for adapting folk-songs from around the world into attractive pop songs.[†] Dusty set out the group's artistic policy most eloquently:

> We're not what you might call authentic folk singers. Ours is a slightly commercial approach to folk music because in this way we hope to win the acceptance of the public as a whole and not just a minority section. . . . Our individual tastes in music are very varied. Brother Tom is a real folk music enthusiast. Tim is mad about Latin American music and my personal taste ranges from jazz and

* *Workers' Playtime* and its sister programme, *Music While You Work*, thirty minutes of uninterrupted lively music broadcast twice a day to stimulate productivity, survived like two radio dinosaurs well into the 1960s.

[†] An interesting comparison might be made with Dorita y Pepe (Doreen and Peter), who were serious and respected students of Spanish and Latin American music but whose uncompromising performances sat uncomfortably in the variety bills of the period. The couple would probably have felt more at home on the concert platform – and, of course, they had no chance whatsoever of coming anywhere near the Hit Parade.

rhythm'n'blues to Latin music. Apart from classical music, folk music is the one thing we all agree on. Also, since there are very few folk groups on the pop scene, the adoption of a folksy-spiritual style has enabled us to create a rather distinctive and easily recognisable sound.

Later she was more frank: 'We were pseudo-everything and we knew it.' Certainly the Springfields were a rich mixture of influences: folk-song, country and western, Latin American rhythms, rock 'n' roll – and skiffle, which was itself a musical mongrel.* Somehow they were able to blend the various elements into a distinctive sound that captured the public imagination.

They were an attractive group, too, with two good-looking boys framing a pretty and vivacious girl. And they were cheerful. 'It was extremely important to be cheerful,' Dusty reflected. 'There was a niche somewhere for cheerful people', and the Springfields were 'absolutely as cheerful as hell' – at least, in public. 'We were successful because there was nobody else around like us then. We were jolly and we looked cheerful and that was it.' According to Mike Hurst, 'Tom used to say all the time: "Just smile." And he hated it anyway, when he had this sort of fixed smile on his face, and his smile never left his face and never changed.' But it worked. The Springfields' career as recording artists would prove inconsistent and unimpressive by today's standards, with only two records reaching the Top Five, so their popularity must be attributed in large measure to personality and their engaging style. They found work as soon as they were ready for it and were quickly absorbed into mainstream show business, with tours, Christmas shows, summer season and radio work. They were even given their own television series before

---

* Even the king of skiffle, Lonnie Donegan, has trouble defining this 'mixture of various folk musics, primarily Afro-American, but not to exclude other things. There are no parameters. . . . My greatest regret . . . is that I used the word "skiffle" at all. . . . I wouldn't have had this endless discussion, "What exactly *is* 'skiffle', Mr Donegan?".'

they had even released their first record. Not even the Beatles could match that achievement.[15]

Their first record was released in May 1961. 'Dear John', a traditional song dating from the American Civil War and arranged by Tom, is bright and businesslike, and in her solo chorus Dusty emerges as an individual personality on record for the first time. Unfortunately, 'Dear John' enjoyed no success at all, which is ironic because it was their performance of this song in Johnny Franz's office that had won the Springfields their recording contract in the first place: 'The three of them sat right here, right in front of my desk, and sang "Dear John". It was a new sound, a fresh sound. I signed them up on the spot.'[16]

The B-side, 'I Done What They Told Me', written by Tom, is the sort of chugging blend of folk music and rock 'n' roll that was commonplace at the time.

The next single, released in August and again featuring songs by Tom, gave the group their first taste of success as recording artists when it climbed into the lower end of the Top Forty. 'Breakaway' is inferior to 'Dear John', but it is more obviously pop-orientated and clearly had something about it that appealed to the public where 'Dear John' had not.

On the B-side, 'Good News', we are treated to our first taste of Springfield humour and the Goonish influence that would intrude into several recordings.

Christmas that year came early for the Springfields when 'Bambino' took them into the Top Twenty for the first time. Adapted by Tom from an Italian carol, 'Bambino' has retained its charm over the years. The B-side, on the other hand, is a very different matter. 'Star Of Hope' was no doubt intended as a gentle contrast to the exuberant 'Bambino', but what we have is a slow and gloomy ballad that has Dusty almost singing baritone.

December brought the release of the Springfields' first LP. Attractively presented, with a sleeve photograph showing Dusty as a vivacious redhead flanked by two handsome young men, *Kinda Folksy* nevertheless exposes the group's musical confusion. On this record they are kinda *everything*.*

'Wimoweh Mambo' – or 'Mambo Wimoweh', depending on whether we believe the sleeve or the label – is an intensely irritating song that has proved so stubbornly resilient that perhaps only driving a stake through the sheet music will finally lay it to rest. Dusty had assured us on one of the television shows that the song had its origins as a 'Zulu war tune', though we may suspect that the song had been no nearer the Zulus than Dusty had.†

From the plains of southern Africa we move to 'The Black Hills of Dakota', a song by Paul Francis Webster and Sammy Fain that had been a big success for Doris Day in 1954. Webster had also collaborated with Dmitri Tiomkin to write 'The Green Leaves Of Summer', which the Springfields lifted from the soundtrack of the John Wayne film *The Alamo* where it was sung as everyone inside the fort waited to be shot. 'Dear Hearts And Gentle People' had provided hit records for Bing Crosby, Dinah Shore and Gordon Macrea; while 'Row, Row, Row' had its origins in vaudeville in the early years of the century. 'Silver Dollar' is a cowboy song that the Springfields perform as kinda rock 'n' roll. The word 'folksy' is truly being pushed to the limit – unless, of course, we subscribe to Louis Armstrong's argument that 'All music is folk music. I ain't never heard no horse sing a song.'

But the Springfields found plenty of reasons to be cheerful.

---

* *Kinda Folksy* (Philips LP, 1961: mono BBL 755; stereo SBBL 674): Wimoweh Mambo · The Black Hills of Dakota · Row Row Row · The Green Leaves Of Summer · Silver Dollar · Allentown Jail · Lonesome Traveller · Dear Hearts And Gentle People · They Took John Away · Eso Es El Amor · Two Brothers · Tzena, Tzena, Tzena.

Kinda Folksy was also issued in 1962, under the same title, as three EPs; and all the tracks were reissued on *Over the Hills and Far Away* (Philips 2CD set, 1997: 534 930-2).

† 'Wimoweh' proved very successful for Scottish singer Karl Denver early in 1962. It is almost impossible to describe Karl Denver's extraordinary voice for anyone who has never heard it. Try to imagine a singing cement-mixer.

'Allentown Jail' was a melancholy lament for an incarcerated lover that found its way into the repertoire of several popular singers at this time, but the Springfields sing with a gusto suggesting that they were the ones who had called the police in the first place and will definitely be pressing charges. They also find the bright side of 'They Took John Away' and 'Lonesome Traveller', though they manage to compose themselves for 'Two Brothers'.

There are two further excursions into foreign languages. 'Eso Es El Amor' is one of those Latin American songs that are only just distinguishable from each other. The song was to be granted an undeserved longevity as a favourite dance-tune on the BBC's *Come Dancing*, accompanying the rhythmic spasms of various sturdily built, overtanned and underdressed young women. 'Tzena, Tzena, Tzena' was apparently an Israeli folk-song.

In January 1962 the Springfields performed a smash-and-grab raid on 'Goodnight Irene', a gentle ballad – or, at least, it *had been* a gentle ballad – by Huddie Ledbetter and Alan Lomax. The Springfields recording is energetic but otherwise uninteresting, and made no impact on record-buyers. The B-side, 'Far Away Places', is pleasant enough.

The Springfields' next disc, 'Silver Threads And Golden Needles', released in April, would turn out to be the most significant of them all, although at first it represented another failure. Quite why the British record-buying public failed to respond to what is one of the group's strongest performances remains a mystery; but the record gave the Springfields their first success in America, and that would prove of far greater importance – not least for Dusty. The B-side, 'Aunt Rhody', has the group giving a rowdy treatment to this traditional elegy for a dead goose.

Shelby S. Singleton of Mercury Records was searching for European artists he thought might do well in America, and when Johnny Franz played 'Silver Threads And Golden Needles' to him he liked it straight away. Following the disc's success in America, the Springfields were invited to record in Nashville.

In the meantime the group reverted to their old habits for their next British release: despite its pseudo-African overtones, 'Swahili Papa', another of Tom's compositions, is a cute comic song that really stood little chance of capturing the imagination of the public. The B-side, 'Gotta Travel On', is a much-travelled song that was in the repertoire of virtually every skiffle group. This strange pairing of titles is yet further evidence of the group's lack of direction.

In the autumn of 1962, Dusty contributed a short article to her old school magazine, in which she treated her readers to a glimpse of her hectic new lifestyle. A typical day began at about 8 o'clock at the hairdresser's, probably followed by 'a press interview, a hasty snack lunch, and an afternoon rehearsal and recording session', with another rehearsal for the evening performance. Lest the nuns should be worried for the spiritual welfare of one of their girls, Dusty informed them that many people in show business were Catholic. She listed Max Bygraves, Joan Turner, Dickie Henderson and Anne Shelton. The list is interesting; wherever Dusty had hoped to be, she had landed squarely in the middle of old-style show business.

In November, Tim Feild's wife was taken ill, and Tim decided to leave the group so that he could take care of her. His departure seems to have been on good terms, although he was quoted as saying that Dusty and Tom 'had thought of nothing but show business since the age of four' and that he was tired of having to carry Dusty's dozens of stiff, frilly petticoats in and out of theatres. He later embraced Sufism, changed his name to Reshad Feild and wrote many books about his spiritual journey. He seems to have kept in touch with the group's progress; and on one occasion, after Dusty had gone solo, he and some Sufi friends went backstage at the Palladium where Johnny Franz found himself surrounded by 'Fellas in sheets' as they chanted for Dusty's success.[17]*

Tom and Dusty needed a replacement. Auditions were held, and eventually Mike Longhurst-Pickworth – 'handsome in a darkly glowing way', as one smitten female journalist described him – was

---

* In 1964, in a questionnaire for the sleeve of *I Only Want To Be With You* (EP), Dusty nominated Tim Feild as her best friend.

chosen.[18] After a brief spell as Mike Pickworth, he eventually became Mike Hurst.

The change in the line-up certainly did the group no harm. In November they had their greatest success so far. According to Tom, 'Island Of Dreams' was successful because it sounded 'vaguely like a lot of other tunes', so that 'people who aren't musical can whistle it after a couple of hearings'.[19] Whatever the reason for the song's appeal, it took the Springfields into the Top Ten for the first time. The B-side, 'The Johnson Boys', is a bit of hillbilly silliness and is allegedly 'traditional' – meaning perhaps that no one is prepared to take responsibility for it.

Tom later recorded 'Island of Dreams' a second time with the Seekers when he was their producer and principal songwriter. Quite why Tom felt that he needed to try again is unclear, but a comparison of the two recordings is interesting. Like the Springfields, the Seekers were driven by a distinctive female singer; but the crystal clarity of Judith Durham's voice lacks that indefinable magic that lifted Dusty above the rest.

Christmas 1962 brought a further seasonal offering from the Springfields in the form of *Christmas with the Springfields*, an EP produced in association with *Woman's Own*.* Like most Christmas records, it had been recorded in the summer, when Tim Feild was still with the group. They plod their way through 'The Twelve Days Of Christmas', become a little 'folksy' with 'Mary's Boy Child', sound rather too polished and professional for the touching naïveté of 'Away In A Manger', and end with the oppressively cheery 'We Wish You A Merry Christmas', which they round off with a multilingual flourish reminiscent of a UNICEF Christmas card.

Following on the success of 'Silver Threads And Golden Needles' in America, the Springfields spent January 1963 recording in Nash-

* *'Woman's Own' Presents Christmas with the Springfields* (EP, 1962): The Twelve Days Of Christmas · Mary's Boy Child · Away In A Manger · We Wish You A Merry Christmas.

All the Springfields' Christmas records have been reissued on a privately produced CD, *We Wish You A Merry Christmas*. See Appendix.

ville with Shelby S. Singleton. On the strength of 'Silver Threads And Golden Needles' their hosts were convinced that the Springfields were a purely country group, and the difficulties this created were exacerbated by the Nashville way of working. According to Dusty:

> it took us three weeks to rehearse one verse and in Nashville at that time, you know, they'd write the song in the morning and you'd go in and start recording it in the afternoon. And they were writing the music parts on the balcony and throwing down the violin part as you're singing. . . . [W]e were hopeless and we just didn't work. They were still very nice to us. . . . [We] just didn't know how to work that quickly and stylistically.[20]

Nevertheless, Dusty later claimed that 'they asked me to stay, but I didn't want to do that kind of music'.[21]

Folk Songs from the Hills, the LP that emerged from these sessions, is not a happy experience.* The garish sleeve, for which the Springfields demonstrated their 'country' credentials by posing self-consciously with some bales of hay, alerts us that all might not be well – and the record confirms our misgivings. The group pounds its way through numbers such as 'There's A Big Wheel', 'Midnight Special', 'Wabash Cannonball' and 'Foggy Mountain Top' with an affected Southern drawl that seems to defy us to take the record seriously – or, indeed, to believe that the Springfields themselves took it seriously – and makes them sound as if they were auditioning for *The Beverly Hillbillies*. Tom was well aware of the difficulty: 'You can never be

---

* *Folk Songs from the Hills* (Philips LP, 1963: 632 304 BL): Settle Down · There's A Big Wheel · Greenback Dollar · Midnight Special · Wabash Cannonball · Alone With You · Cottonfields · Foggy Mountain Top · Little By Little · Maggie · Darling Allalee · Mountain Boy.

All the tracks were reissued on *Over the Hills and Far Away* (Philips 2CD set, 1997: 534 930-2).

Mike Hurst is still called Mike Pickworth on the sleeve; no sooner had he joined the group than he found himself recording in Nashville and had not yet got round to changing his name.

authentic if you're British. It's mimicry.' The problem continues to dog British artists who wish to perform American country music.

None of this would matter in the end. When the record appeared it was already irrelevant. For Dusty, at least, it had been overtaken by events.

'Our trip to Nashville changed everything for us,' she declared. The girl who had sat in cinemas and dreamed of America now found herself looking up at the skyscrapers of New York as the group stopped over on their way to Nashville. For Dusty, 'It was love at first sight'. As the love-affair deepened, it would bring her personal and professional fulfilment yet it would also come close to destroying her; but, for the moment, she was overwhelmed by the experience – and not least by the music she was hearing for the first time. She discovered Dionne Warwick: when she heard 'Don't Make Me Over' on the radio she 'had to sit down very suddenly'. Through Dionne she found the work of Burt Bacharach and Hal David, and this was probably the single most important musical relationship of her career.

Dusty liked to identify turning-points in her life, and all the discoveries of this trip became crystallised for her in the moment when she passed the Colony record store in New York late at night and heard the Exciters' record 'Tell Him' blasting out into the street. 'Tell Him' changed her life completely. 'The *attack* in it! It was the most exciting thing I'd ever heard.' It was 'a revelation'. The Exciters 'got you by the throat'; and – crucially – 'I could approximate the voices'. Indeed, she could; and it is not difficult to imagine her singing 'Tell Him' softly to herself as she went on her way. Suddenly, all her vague feelings of frustration and discontent came into sharp focus: 'I knew I wanted to do something but I didn't know what it was until I heard it.' Dissatisfied with what she dismissed as the 'twanging and nasal noises' of the Springfields, 'extremely awful and noisy', she wanted 'that crispness, the ballsiness in the voice, which we hadn't had in England'. For Dusty at least, the Nashville recording session no longer had any significance.

Dusty never recorded 'Tell Him' – although, as she was aware, it would have suited her voice perfectly. British success with the song fell to Billie Davis, who produced an energetic, if undistinguished, recording. Of more interest is the version by Alma Cogan. Alma was Britain's foremost female singer before Dusty. She had emerged from fifties cuteness to record two outstanding LPs – *With You in Mind* (1961) and *How About Love?* (1962) – with musical director Tony Osborne. When the face of popular music was transformed in the early sixties, Alma tried to make the transition to the new style; she made polished recordings of songs by Lennon and McCartney but was unable to emulate the success of Petula Clark, who had made a similarly drastic change in the direction of her career. Alma adapted 'Tell Him' to her own lively style, but the record was never going to stop people in their tracks as it blasted out of a record shop.[22]*

In March 1963 the Springfields released their first record since their return from Nashville. Once again Tom had performed his musical alchemy, this time transmuting a French nursery rhyme into a Top Ten hit, and 'Say I Won't Be There' would prove a worthy successor to 'Island Of Dreams'. To the accompaniment of French horns, some purposeful percussion and a highly strung guitar, the Springfields deliver another strong performance; but, listening to the record today, the real interest lies in Dusty's solo. There, in the middle eight, soaring clear of the ensemble and sounding almost like a declaration of musical independence, is quite recognisably the voice that in a matter of months would have established itself as one of the great voices in popular music.

The voice that Dusty herself variously described as 'strange', 'smoky' and 'gravelly', and that was once famously characterised as sounding 'as if it were on its way to a prayer meeting and got lost in Tin Pan Alley', was present – in an immature state – even on the early

---

* Alma Cogan died, absurdly young, in 1966. She is perhaps best-remembered as one of the finest interpreters of the work of Noël Coward and Cole Porter: we shall probably never hear a finer interpretation of Porter's 'I Get A Kick Out Of You', in which she even found time to include a mischievous parody of Shirley Bassey.

recordings she made at home in her teens.[23] 'Dusty has always had that strange grown-up voice,' recalled Tom.

In the light of Dusty's early ambition to become an actress, which had no doubt been reinforced by all the Hollywood musicals she had seen in Ealing's cinemas during the 1950s, it should come as no surprise that at first she wanted to go into musical comedy. 'I was singing Rodgers and Hart when I was ten', and 'When no one else was looking, I was leaping off desks doing Gene Kelly routines. I really wanted to be Cyd Charisse, but I have very short legs.'[24]* Even worse, her voice was inadequate. 'I am not being modest but realistic.' Hers was only a 'microphone voice'; while 'Singers like Ethel Merman have voices of tin'. The comparison was perceptive. Cole Porter's infatuation with Ethel Merman sprang directly from the ease with which she was able, at a time when there was no stage amplification, to send every syllable of his elegant lyrics to the back of the upper circle. In the words of his biographer: 'Upon hearing her siren song blasting a brassy comedy line across the proscenium or pushing a quiet sentiment to the highest reaches of the second balcony, he placed her among the living divinities.'[25] The situation had changed little by the early sixties; whereas with today's technology, of course, even the smallest and least distinguished voice can survive on stage.

Dusty was well aware of her lack of technical expertise. 'I'm always forcing my voice to do things it's not educated to do. I don't breathe properly and I've got a weak throat.' She had had no formal training, and she abused her voice. 'I mean well when I go onstage, but I lose contact with any form of discipline. I've always gone for the end effect and to hell with the cost.'[26] Her standard remedy for a croaky voice was onion juice, but generally 'I just hope for the best – and eat throat sweets'.[27] The price of this neglect was recurrent throat problems, which were often aggravated – and possibly even caused – by the stress of the big occasion.

'Little Boat', the song on the B-side of 'Say I Won't Be There', was

---

* Compared with Cyd Charisse, of course, *every* woman has short legs.

written by Tom in collaboration with Clive Westlake, a songwriter who would play a significant role in Dusty's career.

In the same month, Dusty made her television solo début with an appearance on *Juke Box Jury*. Hosted by David Jacobs, the weekly show invited the famous and the not so famous, the musical and the not so musical, to pass judgement on a selection of the latest record releases. All too often it provided an opportunity for popular music's old guard to make a last defiant stand against the onward march of the new, young music – most notably when the 'jury' included veteran bandleader Henry Hall, who loathed everything he heard. Other guests linger in the memory: American musical star Stubby Kaye chewed gum as if his life depended on it, and occasionally blew a bubble to raise the tone of the proceedings; while Italian starlet Lisa Gastoni appeared on the show in a strapless dress cut so low that on screen she appeared to be naked – prompting David Jacobs to ask her to stand up and prove to the viewers that she really did have some clothes on.*

In July the Springfields released what would be their last record as an active group. 'Come On Home' is energetic but undistinguished and failed even to make the Top Thirty. On the B-side was 'Pit-A-Pat' – another 'traditional' song, but arranged on this occasion by Clive Westlake. 'Pit-A-Pat' is a charming performance that displays a belated musical maturity which is also evident on 'No Sad Songs For Me', the final, valedictory track ('It's all over') on the retrospective *Springfields Story* released in 1964.[†] It came too late.

* David Jacobs very kindly confirmed the accuracy of the author's recollections.

[†] *The Springfields Story* (Philips 2LP album, 1964: BET 606 A-B): Dear John · Breakaway · Bambino · Far Away Places · Silver Threads And Golden Needles · Two Brothers · Aunt Rhody · The Green Leaves Of Summer · Allentown Jail · Gotta Travel On · Pit-A-Pat · Island of Dreams · The Johnson Boys · Little Boat · Cottonfields · Foggy Mountain Top · Maggie · Alone With You · Settle Down · Say I Won't Be There · Come On Home · Maracabamba · If I Was Down And Out · No Sad Songs For Me.

Virtually the entire Springfields catalogue was reissued in 1997 on *Over the Hills and Far Away* (Philips 2CD set: 534 930-2).

Dusty later chose to portray the end of the Springfields as part of a well-laid plan – 'When we started the act we arranged to pack it up after three years' – but it was not so neat and tidy. There had always been tensions behind the cheery image that the Springfields presented to the world; in particular the relationship between Tom and Dusty was never easy. Mike Hurst, the youngest member of the group, was less willing than Tim Feild had been to act as peacemaker in the rows between brother and sister that were becoming more frequent. 'We weren't even friendly with each other, let alone with the world,' Dusty recalled.[28]

Such discord might have been manageable if they had been united by the music, but they were not. According to Dusty, 'I wasn't enamoured of what we were doing. None of us were. Singing all that pseudo folk-country.' It was merely 'a means to an end', with everyone in it to 'sort of gain experience and try to enjoy it as much as we could'. Dusty herself was 'just doing it to get famous' and acknowledged that 'It served us very well'.[29] Dusty's sights were set firmly on a solo career, and the musical discoveries she had made in America served to add urgency to her ambition. 'We were all chafing at the bit, but I suppose my feeling that I could make it alone was the primary factor in our breaking up.' She felt that success mattered more to her than to the others:

[W]e'd change trains in Crewe and the boys would leave their mikes on the station and their guitars and go off and have a cheese sandwich whereas I would sit with the mikes and guitars because I knew someone was going to steal them. . . . And I'd say, 'But if they were stolen, we wouldn't have been able to do the show,' and they'd say 'Great!'

'I was the one who always wanted to get it right and that's the way I continue to be. . . . Conscientious to the end.'[30] All the ingredients were there for a slow and increasingly acrimonious demise; but, when it came, the end of the Springfields was both sudden and casual. Mike Hurst recalls:

Winter Gardens, Blackpool. We were sitting there having a cup of tea, having done a rehearsal for that Sunday night's concert, and . . . Tom says, 'Why don't we break up?' And Dusty says: 'Yeah. OK.' And they both looked at me . . . and like an idiot I said: 'Yeah, it sounds like a really good idea.' If only I'd thought about it more![31]

In fact, it was the right decision. Lacking the capacity for musical development, the Springfields had nowhere to go; and they had been to the Cavern Club in Liverpool and heard the future of pop music – and knew that, as things stood, they could have no part of it. 'I was always amazed that we got as far as we did,' admitted Dusty frankly. They had gained experience but little else: 'We made absolutely nothing by the time we had paid everything. Our expenses were too high.'[32]

Nevertheless, the Springfields had had their moments. Long before Bob Dylan 'went electric' at the Newport Folk Festival in 1965 and – so the story goes – changed the face of pop music for ever, the Springfields effected their own electric revolution – at the Winter Gardens, Blackpool.

'We had amplifiers three feet high and we thought it was great,' Mike Hurst recalls.

Unfortunately, impresario Harold Fielding was less than impressed, believing that the amplifiers spoiled the look of the stage, and demanded that they be removed.

Dusty stood firm, and ugly words were exchanged.

Harold Fielding's wife felt moved to intervene. 'Don't let her talk to you like that!' – a remark that can always be relied upon to raise the temperature of any argument.

Dusty summoned up all the benefits of a convent education. 'Tell that bloody cow to shut up!' she snapped.

This provoked the inevitable 'You'll never work in one of my shows again' from Harold Fielding. But the amplifiers stayed.[33]

Once the decision to disband had been made, events moved quickly. The Springfields played their official farewell concert at the Palladium in October, and in the following month Dusty was in the Top

Ten with 'I Only Want To Be With You'. According to Dusty, 'it took three weeks to go from being a Springfield to being a solo.'[34] Few artists can ever have made such a transition so smoothly. 'I didn't exactly have to claw my way to the top,' Dusty conceded.[35]*

No sooner had Dusty declared her intention of going solo than she went into a recording studio with Johnny Franz. According to Vic Billings, her new personal manager, 'we originally did nine tracks, and picked "I Only Want To Be With You" from them. It became a big hit, and from then on it was merely a matter of finding the right songs at the right time.'[36] Dusty had fallen in love with the song straight away: 'I heard that and went Yes! we could do that à la Phil Spector sound. . . . That was a gift. I didn't ask for that song. It just came into my life.'[37]

'I know I can sing better on my own,' Dusty said confidently. 'Much wilder.'[38] And as we listen to her exultant performance of this song by Mike Hawker and Ivor Raymonde it is as if she has shaken off her fetters and is at last free to stand alone.

There was a further surprise: for the B-side Dusty recorded a song she had written herself. Once Lennon and McCartney had shown the way, a growing number of performers tried their hand at writing their own songs – all too often with embarrassing results. 'Once Upon A Time' is a cute little pop song for which Dusty's voice already sounds too mature, but it does demonstrate that she was now tuned in to a completely different type of music.

Few singers have announced their arrival so emphatically. 'I knew it was going to be all right. Now, I don't know how I knew. . . . I just knew somehow it would all work out.'[39]

---

* Following the demise of the Springfields, 'Tom wrote songs and made a lot of money' (*Radio Times*, 30 April 1994); he went on to become songwriter and producer for the Seekers and Anita Harris. After an attempt at a solo career of his own, Mike Hurst also became a producer, most notably for Cat Stevens.

3

A Girl Called Dusty

DUSTY WAS FINALLY where she wanted to be. As one of the Lana Sisters, a close-harmony group, she had been unable to develop an individual musical identity and was merely 'the one on the end'. With the Springfields she had been the pretty girl framed by two good-looking boys, and the group's success with records and on television had made her face and her voice familiar throughout the country, as well as establishing useful contacts in America; but the Springfields had never really been a happy group and had lacked musical direction. Now she had broken free, knew the kind of music she wanted to perform and was enjoying remarkable success with her very first record.

But she had little opportunity to savour the moment. She was caught up in the revolution that was overtaking popular music and sent out on tour with the likes of the Searchers, Brian Poole and the Tremeloes, Freddie and the Dreamers, and the Swinging Blue Jeans. Her life became centred on the race to catch the tour bus that left Alsop Place, adjacent to Madame Tussaud's in Baker Street, at eight o'clock in the morning. This meant being at the hairdresser's at six. Dusty was frequently the only girl in the party; and, while the boys could crawl on to the bus with hangovers, Dusty had to arrive 'rigidly together' and looking her best. This need to appear beautiful and 'rigidly together' in public at all times created pressures of its own, and prompted some strange behaviour: for example, if room service brought a meal to her hotel room, Dusty would shut herself in the bathroom until the meal was served and she was alone once more.[1]

Derek Wadsworth, trombone-player with the Echoes, observed that Dusty 'worked at her beauty just the same way that she worked at her voice and worked at the other aspects of her craft', and recalled that only once did he catch a glimpse of Dusty without the full makeup and was struck by the 'fresh-faced country girl underneath it all'.[2] But such sightings of the famous image 'off duty' were very rare indeed. On the one occasion when she was too tired to put on her full makeup before rushing to catch the tour bus, 'the bus pulled up backstage and I had a scarf on and I hadn't done my makeup properly and I heard two people say, "Oooh, she doesn't look good, does she?" I never did it again.'[3] Asked to nominate her most embarrassing moment, Dusty recalled an occasion on tour in Australia when a group of fans burst into her dressing-room when she was still without wig, makeup and, indeed, much else. She sought refuge with Brian Poole and the Tremeloes, and 'I'll never forget the face of the guitarist of the Tremeloes when I rushed in'.[4] In the relaxed and casual atmosphere of a Memphis studio in 1968, producer Tom Dowd was amazed by her appearance. 'She had her hairdresser John Adams with her, and she'd have her hair blown, dried and cut every day. She had a Memphis beehive and looked like the queen of the Southern contingent.'[5] He clearly failed to appreciate the daily process of *becoming Dusty Springfield*.

We have to understand what was happening. The elaborate fiction called Dusty Springfield was the means by which shy little Mary O'Brien was able to realise all her dreams of stardom. 'I was nothing as Mary O'Brien. Years of hard work and pushing got me to be Dusty Springfield.'[6] But the talent was Mary's own. She had had that voice, in an undeveloped state, when she was 12 years old – we can hear it on the recordings her father made at home – but lacked the self-confidence even to hope for a career in show business. The decision to create a new identity for herself changed everything. It enabled her to get on stage; and, not least, it enabled a white middle-class English convent girl to champion the music of black Americans who were still subject to prejudice in their own country. Dusty Springfield was Mary O'Brien's salvation, and she must not be al-

31

lowed to fail. Above all, she must not be found out. No one must be allowed to suspect that behind the confident image of the glamorous singing star was a frightened little girl; for her obsessive pursuit of perfection and her reluctance to leave anything to chance masked a profound insecurity that was only just being held in check:

> [T]he fat convent schoolchild that suddenly became someone else . . . is still there, the person that I have to smash down and say: 'No! you're not too shy to do it, you're not, you *are* good enough.'

'Without the face I was a quivering wreck', so 'I developed this front so they wouldn't know. Because if they knew the real me they wouldn't like me', even though 'I have to spend an inordinate amount of time becoming that person'. Fortunately, 'the bigger the hair, the blacker the eyes, the more you can hide'. There could be no chinks in her armour. The image had to be perfect; and the performances had to be perfect, too. 'I worry about my photographs, about the way a record is being made, about my clothes, everything. It obsesses you. If it doesn't – then you don't make the grade.'[7] She hated being photographed from the left, because that was her bad profile.

On stage 'I really come alive'; it was 'some kind of growth that happens, and I know this is what I'm meant to do'. Although she was only 5 feet 3 inches tall, her piled-up hair, high heels and, above all, the 'big expansive gestures', dramatic, elegant and perfectly timed to complement the music, helped to give her a commanding presence on stage. Penny Valentine has captured perfectly the irresistible magic of those moments when Dusty's hand 'would suddenly reach up mid-song and pluck the air to draw down the notes or turn sideways as though to ward off the grief of the lyrics'.*

---

* While it may be true that Dusty sometimes wrote the words of songs on her arms, this was surely prompted by a last-minute dressing-room panic rather than by any serious intention to read the words as she went along, which would hardly have been practicable. At the San Remo Song Festival in 1965, when she experienced genuine difficulty with a song, Dusty took the sheet music on stage with her.

Dusty never really enjoyed performing – 'I have to run from the dressing-room to the stage, because I might run the other way if they gave me five seconds' – but her anxieties became part of the performance:

that *edge* . . . creates an atmosphere of 'God, is she going to make it? Or is she even going to get through the song? Is she going to finish this set? What's going to happen next?' And I think that that living-on-the-edge quality is what makes audiences quite enjoy themselves. They may come out sweating . . . and exhausted, but they think they've had a good time! And I'm there to give them a good time, no matter what the cost to me.

Not surprisingly, 'I'm a wreck after a performance'.[8]

At what precise point the final phase in the emergence of Dusty Springfield began is unknown – 'one day, my brother tells me, I just went out to Harrods, bought a black sheath dress, a string of pearls, put my hair up in a chignon and was a different person'[9] – but on the sleeve of *Kinda Folksy* (1961) Dusty is still the red-haired girl next door while *Folk Songs from the Hills* (1963) presents us with a Hollywood-inspired blonde bombshell (although the ghastly tartan creation she has chosen to wear does make her look like one of the little dolls to be found in gift shops). Even that decisive transition from red crop to perhaps the world's most famous blonde beehive was not achieved without pain. Madeline Bell recalls that Dusty would sit for hours in Vidal Sassoon's salon having her hair bleached. She would have tears in her eyes, and two junior employees would stand on either side of her with hairdryers, blowing cool air on to her head.[10]

Her own hair was augmented by wigs and extensions. There were three basic wigs, nicknamed 'Cilla', 'Lulu' and 'Sandie'; but, despite their vital importance to the creation of the image of Dusty Springfield, they were accorded no respect. On one occasion, when journalist Keith Altham went to the *Ready Steady Go!* studio to interview Dusty, he found her 'tossing one of the wigs all around the dressing room'. She explained: 'I'm just giving Cilla a good kicking!'

Vic Billings witnessed a similar spectacle in Australia when 'Cilla' was suffering badly from the humidity. Dusty was very agitated, 'pulling bits off Cilla, but it just wouldn't go right'. Finally, she gave up and threw 'Cilla' into a corner. When Vic returned ten minutes later, 'Dusty was sitting with Cilla stuck on her head, all covered in fluff'. He burst out laughing. 'She gave me a glare and then started laughing too.' Many years later, when Dusty was making a video with the Pet Shop Boys, one of her hairdressers fled from the dressing-room shrieking: 'It looks like she'd had that wig in the washing-machine!'[11]

Then, of course, came the lacquer. And more lacquer. And yet more lacquer. Mike Hurst, who stood next to Dusty on stage with the Springfields, was almost overcome by it: 'The hair was amazing. . . . [S]he used to lacquer, lacquer to build this layer up and up and up, and if you are singing in close proximity to this, your nose almost stuck into her hair, the power of that lacquer. . . . I swear I used to suffer from it actually.' Having achieved the desired effect, it was necessary for Dusty to sit upright and even to sleep in a sitting position, otherwise her creation would become misshapen and 'I'd have to go on stage with this dented head'.[12]

Dusty's hair would remain in development for the rest of her life. In the mid-eighties she admitted: 'My hair doesn't know where it's going yet. Or let's say it hasn't arrived where it wants to be.'[13]

The most famous makeup of the decade was originally a 'giant mistake'. Dusty tried to copy the models in French *Vogue*, who had black eyelids ('Not naturally, as far as I am aware'), but she never quite got it right. 'I never knew how to blend it.' Dusty's own recipe was a blend of mascara and kohl, 'a metallic powder used in the East for darkening eyelids'. Once applied, it stayed on for weeks at a time because 'it took about six days to get a good build-up by using talcum powder and more eyeblack' and, in any case, 'it was such hell getting it off'; so it stayed where it was, and Dusty simply washed round the edges. 'When you finally took it off you needed an ice-pick.' The false eyelashes were put on only for television or live performances. Underneath it all, 'my eyes are greenish khaki, sort of Army surplus colour' – a striking image that refers back to Dusty's early years in postwar Ealing where there had been at least one large Army-surplus store not far from her home.*

The whole effect was completed with 'hot pink' lipstick. Pink was 'the best colour in the world. It really is erotic.'[14]

There could be unfortunate consequences. Ivor Raymonde recalled that, while recording one ballad, Dusty was so moved that she rushed from the studio in tears. 'When she came back all her make-up had run and it looked like a ton of soot had fallen down her face.'[15][†]

Yet, paradoxically, having taken such pains to create and maintain this image of glamorous perfection, Dusty lost no time in debunking it. Knowing that behind this beautiful confident image there was a plain and frightened little girl, perhaps she was guiltily trying to draw attention to the fact that it was all a performance, pointing it out herself before she was found out by someone else. What-ever the reason, she was more than happy to draw attention to her imperfections.

First, of course, there was her notorious short-sightedness. She had tried contact lenses briefly but without success. (We can only imagine what fresh levels of backstage anxiety contact lenses would have brought.) Onstage she could not even see her audience. 'There's no denying I get a bit panicky on the stage with being virtually blind.'[16] When she was offstage or away from the cameras she wore specta-cles, favouring prescription sunglasses; but 'I keep sitting on them. Never see them . . . because I'm not wearing glasses, I guess!'[17] Later, when she had her own television series, a large white card would be attached to the camera to which she was meant to be working; and,

---

* The term 'panda-eyed', which has now become a tedious piece of journalistic shorthand to be used automatically whenever Dusty's name is mentioned, was coined by someone who had obviously never looked at a panda.

† In later years, when she was playing up to representatives of the gay press, Dusty liked to claim that she had acquired her makeup tricks from drag queens; but at this time it is unlikely that she even knew what a drag queen was. The Dusty Springfield who emerged in 1963 surely owed more to private experiments at a dressing-table in an Ealing bedroom.

because cue-cards and autocues were of no use to her, she had to learn all her lines by heart. Much of Dusty's career was quite literally a blur.

She thought her nose was too long and she hated her legs. She had varicose veins – 'Certainly you may say I have varicose veins' – and wore dark stockings to cover them up and to make her legs look slimmer. Furthermore, 'I don't cut my toe nails, but I pull at them and tear them off.' During her time with the Lana Sisters, she had torn a dress with her *knee* – 'I was never known for having dainty knees' – and she once went so far as to describe herself as being 'as sturdy as a Shetland pony'.[18]

As for clothes, at this early stage in her career Dusty felt that the 'secret' was to dress 'in much the same style as your fans . . . but with just a little bit better quality'. This could involve a last-minute dash along Oxford Street, usually to C & A or Marks & Spencer, to find something to wear on *Ready Steady Go!* – only to spot a girl in the audience that evening wearing an identical dress.[19] If Dusty's hair was uncertain where it was going, then her wardrobe seems to have lost its way completely. The young woman who could look stunningly beautiful in a discreet matching jacket and skirt never managed to find a style of dress that satisfied her. During her days with the Springfields she would drift from a homely pinafore dress to some extravagant hooped construction that scattered all before it. As a solo artist she was to be seen at one moment shuffling urgently on-stage at Wembley Arena in a full-length tight skirt and high heels to sing 'Dancing In The Street' and the next moment leaping around in a perilously short mini-dress. Later in the decade she favoured a high-waisted full-length shift, like a rather expensive nightdress, from which her feet 'Like little mice stole in and out/As if they feared the light'.[20] For the big occasion she was apt to appear in what she seemed to feel was the kind of elaborate spangled confection that an international star should wear. And when 'flower power' overran the sixties the beads and bells did as little for Dusty as they did for any other woman (or man). Yet by the end of the decade she felt that she had become too 'sedate' and that perhaps she should return to wearing 'purple and magenta and all the tarty colours'. After all, 'I've got very erotic tastes'.[21]

On New Year's Day, 1964, at 6.35 in the evening, with 'I Only Want To Be With You' still riding high in the Top Twenty, Dusty joined the Rolling Stones, the Dave Clark Five, the Hollies and the Swinging Blue Jeans for a piece of television history when they all took part in the very first edition of *Top of the Pops*. Although the show was obviously the BBC's answer to *Ready Steady Go!* and *Thank Your Lucky Stars*, it also owed a large debt to Alan Freeman's radio show, 'Pick of the Pops', which was linked directly to the current hit parade and had become required listening for young people. *Top of the Pops* followed the same formula; and, as if to suggest that the show was being broadcast directly from a disco, the records were 'played' by a pretty girl sitting at a turntable. Denise Sampey performed this function on the first show, but she was replaced by the legendary Samantha Juste until this gimmick was dropped altogether and *Top of the Pops* was allowed to become a straight-forward television show. *Radio Times* warned viewers that the artists 'will mime their songs. This is a departure from normal BBC practice, but the rule is being relaxed because the purpose of the programme is to let you hear the discs exactly as recorded, though within the setting of a television programme.'[22] (Eventually, under pressure from the Musicians' Union, *Top of the Pops* was obliged to follow *Ready Steady Go!* and go live – though the question 'How live is "live"?' lingers to this day.)

There was no attempt to match the presenters to the audience; the show's original hosts – Jimmy Savile, Alan Freeman, David Jacobs and Pete Murray – were all approaching middle age. Unfortunately, this was typical of the time. Television producers were still trying to come to terms with the new teenage phenomenon, and the idea of recruiting young presenters for the new young music still lay in the future. Consequently, the few outlets for pop music on both radio and television were put into the hands of a generation who had spent their own teenage years in the big-band era, had in some cases gained their first broadcasting experience in the armed forces, and tended to preside over pop-music shows like a schoolmaster supervising a school dance. Interviews could often seem like a summons to the headmaster's study.* The struggle to match pop-music presenters to the age and experience of their audience would be long and painfully slow.

The key figure in this process was a 19-year-old secretary called Cathy McGowan, who answered an advertisement for a teenage adviser for *Ready Steady Go!*, Associated-Rediffusion's new pop music programme which had begun on 2 August 1963 and quickly become essential Friday-evening viewing for the nation's teenagers. With what one contemporary critic described as 'disarming artlessness and powder-room chatter', and continually flicking her long, straight hair out of her eyes, Cathy triumphed over 600 other applicants to find herself as the show's new, young presenter – although initially she was supported by the reassuring maturity of Keith Fordyce. According to the show's producer, Elkan Allan, 'She was awfully gauche and raw and desperately nervous but she was worth taking on because she was obviously terribly switched on in a teenage way'.[23] With 'cameras sweeping back and forth like robot jivers, tangled black leads from the guitars, and Pop Art décor', and with the studio floor packed with young dancers, *Ready Steady Go!* established a completely new style for pop-music programmes. The dancers were recruited from London clubs and had to pass a short audition, but 'The producers presumably felt that the subsequent loss of spontaneity is a small price to pay for the stylish, fast-moving character which they give the programme'.[24] Unmoved, the BBC doggedly continued to put its faith in schoolmasters.

Dusty's own television experience at this time was considerable. Indeed, it was one of her most valuable legacies from her time with the Lana Sisters and the Springfields. When the BBC gave the Springfields their own series Dusty had to learn to work with

* Even so, Cliff Michelmore introducing Bob Dylan to viewers of *Tonight* remains in a class of its own. And who could forget Victor Sylvester, the king of ballroom dancing, resplendent in evening dress, teaching the nation to twist?

cameras and address her television audience directly – and all this at a time when performers who were soon to become household names were still playing in pubs, clubs and church halls for a few pounds, so that when they had their first hit record they suddenly found themselves on television with a lot to learn.

Although the male groups dominated the pop music explosion of the early sixties, on television a solo performer as accomplished as Dusty held the advantage. She was the only focus of attention for both director and audience, and she enjoyed freedom of movement. Anchored by their guitar leads, and obliged to form a tight unit for the cameras, the groups could do little but stand in a line, wear a vacant expression, glance self-consciously at the monitors to see if they were on camera, and try hard to resist the urge to wave to mum.

In the late fifties Britain's first successful male group, the Shadows, had recognized the problem and had evolved the 'Shadows walk', that legendary piece of choreography that became the Shadows *kick* in the livelier numbers. Among the new wave, only Freddie and the Dreamers took the hint, with the Dreamers performing a lunatic parody of the Shadows walk behind Freddie as he executed his own extraordinary series of gyrations. What else was there to do?

Dusty's advantage, and her readiness to use it, was made vividly apparent in an intriguing television performance in 1964. Both Dusty and the Merseybeats had recorded 'Wishin' And Hopin' ', and an adventurous director had what was – for its time – the bold notion of having both versions performed together, while the camera cut from one to the other. With their matching clothes, guitars and hairstyles the Merseybeats, who were never the most cheerful-looking souls, could only stand dolefully in a row and allow themselves to be upstaged by Dusty, who was free to move around, work directly to camera and sell the song – and herself. By the final chorus the Merseybeats had been virtually forgotten, stranded in silhouette at the back of the studio, leaving Dusty in full command.

Dusty had even presented *Ready Steady Go!* for a few weeks, and recalled the 'warts and all' style, 'but that's what gave it its atmosphere'. The audience were desperate to be on camera and were 'so close they used to goose you and I was really incredibly shy and to have to perform with people in your face was totally unnatural'.[25]

Vicki Wickham, the show's co-producer, would become Dusty's closest friend; and Dusty herself would have a crucial influence on the show's musical development.

In the middle of January, Dusty was involved in a minor accident in the minicab that was taking her to the airport. She suffered no physical injuries; but, as Vic Billings explained, 'the incident shook her. She's had a hard time lately, virtually living in aeroplanes and dressing-rooms. She is pretty exhausted.'[26] She was ordered to rest for a week. It was a warning of worse to follow: as her career gathered momentum, and she pushed herself ever harder, with the daily pressure of simply *being* Dusty Springfield becoming increasingly intense, she suffered more such crises. Her mother was worried about her:

> It's only natural, I suppose, when a mother finds her daughter working in a world which is completely foreign to everything she has known. She often says to me: 'Mary, what's become of you?'[27]

Later in the year, she would suffer another, more serious breakdown. On tour in America, she collapsed backstage and was sent to recuperate in the West Indies.

> I live totally on my nerves. My mother always said I didn't have much stamina, and I've found out she was right. I wasn't ill. . . . I just became exhausted. Stupid things began to upset me. I would lose a pair of false eye lashes and go into a complete tantrum. It got so bad I didn't know what I was doing. I was no longer in control of anything. I was living in a complete dream. My voice didn't fail me – but when I gave a very bad performance one night I just went backstage and collapsed in a heap. . . .[28]

She was aware of the dangers – and of an obvious comparison, too.

I think of people like Judy Garland, with her bust-up of a life and her bust-up marriages, and I say to myself: '*You* might well end up like that.' It is frightening.

Soon others would be drawn to similarities between the two women, and George Melly would describe Dusty as 'the Judy Garland of the "in" set', but for the moment she was confident that everything was under control.

I don't see myself as a legend. I'm not the legendary type. You have to be a bit of a tragic figure to become a legend – like Judy Garland and Edith Piaf. I don't have that quality. I don't particularly want it – not if you've got to slash your wrists two or three times in your life to get it. That seems to be the rule. . . .

Her words were to prove horribly prophetic.[29]

Dusty's recording career was steadily gathering momentum; but, first, there was some unfinished business. January saw the release of the film *It's All Over Town*, in which the Springfields had made a brief appearance before they broke up; and the two songs they performed in the film were also released on record. 'If I Was Down And Out' is an impressive final flourish, with the group making an obvious move towards the tougher sound of the beat groups that had started to emerge in the previous year; but, turning the record over, we find 'Maracabamba', a piece of Mexican nonsense with Goonish touches that offers the last example of the way in which any musical progress the Springfields tried to make would be followed promptly by a return to the cute chirpiness with which they felt safe and comfortable. Confused to the end, the Springfields never really knew where they were going.

In the following month Dusty's second solo single, 'Stay Awhile', another song by Mike Hawker and Ivor Raymonde, was released. Driven by tumultuous percussion, sounding 'as though the Household Cavalry had just gone by', and with the backing singers, the

Breakaways, sounding like no British girl backing singers had ever sounded before, 'Stay Awhile' is Dusty's finest attempt to 'copy Phil Spector's sounds': 'I knew . . . there was going to be a space for that in this country . . . and I was the one to do it'.[30] The record confirms Dusty's confidence: released only three months after 'I Only Want To Be With You', it marks a definite development from that initial effort and demonstrates that Dusty had a very clear idea of where she wanted to go. Thirty-five years later, 'Stay Awhile' has lost none of its impact.

Once again, the B-side is one of Dusty's own compositions. 'Something Special' is actually a rather pedestrian early-sixties pop song; but, like 'Once Upon A Time', it is definitely not a Springfields number, and is yet further evidence that Dusty was now firmly committed to a new kind of music.

March brought Dusty's first solo EP, *I Only Want To Be With You*.* Together with a fresh outing for Dusty's first single, the selection included 'Twenty-Four Hours From Tulsa', a strangely popular Bacharach-and-David song which brought great success to Gene Pitney, as well as two solid but otherwise unremarkable numbers: 'He's Got Something' by Ian Samwell and Kenny Lynch, and 'Every Day I Have To Cry', an Arthur Alexander song that was recorded by several people but brought success to none of them. The record's sleeve-notes included a long questionnaire in which Dusty revealed, among many other things, that her favourite singers were the Shirelles – quite a few people's favourites at this time – her favourite composer was Richard Rodgers, her personal ambition was 'to be happy', and her professional ambition was 'to be an international star'.

She took a big step towards realising her professional ambition in April with the release of her first LP, *A Girl Called Dusty*. Most, if not all, of the tracks were recorded when Dusty was still with the

---

* *I Only Want To Be With You* (Philips EP, 1964: BE 12560): I Only Want To Be With You · He's Got Something · Twenty-Four Hours From Tulsa · Every Day I Have To Cry.

Tracks 2–4 are to be found on the 1997 reissue of *A Girl Called Dusty*, which also includes an alternative version of the title track.

Springfields. According to Johnny Franz, when Dusty chose to go solo 'I decided right away to make a lot of titles and release an LP'. At this time, when groups came to record their first LP they usually fell back on the songs they had been performing regularly in the clubs – this is what made it possible for the Beatles to record their first LP, *Please Please Me*, in a single day – but for Dusty, who had no solo career behind her, there was really no option but to cover other people's records that had taken her fancy. 'Even then she knew the kind of numbers she wanted to record. She had always been an avid disc collector. She really knew what was going on.'[31]*

'Mama Said' and 'Will You Love Me Tomorrow' were cover versions of Shirelles records. Four girls who began singing together at high school in the late fifties and went on to a professional career, the Shirelles were one of the most successful American groups of the early sixties, and their records were a rich source of material for many British artists – not least the Beatles, who covered two Shirelles numbers on their own first LP.

'You Don't Own Me' had been recorded by Lesley Gore in the previous year, and Dusty's version follows the original arrangement very closely. It is a powerful performance and perhaps deserving of more attention than it has received.

'My Colouring Book' is the outstanding performance in the collection and offers an early demonstration of one of Dusty's most distinctive talents: her ability to read a lyric and get to the heart of a song. (Working with Dusty many years later, Neil Tennant remembered her arriving at the studio with the lyric-sheet 'annotated and

---

* *A Girl Called Dusty* (Philips LP, 1964: mono BL 7594; stereo SBL 7594): Mama Said · You Don't Own Me · Do Re Mi · When The Lovelight Starts Shining Thru His Eyes · My Colouring Book · Mockingbird · Twenty-Four Hours From Tulsa · Nothing · Anyone Who Had A Heart · Will You Love Me Tomorrow · Wishin' And Hopin' · Don't You Know.

A Girl Called Dusty has been reissued twice on CD, in 1990 and in 1997. The earlier version offers a more faithful transcription of the original vinyl LP; unfortunately, like a well-meaning cleaner taking Vim to the family Rembrandt, the producers of the 1997 transcription nullified the effects Dusty was struggling so hard to produce and sapped all the vitality from the disc.

underlined'.) Written by John Kander and Fred Ebb, 'My Colouring Book' describes the progress of a love-affair in terms of different colours, and it would be easy to dismiss it as merely a novelty song; but the vulnerable quality in Dusty's voice – complemented by a beautifully understated arrangement by Ivor Raymonde – brings out the song's underlying sadness.

'Do Re Mi' and 'Mockingbird' are simply catchy novelty songs of the period that had evidently taken Dusty's fancy. 'Mockingbird', composed and first recorded by Charlie and Inez Foxx, offers Dusty the chance to sing a duet with herself, and adding the 'second voice' she seizes the opportunity to explore the black American influences she was beginning to absorb. She would later perform the song with Jimi Hendrix in a television performance of which only a tantalising fragment has survived.

'Nothing' is an example of the gutsy numbers that Dusty loved to sing and which she continued to record throughout her career. On 'Don't You Know', which is in the same vein and provides the Big Finish that was considered essential on LPs at this time, Dusty risks damage to her voice with a series of screeches and yelps, and no doubt required a lot of onion juice afterwards, but no British girl singer had ever sounded like this.

'Anyone Who Had A Heart' has earned a small place in the history of pop music because of the ill-feeling which it created in certain quarters and which lingers to this day. As with so much Bacharach-and-David material at the time, the song was recorded originally by Dionne Warwick, who hoped that it would provide her first big success in Britain. However, Cilla Black also recorded the song, her version was released first and was a great success, and Dionne was obliged to wait until her next record, 'Walk On By', before she was able to break into the British market.* But Dusty sneaked in and did a better job than either of them. She posed no commercial threat because

---

* It is possible that Dionne Warwick would have been denied British success a second time if Helen Shapiro's recording of 'Walk On By' had been released as a single.

her recording was not released as a single, but she had the range of vocal colouring that Dionne lacked; while Cilla could only handle the song's gathering intensity by producing an ugly Scouse squall.*

'Wishin' and Hopin' ', which is reputed to have been the first solo recording Dusty ever made, was also a cover of a Dionne Warwick record, but on this occasion she professed not to mind.[32]

With this first LP, Dusty established musical relationships that would endure for the rest of her career. Carole King and Gerry Goffin provided 'Do Re Mi' and 'Will You Love Me Tomorrow'; while from Burt Bacharach and Hal David she took 'Twenty-Four Hours From Tulsa', 'Anyone Who Had A Heart' and 'Wishin' And Hopin' '. She would return to these composers again and again, and become the finest performer of their work.[†]

To listen to *A Girl Called Dusty*, with its wide variations in sound-balance from one track to another, is to be made aware of the challenge faced by many British artists at this time as they struggled to reproduce, in British studios staffed by technicians accustomed to recording very different types of music, and with musicians used to working within the narrow constraints of a Norrie Paramor arrangement and the deadly harmonies of the Mike Sammes Singers, the sounds they had heard on American records. On one track, 'When the Lovelight Starts Shining Thru His Eyes', which is a

---

* In fact Dusty had discovered the song before Cilla: 'I heard Dionne Warwick singing "Anyone Who Had A Heart" in Paris. . . . I brought the disc home and played it over and over. I kept thinking: "It must be a hit. But is it too good?" I just didn't dare record it – in case it was a flop – and in the end I plumped for something safe, "Stay Awhile" ' (*News of the World*, 25 August 1964).

† Dusty was almost unique among sixties singers in not recording any songs by Lennon and McCartney. No doubt she felt they were not right for her. If so, her judgement was vindicated in the early seventies when, in the course of a guest appearance on a Burt Bacharach television show, she joined Burt, Juliet Prowse and Mireille Mathieu in a Lennon-and-McCartney medley. In an embarrassing mismatch of songs and singer, Dusty was lumbered with 'Come Together' and 'Let It Be', and the whole performance is best forgotten. Dusty's only obvious musical link with the Beatles is that she, too, recorded a cover version of the Miracles' 'You've Really Got A Hold On Me' – *fifteen years later*.

cover version of the record that had given the Supremes their first success, but which here owes more to Phil Spector's 'wall of sound', Dusty's voice is in danger of being swamped by the backing.

Human ingenuity often compensated for technical limitations, and Dusty found some interesting solutions:

> I wanted to get these sounds on very limited equipment, and one of the things that drove me crazy about recording in that particular place [the Philips recording studio at Marble Arch] was that it was so *dead.* I mean, you would sort of sing, and the sound would *stop.* . . . I like much more ambient sound and wilder sound, and so I used to record in the corridors mainly; there was some ambience to it. And the best place was the ladies' loo; that was great. . . . It really was the best sound in there; it was a little echoey, and there was no control over it, but it gave it that sound.

The 'ambient' sound of 'Some Of Your Lovin' ' was produced in these unusual surroundings; while Dusty sang 'I Close My Eyes And Count To Ten' at the end of the corridor – 'Much to the surprise of the cleaners one morning. About six . . . I heard all this clanking down the end of the corridor, and they were just standing there in their sort of print pinnies going "What's *she* doin', then?" ' The classic 'You Don't Have To Say You Love Me' was recorded in the stairwell, with Dusty standing halfway up it, singing into a microphone dangling in front of her.[33]

Her father's interest in radio, and her early performances at home with brother Tom, had encouraged Dusty to develop an interest in the *process* of recording her voice almost as soon as she had started to sing.

Peter Jones watched her at work in the early days: 'She simply knows what she wants, even if she can't explain it strictly in musical terms. She imitates musical instruments – energetically sizzling like cymbals, boom-booming like bass drums, tarrah-ing like whole brass sections.'[34] But the world is a hard place for perfectionists, and in her relentless pursuit of her ideal sound Dusty encountered considerable resistance from musicians who did not appreciate being told how to play by a young pop singer – and a woman at that.

> I was asking musicians to play sounds they'd never heard before. . . . Motown hadn't released any records in Britain but I'd heard them on tour in the States. I wanted to use those influences in a country where they were still playing stand-up bass and the only black music they knew about was jazz. So I would scowl a lot. They knew what I wanted but the last person they were going to take it from was a beehived bird.[35]

Session men were 'extremely nice individually, but rather Prussian together. They run in packs. They don't like you suggesting things about the music to them.'[36] Resentful musicians no doubt aired their grievances with colleagues in the pub, and Dusty quickly acquired a reputation for being 'difficult'; it stayed with her for the rest of her life. For the session musicians it was merely another job – they played the notes and collected their money – but for Dusty it was vitally important to get it right, 'because once it's recorded, you are stuck with it, you know'.[37]

> I was aware there was a wall of resistance on occasion. But I didn't realise what it was about, and I was far too busy to realise the resentments. I weeded out the ones I felt unspoken resistance from, and kept the ones I felt wanted to genuinely help me. . . .[38]

For Dusty, the issue was straightforward: 'I know when it sounds right and I know when it sounds wrong – and it's only when it sounds wrong that I make a fuss.' After all, 'I've got ears, you know. I've got really good ears – terrible eyes, great ears'.[39] But she did little to help her cause: 'I knew no tact. I mean, if it was wrong, I just used to go flying into the studio'; and on one occasion she was seen 'crashing into the orchestra pit like a smouldering tigress and pointing an accusing finger at a quaking musician'.[40]

Dusty liked to put her voice on last. 'I never thought of myself as a singer with an orchestra. I am part of the orchestra, part of the ensemble. I'm another instrument, and that's why I like "surround sound"; I like to be part of it':

> I bounce off what the musicians do. . . . If they play a great lick or if there's some emotion in the strings at a certain point, a colour I want to hear, then my voice will do things I didn't even think about. It reacts to emotional and symphonic qualities in things.

For Dusty, 'The putting together, the playing, the ideas that flow . . . that's joyous to me. It's probably hell for the musicians.'[41]

Her own preparations were meticulous. Her sheet music was always heavily annotated. As for the sheet music itself, 'It's always wrong'.[42] For Dusty, the score was merely the starting-point for musical negotiations – and she was a very tough negotiator. Through this process, for which Neil Tennant later coined the term 'dustification', she made a song so entirely her own that it can still come as quite a shock to discover that someone else had actually recorded it before her.

According to Brooks Arthur, who worked on the recording of Dusty's first LP, she had begun to explore microphone technique, too, 'making great sounds . . . by moving in and out on the mike and singing sideways. When she sang "You Don't Own Me" she moved her hands and head as if it was a stage show. She knew the science of recording.'[43]

This sensitive attention to detail seems all the more remarkable when we consider that Dusty demanded that the playback through her headphones be 'on the threshold of pain' – so loud that she could not possibly have heard herself singing. Jerry Wexler is surely not alone in finding it hard to understand 'how she stayed in tune, stayed in time, and also sang with Dusty Springfield's personality and created these marvellous vocals'.[44]

It should have become clear by now that Dusty was able to exercise far greater creative control over her recordings than any other British singer – male or female – at this time, yet it had to remain unacknowledged. All Dusty's recordings from this period bear only the name of Johnny Franz as producer; but, as she admitted later, 'I just said, "I don't really care about the kudos, I just want to get it right".'

Seventeen of them I gave over the credit to someone else. I did all the work, I did all the mixing, I did all the singing, I did all the backgrounds, I did all the working with the string arrangers. I did everything.[45]

And what was Johnny Franz doing while all this was going on? Dusty liked to paint a portrait of Johnny sitting quietly in a corner reading *Popular Mechanics* while she got on with the business of making the records – he 'knew that I knew what I was talking about and he knew he didn't', so he 'more or less used to let me do anything I wanted' – but this is hardly fair. It was a genuine partnership. Dusty had no formal training and could not read music; so, no matter how much she scowled and ranted, she still needed Johnny to give the musicians precise directions. 'He had perfect pitch, so he would say: "That should be a B not a B flat," which I couldn't do. I could only sing it. I'd have to take the chord apart, and that takes a very long time to explain to a musician.'[46]

The technical challenges continued on tour:

I just couldn't stand the fact that people couldn't hear, and I would spend half my time at sound-checks, for what they're worth, running around into the audience but never being able to explain it and being a troublemaker for even mentioning it. . . . But they would think they'd got it right. Never took into account that two thousand people would deaden it. But they never bothered to alter it once it was set at four o'clock in the afternoon.

Not surprisingly, 'I can't say "Those were the days!" because they were bloody awful'.

Yet Dusty's feelings of insecurity and her determination not to leave anything to chance could blind her to the goodwill and support around her. Fred Perry, who became the technical director for Dusty's stage shows, acknowledged that she was 'vulnerable, like an exposed nerve, which is why everyone bends over backwards to keep her happy. Sometimes she doesn't realise the loyalty she inspires'; while Stanley Dorfman, who directed her BBC television shows, concluded that 'Her big fault is lack of faith in all the technicians who work with her. She seems to think they're not going to bother when in fact everyone's knocking themselves out. She doesn't want to leave anything in anyone else's hands.'[47]

In May, Dusty flew to America to make her first appearance – after a small problem with her work permit – on *The Ed Sullivan Show*. Entirely devoid of any on-screen charisma, Ed Sullivan fluffed most of the lines he uttered, sometimes seemed unsure of the names of his guests, and conducted inept brief 'interviews' with singers after their performance, but his Sunday-evening show was an American institution and was to become an important showcase for pop music in the sixties – not least for British acts trying to establish themselves across the Atlantic. The show mingled pop singers with acrobats, jugglers and animal acts; and, although frequently narrow-minded in its outlook – Elvis Presley was shown only from the waist up, lest his gyrations excite impressionable American womanhood, and the Rolling Stones were obliged to rewrite the lyric of 'Let's Spend The Night Together' as a condition of their appearance – it gave equal consideration to both black and white artists.[48]

As if to confirm Dusty's growing reputation as an international singing star, in June she was invited back to her old school in Ealing to open a fête organised to raise funds for a new chapel.

Dusty's big hit that summer was Bacharach and David's 'I Just Don't Know What To Do With Myself'. According to Vic Billings, 'We did records two by two', and after two up-tempo hits Dusty was due for a ballad. Dusty felt that her voice 'certainly wasn't such a good marriage to Burt Bacharach's music as Dionne Warwick's was, but there were certain songs . . . that were totally right'. Beginning quietly, the song builds steadily into one of the dramatic chest-expanding ballads that will forever be associated with Dusty. 'My Colouring Book' was lifted from *A Girl Called Dusty* for the B-side.[49]

On 16 July, Dusty joined the Beatles and others on the first edition of *Top Gear*, BBC radio's new pop music programme. Her performance included a brave, if not entirely successful, attempt to sing 'The House Of The Rising Sun', with which the Animals were enjoying enormous success at the time. Dusty's interpretation had a distinctly 'country' flavour reminiscent of her days with the Springfields.

Yet the girl who had quickly become notorious for her relentless pursuit of perfection was also acquiring a reputation of a rather different kind. As we have seen, tensions within the O'Brien family often found release in what Dusty called 'slapstick' – principally, in spontaneous outbursts of food-throwing. When they left home, Tom and Dusty took the 'slapstick' to a wider audience; indeed, Dusty talked of it almost as if it were a family business, reporting airily: 'My brother Tom is a thrower, my mother just a bit, but not too much. And my father not at all.'[50] The practice really came into its own at the parties Dusty gave at her new flat in Baker Street.

At first the parties were no different from any others; but then 'Something would just go hurtling across the room' – a slice of cold meat aimed at the bare back of the Seekers' manager, perhaps, or a sardine lobbed into the cleavage of one of the Shangri-Las – and the 'second party' would begin, with food flying to and fro. Kim Weston, the Motown diva, made a grand entrance – 'Hi, honey!' – only to take a direct hit from a large portion of sauerkraut and find herself almost back in Baker Street again; while Gene Pitney was not too pleased when his new suit was covered in flour. Martha and the Vandellas sheltered in bewilderment behind the couch until they plucked up the courage to join the fray and 'came out swinging with these huge long French loaves'.[51]

No sides were taken, anyone was fair game, and sometimes Tom and Dusty did not even need a party as an excuse to indulge themselves:

> Once we threw the remains of a very badly made trifle onto Mike Hurst's E-type Jaguar. There was green gunge all over the windscreen. He laughed and got his windscreen wipers going trying to move the stuff off. But he didn't really think it was funny. Half way down the road, when he thought we couldn't see, he got out and started rubbing at the windscreen like a lunatic. He was rather cross.[52]

This was all very childish and harmless, but Dusty could find herself embarrassed when these private antics were repeated in public. On one occasion, at an awards ceremony in the restaurant at the top of the Post Office Tower, Dusty took exception to the manner in which the assistant manager, Stanley Drake, was treating one of the waiters. First, she threw a cheese roll at the back of his neck and then, as she bade him farewell, squashed some shrimp concoction into the palm of his hand. Mr Drake dismissed the incident with almost Jeevesian sang-froid – 'Miss Springfield is a charming person. I cannot tell how all this came about' – but with so many journalists present it was inevitable that the story would reach next morning's newspapers.[53]

There were practical jokes, too – arranging a babysitter for people who did not have a baby, ordering Chinese meals for unsuspecting friends, tipping bags of flour over Brian Poole and the Tremeloes just as they were about to go on stage, removing her brother's furniture from his flat while he was away on holiday – but all this was as nothing beside the crockery-smashing.

Breaking china had begun with the Springfields: 'We used to smash them by the dozen to relieve the boredom and pressure.'[54] According to Mike Hurst: 'She'd send out to Woollies when we were on tour, and she'd buy four sets of the cheapest china – full sets.' In Weymouth, at a civic reception to mark the end of a successful season, apparently at Tom's suggestion – Dusty always liked to blame others – they bought a gross of cheap cups and hurled them over the theatre balcony. 'The look on people's faces was better than pantomime.' On another occasion, when they happened to find themselves on the same bill as her old singing partners, Riss Chantelle and Lynne Abrams, Dusty stood in the wings and tossed a trayful of crockery into the air just as the girls began their next number. She put the blame on Mike Hurst, who was promptly ejected from the theatre![55]

When Dusty began her solo career she took the crockery-smashing habit with her. She liked to dismiss it as merely a form of relaxation – 'Some people smoke. Others drink. I do neither. I throw teacups'[56] – but it was clearly more than that. It had become an important emotional safety-valve: for the girl who could not allow herself to fail, and for whom only perfection was acceptable, the complete opposite – wanton destruction – provided a means of releasing the intolerable pressure that was building up inside her. 'I love to see things toppling over.'[57] According to Frank Allen, who witnessed some of these sessions, Dusty would 'spend as long as it took to either exhaust the supplies or purge her demons by hurling [china] at the walls of the corridor outside her dressing room. Anyone around would be invited to join in the orgy of destruction.'[58]

That such behaviour might have a darker side became evident when Dusty was invited to take part in the summer shows presented at Brooklyn's Fox Theater in New York by disc jockey Murray 'the K' Kaufman. When Beatlemania had hit America, Murray had unilaterally declared himself 'the fifth Beatle'; and, according to Dusty, he only booked her for his shows because he thought she was from Liverpool.[59] Lonely, friendless and a long way from home, as she sat in her dressing-room at the Fox, Dusty reverted to her usual method of relieving pent-up anxiety: she smashed crockery.

Now, this was hardly a spontaneous outpouring of emotion. Instead of grabbing the nearest thing to hand and throwing it at the wall – after all, as a well brought up young lady she could not possibly damage someone else's property – Dusty had gone to the trouble of seeking out cheap china, had locked herself in the dressing-room and begun steadily smashing all the crockery, piece by piece, against the wall. Alone in a theatre full of strangers, and too shy to introduce herself to anyone, she had chosen a favourite method of drawing attention to herself to make the others come to her.

And it worked. Knocking at her door was not an irate stage manager yelling at her to pull herself together and get on stage, but Martha Reeves, lead singer with Martha and the Vandellas, who had been dispatched by Murray the K to befriend Dusty, who was 'homesick and upset'. When Martha reached the dressing-room she could hear that 'Dusty was having this fit'. Eventually, Dusty agreed to open the door and let her in, and Martha saw that she had been crying; her makeup was a mess, 'with black streams of mascara running down both of her cheeks'. Asked what was going on, Dusty said, 'I'm having a party,' and continued to throw crockery at the wall. 'I'm bored and I'm lonely and I want to go home.' Slowly Martha won her confidence, and Dusty explained that in her family, 'when they felt anxiety they couldn't contain, they broke things until their feelings changed'.

Eventually Dusty grew calm, repaired her makeup, and 'her attitude brightened like clouds parting after a storm'. The two women became close friends. 'For the rest of the Brooklyn Fox engagement, she was just fine, and I had fun with my new friend.'[60]

The work-schedule was formidable. The Fox was actually a cinema, and the stage show would alternate with the films throughout the day, beginning at ten in the morning and finishing in the early hours of the following morning. Fortunately, even the top acts were required to sing no more than three songs, with most artists performing only one number before hurrying off one side of the stage as the next act came on at the other. And acting as ringmaster, controlling the whole musical circus, was Murray the K. According to Frank Allen, who went to the Fox as a member of the Searchers, Murray was a 'dyed-in-the-wool Sinatra-influenced fogey' with an 'appalling line in the kind of sweater that would embarrass even a golfer' and a silly Sinatra-inspired hat. As we have seen, such a generation-gap between presenters and performers was quite normal at this time, and as for the silly hat – well, when the Motown Revue arrived in London early in 1965 many of the male members of the party were wearing one.[61]

Dusty found the early-morning shows difficult, but there was one great compensation. One of the Vandellas would usually have over-slept, so Dusty was drafted into the group as an honorary Vandella when they were the offstage backing singers for Marvin Gaye, and that was 'the biggest thrill of my life'.[62]

As for their working environment, Frank Allen remembers 'a hell hole that would have been enforceably closed by the health depart-ment had it been the workplace of any other profession than the music fraternity'. With the tiny dressing-rooms 'crammed to burst-ing point with human flesh and with all the smells that go with it' – including 'the herbal smells that accompanied the more private pastimes' of the musicians – it was 'reminiscent of a third world sweatshop'.[63] Dusty shared a dressing-room with the Ronettes – 'an extraordinary experience'. It was very hot, 'and all our beehives were in there – three black beehives and one white one. It was collisions constantly.' Next door were Martha and the Vandellas on one side and the Supremes on the other. 'I remember Mary Wilson [of the Supremes] always reading Latin books, and Diana Ross's mum helped me turn up my hems because I was always buying things that were too long.'[64]

Conditions on stage, too, were far from ideal, and Dusty did not enjoy performing there. The sound system was fairly unsophisticated, using only the cinema speakers; and, because the members of the Earl Warren Orchestra were crammed into any available space back-stage, there was a time-lag: 'the drummer appeared to you to be half a beat behind because he was so far back in the bowels of the Brooklyn Fox'. But none of this mattered in the end. 'I was just in awe.' Dusty wanted nothing more than to be able to stand in the wings and absorb all these exciting new musical influences. 'It was a dream come true. It was priceless. I would've *paid* to do it.' After all, 'what could be more stimulating than listening to the brass arrangements of the Temptations from the side of the stage? That was heaven for me.'[65] With all this new music overwhelming her, Dusty was almost spoilt for choice, 'But I'd copy them all; one day I woke up wanting to be Dionne Warwick, the next day the Ronettes. It took some time to find my own style – which came with the ballads. . . .'[66]

We should not be surprised to learn that all the tensions and anxieties of this new experience brought on Dusty's laryngitis; but on this occasion she was offered a new cure. Alcohol. According to her own accounts, she was offered a plastic cup of vodka by the Temptations:

> And of course it was 88 per cent proof, because that's what those boys liked. It never occurred to me to sip it. I drank it down, gagged a few times, and five minutes later I went, *Yes* – this is the answer to life. I was no longer shy; I was no longer afraid; fuck the Brooklyn Fox – I can deal with it all.[67]*

Obviously, anyone who comes to rely on vodka to help them through life's trickier moments has a problem, but at what point vodka replaced hot chocolate in Dusty's life remains unclear. Dusty's secretary, Pat Rhodes, is emphatic that Dusty 'never drank, never smoked when we were on tour in the sixties. . . . People used to send bottles of champagne backstage and we quietly used to give them away. It seemed a shame to waste them.'[68] Despite a throwaway reference to 'that time I was smashed but still had to go on and do *Thank Your Lucky Stars*', it is unlikely that Dusty's drinking was out of control in the sixties; while she may have taken a drink to steady her nerves, and may occasionally have taken too much, her career was at its most intense, and only towards the end of the decade was she beset by anxiety about the future.[69]

As her love-affair with America deepened, Dusty even took her parents across the Atlantic to share the experience. Her mother had never been on a plane before, but 'We filled her full of brandy and

---

* In her autobiography (p. 116), Martha Reeves takes upon herself the guilt for having introduced Dusty to serious drinking, but she is being unfair to herself: in her own recollections Dusty never mentions Martha at all.

she was fine!'[70] Her visits to America had also become important buying trips. 'I just swiped anything I heard from the States that wasn't going to be released here. That's the truth of it.'[71] She had already fallen in love with the work of Gerry Goffin and Carole King – 'I knew that if Carole King wrote it I was going to be able to sing it right'[72] – while Burt Bacharach and Hal David's 'Wishin' And Hopin' ' had been a great success for her in America in the summer and had brought her to the attention of the song's composers. If 'Wishin' And Hopin' ' was indeed the very first song that Dusty recorded as a solo artist, then her choice could not have been more fortunate. It marked the beginning of a rich musical relationship. Hal David recalled hearing the record on his car radio one evening:

> I didn't even know who she was, and I called the disc jockey when I got home, and he said, 'That's Dusty Springfield.' And I was just bowled over by her, and she did so many of our songs. I think she's one of the great interpreters of our material or of anyone's material.[73]

The admiration was mutual. For Dusty, a Bacharach-and-David song 'didn't do what you expected it to. I'd never heard anything like it before, and that was its charm and its impact.' The songs were 'gossamer'; Burt Bacharach 'was using time signatures no one had used in pop music. . . . I thought I'd died and gone to heaven! . . . I knew I hadn't heard that before.'[74]

There were other important discoveries, too. In America, Dusty heard recordings by black artists who were completely unknown in Britain: Maxine Brown, Mitty Collier, Jimmy Radcliffe and, most significantly, Justine 'Baby' Washington, whom Dusty once nominated as her favourite singer.

All these musical influences would blend for the first time on her next LP, *Ev'rything's Coming Up Dusty*.

Meanwhile, back home, September brought Dusty's second EP, called simply *Dusty*. On her cover version of Marvin Gaye's 'Can I Get A Witness', Dusty pushes her voice to the limit as she tries to do the work of an entire gospel choir; while 'All Cried Out' is yet another of the powerful performances we had already come to expect from her. 'I Wish I'd Never Loved You', a soulful ballad by Mike Hawker and Ivor Raymonde, falls beautifully for Dusty's voice and is the outstanding track in the collection.*

During this hectic year Dusty also acquired a backing group. The Echoes had been together since 1958, although there were several changes in the line-up. Finding a drummer seemed to present particular difficulties. Ringo Starr was with the band for a while, as was the aptly named Bob Wackett – surely a man born to be a drummer in a pop group! The Echoes backed visiting American artists such as Gene Vincent, Eddie Cochran, Jerry Lee Lewis and Freddy Cannon, and also British artists including Susan Maugham, Matt Monro and the Mudlarks (arch-rivals of the Lana Sisters). By 1964, however, the work had dried up, and there was no immediate prospect of any more on the way. Then Doug Reece, founder member and bass guitarist, heard from his mother that Dusty was looking for a backing group. Auditions were held at the Granada cinema, Kennington, and the Echoes succeeded against a lot of opposition.

They would stay with Dusty for seven years – although at least one person failed to appreciate their contribution. When Dusty appeared in *Merry King Cole* at the Empire Theatre, Liverpool, in December 1966, the theatre critic of the *Liverpool Echo* was irritated by the 'guitar and brass barrage' of this 'large and heavily over-amplified backing group' as first Paul and Barry Ryan and then Dusty were 'drowned out by the ironically named "Echoes" '. (As the show also included a 'foam and water slapstick routine' and a 'crazy xylophone act', it would appear that the Echoes drowned out the wrong artists.)

The Echoes also released eight records of their own; and Dusty may be heard, along with Madeline Bell and Lesley Duncan, as a

---

* *Dusty* (Philips EP, 1964: 12564): Can I Get A Witness · All Cried Out · Wishin' And Hopin' · I Wish I'd Never Loved You.

All four tracks were included on the 1997 reissue of *A Girl Called Dusty*; but the American transcriptions on *Dusty* (Mercury CD, 1999: 314 538 909-2) are to be preferred.

backing singer on two of them: 'Got To Run' (1966) and 'Searching For You Baby' (1968). On 'Got To Run' Dusty also contributed to the percussion, playing tambourine and ashtray![75]*

Dusty's next single, 'Losing You', released in October and another ballad, marked her first association with composer Clive Westlake, who wrote the song in partnership with her brother Tom, whose own talent as a songwriter had blossomed since the demise of the Springfields. The song has a pleasant lilt and builds to a powerful chorus. Dusty's readiness to push herself to the limit to achieve the performance she was seeking is made apparent in the final fade where her voice is clearly tiring and starting to break up.

The B-side, 'Summer Is Over', another fine ballad by Tom and Clive, was also a success for Frank Ifield in the same month.

In November, Dusty released her only solo Christmas record. 'O Holy Child' is a pleasant approximation to a Christmas carol, and was written by her brother Tom in collaboration with Peppi Borza, an American dancer who had settled in Britain and become a close friend of both Tom and Dusty.[76] 'O Holy Child' was coupled with an old recording of 'Jingle Bells' by the Springfields.† Although it was issued to raise money for Dr Barnardo's London Centenary Fund, Dusty can only have regarded the disc as an unwanted diversion in her musical progress – especially if she was aware of Phil Spector's thundering classic of the previous year, *A Christmas Gift for You*, which was probably the kind of Christmas record she would rather have made.

Dusty could look back on a remarkable first year as a solo artist; but her career was about to receive its first serious jolt.

---

* The Echoes are to be heard on twelve of Dusty's recordings: 'Can I Get A Witness', 'In The Middle Of Nowhere', 'It Won't Be Long', 'La Bamba', 'If It Don't Work Out', 'I Can't Hear You No More', 'Packin' Up', 'Little By Little', 'Every Ounce Of Strength' (on which perhaps they are heard to best advantage), 'Go Ahead On', 'Take Me For A Little While' and 'Needle In A Haystack'.

† 'O Holy Child' and 'Jingle Bells' have been reissued on the privately produced CD, *We Wish You a Merry Christmas*. See Appendix.

4

South Africa

'SOUTH AFRICA was a real muddle. I suppose I had ideals, but I was also politically very naïve. . . . I didn't do an ounce of good; but I didn't really go there to do good – I went there to sing.'[1] Naïve or not, Dusty surely cannot have believed that her tour of South Africa in December 1964 could ever be so uncomplicated. The South African doctrine of apartheid, and the oppression of the black population by the white minority in that country, was one of the most emotive and divisive issues of the decade. The Sharpeville massacre of March 1960, when South African police had opened fire on unarmed demonstrators, killing fifty-six and wounding many others, their commanding officer declaring that the blacks 'must learn their lesson the hard way', was still a recent memory. South Africa had withdrawn from the Commonwealth in 1962 and was well on the way to becoming an international outcast – which in turn raised the question of whether other nations, companies or even individuals should continue to have any contact with that country, giving tacit support to injustice and inhumanity. The debate would rumble on, at varying levels of intensity, for more than thirty years.

Entertainers found themselves in the front line. In South Africa at least, show business had now become a political issue.

The old guard had their own answer to the problem. They ignored it. They flew into South Africa, told their jokes or sang their songs or gave their performances of *Rookery Nook* in comfortable whites-only clubs and theatres – no doubt finding time along the way for a little sunbathing to darken the skin – collected their money and flew home

again. After all, there was always that neat formula, 'I'm an enter-
tainer, not a politician', to fall back on; and, anyway, life must look
rather different from inside the Garrick Club.*

However, for the younger generation – and especially for a singer
like Dusty, who identified strongly with black music and the experience from which it had emerged – South Africa *was* an issue, and
when Dusty eventually agreed to undertake a short tour she did so
only after she had obtained a written assurance that she would be
playing to mixed audiences. And she made it quite clear that she
expected the South Africans to honour the contract: 'If they try to
alter the agreement, I shall be home on the next plane,' she announced at Heathrow as she prepared to leave.

Hendrik Vervoerd, the principal architect of apartheid, had declared that the doctrine was 'relevant to every sphere of life'. Not
only were blacks not allowed to live in the same streets as whites; they
were also forbidden to sit under the same roof and watch the same
show as a white audience. With one exception. Dennis Wainer, the
Jewish lawyer who arranged Dusty's tour, discovered a loophole in
the law. Mixed audiences were still permitted in cinemas that also
offered live entertainment – though even 'mixed audience' meant no
more than that blacks and whites were under the same roof, sitting in
separate blocks of seats. The authorities were apparently unaware of
this anomaly, so Wainer chose the venues carefully, and – naïvely
perhaps – believing that everything had been arranged within the
law, and that the terms of her contract would be honoured, Dusty
and her party left London.

Their troubles began almost as soon as they arrived in South
Africa. The authorities may have been ignorant of the legal loophole when Dusty's tour was first arranged, but they were well aware

---

* At this time, of course, the pop music industry had yet to establish an individual
identity; it was still part of old-style show business, and there were inevitably some
cultural clashes along the way. When the Rolling Stones appeared on *Sunday Night at the London Palladium*, their refusal to join the other artists on the
revolving stage at the end of the show and wave stupidly at the audience as
they travelled round was greeted by some elements of the press and of
mainstream show business as the greatest national humiliation since Suez.

of it now and were intent on closing it. According to Dusty's manager, Vic Billings, officials from the Ministry of the Interior presented them with an ultimatum, which everyone in the party was expected to sign, 'to the effect that we would not perform before mixed-race audiences. Needless to say, we did not sign. It would have been a breach of contract.'[2] Thereafter they were followed everywhere by men from the ministry. Even in the unlikely event that Dusty herself had been prepared to compromise, it would still have been impossible to continue the tour on those terms: while Dusty was a member of both Actors' Equity and the Variety Artistes' Federation, which were still dithering on the question of South Africa, her backing group, the Echoes, belonged to the Musicians' Union, which was unequivocally opposed to its members playing to segregated audiences.

The first four shows were performed before mixed audiences and went off without incident. During the fifth concert, at the Luxurama cinema in the Wynberg district of Cape Town, ministry officials walked around the auditorium as Dusty sang, observing the mixed-race audience. When she returned to her hotel after the show, she was served with a written notice to leave the country within twenty-four hours.

Back in London her agent, Tito Burns, fielded questions from the press and defended Dusty's actions. 'We made it absolutely plain that Dusty would not tolerate being made to sing to segregated audiences,' he insisted, adding: 'She has pretty strong feelings about this colour business.' Later he even disclosed that Dusty had not wanted to go to South Africa in the first place: 'It took me six months to persuade her.' Brother Tom pointed out that 'Dusty is the sort of girl who will stick up for what she thinks is right'; while her mother, speaking from her home in Hove, had other concerns: 'I have been a bit worried with all the trouble there is in South Africa that someone might take a pot at her.'[3]

But the party returned safely to Heathrow on 18 December. For Dusty there had been one small consolation: as she had boarded the plane in Cape Town the black airline workers had raised their hats. 'I thought oh, you did notice, even though I fucked it up.'[4]

She later donated her £2000 fee to a charity for coloured orphans.

At Westminster fifteen MPs signed a Commons motion supporting Dusty's stand against 'the obnoxious doctrine of apartheid in South Africa'. South Africa's Ministry of the Interior responded by issuing a statement asserting that Dusty was 'not being deported as stated in the press'; in fact she was 'leaving the country because the validity of her permit expires today'.

> She was on two occasions warned through her manager to observe our South African way of life in regard to entertainment and was informed that if she failed to do so, she would have to leave the country. She chose to defy the Government, and she was accordingly allowed to remain in the country for a limited time only.[5]

Dusty's records were banned from South African radio. Even South African promoters criticised her, claiming that she was merely trying to create publicity ahead of her forthcoming trip to America: 'the singer who defied the South African government is likely to go down well in some places there'.[6] Dusty pointed out that she had already been to America four times and did not need this kind of publicity.

The incident was even raised in Cabinet. Harold Wilson, who revealed himself as a Dusty Springfield fan, asked the Foreign Office: 'Are we protesting?' The Foreign Office position was that 'Miss Springfield was not arrested and on a strictly legal view the South Africans appear to have acted within their rights'.[7]

Early in the new year Adam Faith, too, embarked on a tour of South Africa. His attempts to play only to unsegregated audiences failed, and he cancelled the rest of the tour.

For the Foreign Office this was all too tiresome. Such situations were bound to arise 'if artists embark on foreign tours without first ensuring that the arrangements comply both to the requirements of local law and custom'; Dusty and Adam 'got into trouble as a result of statements published in the press which made an issue of apartheid'. The circumstances did 'not provide grounds for government intervention on their behalf'.[8]

That seemed to be the end of the matter, but in fact it was not quite over. The following April, Dusty was confronted by the full moral and intellectual authority of Actors' Equity at their annual general meeting. The luvvies were not pleased. Dusty's principal accuser was Derek Nimmo, who insisted that she had brought the trouble on herself by her 'foolish and irresponsible behaviour' and her 'ill-considered action', making it difficult for other performers – such as Nimmo himself – to work in South Africa. Marius Goring tried to cast himself in the role of peacemaker; with all the glorious pomposity of an old ham, he declared: 'We are all servants of the public, both black and white.'[9]

This betrayal by fellow professionals seems to have irked Dusty far more than had the behaviour of the South African authorities. Her resentment rankled for years, and when Derek Nimmo's name was mentioned in an interview *twenty-five years later* she reacted as if stung: 'What a prat! Is he still alive? Well, he's still a prat, I would say it to his face.'[10]*

Nevertheless, if the great and the good of Equity had hoped that Dusty would suffer some awful divine retribution for her unsporting behaviour in South Africa, they were to be disappointed. She was about to embark on the most intensely creative period of her career. Over the next four years she would produce a body of work that would not only put beyond doubt her pre-eminence among British singers but also place her among the very best in the world.

* By a curious quirk of fate, Derek Nimmo died only a few days before Dusty. We must pray that they are reconciled and both playing to mixed audiences in heaven.

5

Everything's Coming Up Dusty

IN JANUARY 1965, Dusty joined Anita Harris, Petula Clark and Kiki Dee to represent Britain at the San Remo Song Festival. Dionne Warwick and Connie Francis provided a strong American presence that year. Dusty was to sing two songs, 'Di Fronte All' Amore' ('Face To Face With Love') and 'Tu Che Ne Sai' ('What Do You Know About Love'), but throat problems – induced, no doubt, by anxiety about the big occasion – and some difficulty learning the words of the songs robbed the event of any pleasure for her. Despite staying up most of the night in a last desperate effort to master 'Di Fronte All' Amore', Dusty had to take the sheet music on stage with her. Well aware that she had given less than her best, at the end of the performance she flung the music to the floor and walked off. She had to repeat the experience the following day with her second song.*

At this point she might have written off the event as something best forgotten but, listening to some other performances, one particular Italian song caught her attention. She was not alone: when the singer reached the middle eight the audience rose to applaud. Dusty managed to acquire a recording of the song, 'Io Che Non Vivo . . . Senza Te', and brought it back to London. 'Praying that no one else would do it', she hid the record under the couch. It would remain there for almost a year.[1]

* Dusty recorded an English version of 'Di Fronte All' Amore', with the title 'I Will Always Want You', but it was not released until 1996 when it appeared on *Something Special*, together with recordings of the two original Italian songs. See Appendix.

In February, Dusty's record company gave her four tickets for the carnival in Rio de Janeiro. She invited her brother Tom, with whom she had shared a passion for Latin American music since their early folk-singing days, together with Martha Reeves ('Do you *really* want to see people dancing in the street?') and Madeline Bell. Madeline had come to London from America in 1962 as a member of the cast of *Black Nativity*, a gospel show, and had decided to stay. Dusty had seen the show – 'I was thrilled. I thought it was fantastic' – but the two women first met at a *Ready Steady Go!* party. Madeline was to become an important element in Dusty's recording career.

Martha Reeves recalls the non-stop music. 'Up and down the strip there was one band after another. Conga rhythms were heard each time they came and danced by, everybody joining in the parade of colorfully dressed natives and tourists with the same festive spirit.' They had their photograph taken on Corcovado, Martha wearing gold lamé pants and Dusty with her beehive wrapped in a scarf to prevent the wind from sending it 'flying down to Rio'. For Dusty, 'It was like everybody suddenly turned to music; you know, yesterday's bus conductor would turn out to be a brilliant drummer. It was so free and relaxed.' She was 'incredibly high on the music', and stayed up dancing for three days and nights. 'It was great until I was dancing in bare feet and I trod on a broken bottle, and that was the end of my trip to Rio'; but 'there is nothing will make me get crazier or dance more than hearing a samba band. . . . It's unlike anything else. Nothing else like it in the world.'[2]

February also saw the release of Dusty's new single, 'Your Hurtin' Kinda Love', which was another song by Mike Hawker and Ivor Raymonde, although it sounds rather laboured and lacks the spark of earlier records. But 'Don't Say It Baby', written by Ted Daryll and Chip Taylor, provided Dusty with another of those delightful B-sides that are easily overlooked.

Dusty's growing commitment to work on the other side of the Atlantic was highlighted in April by the release of *Dusty in New York*. Recorded under the musical supervision of singer Ray Stevens the previous summer, the new EP offered four strong performances that could only serve to consolidate Dusty's position as the White Queen of Soul.*

But the spring of 1965 was dominated for Dusty – and, indeed, for Vicki Wickham, producer of *Ready Steady Go!* – by Motown. Right from the very beginning, when she had actually presented some of the shows, Dusty had become a regular guest on *Ready Steady Go!*, and she and Vicki were now close friends. When Dusty discovered – and was overwhelmed by – the new black music in America, she talked about it constantly, and she quickly managed to communicate her enthusiasm to Vicki, who acknowledges that 'If it hadn't been for Dusty, I would not have known about Motown, Stax, Atlantic'. Vicki proposed a *Ready Steady Go!* Motown special, presented by Dusty, as a showcase for this new music that was as yet virtually unknown in Britain. But things were happening on the other side of the Atlantic, too. Berry Gordy, the founder of the Motown label, was putting together a Motown Revue tour of Britain for March and April, and the television show became a focal point for this American 'invasion' by the Supremes, Martha and the Vandellas, Stevie Wonder, Smokey Robinson and the Miracles, and the Temptations. The show was transmitted on 21 April. Internal rivalries within the Motown stable were becoming apparent, with Berry Gordy seeming to favour the Supremes above the others; but Martha Reeves was Dusty's particular friend, and she was invited to join Dusty on a performance of 'Wishin' And Hopin' '. As they sang, Martha could see Diana Ross in the wings 'eating her heart out because she hadn't been chosen to do it'. This preferential treatment did not go unnoticed: according to Mary Wilson of the Supremes, Dusty and the crew 'treated each one of us like a star, but it was also clear that Martha and the Vandellas were their favourites'. Martha Reeves is in no doubt that what the show did for Motown in Britain 'was comparable to what the Beatles' appearance on *Ed Sullivan* had done for

* *Dusty in New York* (Philips EP, 1965: BE 12572): Live It Up · I Want Your Love Tonight · I Wanna Make You Happy · Now That You're My Baby.
    All four recordings were included as additional tracks on the 1998 reissue of *Ev'rything's Coming Up Dusty*.

them in America a year earlier'. 'I suppose my enthusiasm for it helped push it,' Dusty reflected matter-of-factly.[3]

Perhaps all the excitement had taken its toll, or perhaps Dusty was simply beginning to rebel against the annual ritual of 'summer season', which she loathed, but at the end of May she obtained written confirmation from a Harley Street specialist that she was too ill to open in her summer show in Bournemouth. Cleo Laine deputised for two weeks.

Presumably Dusty recovered sufficiently to promote her new single, 'In The Middle Of Nowhere', written by Bea Verdi and Buddy Kaye, which was released in June. On this record Dusty worked for the first time with her friend Madeline Bell, together with singer and songwriter Lesley Duncan; they would be her backing singers for the remainder of the decade. On this occasion they were also joined by Doris Troy. Dusty had apparently been dissatisfied with the backing singers she had and had rung Madeline to ask if she would help. The presence of these new voices may account for the remarkable energy and exuberance of the record. The magic was carried over on to the B-side, 'Baby Don't You Know', from the same composers.

Dusty herself began to develop a career as a backing singer and worked under the Goonish name of Gladys Thong.

It all started when I made some demo records for Doris Troy when she was here and then I started to sing on Madeline Bell, Lesley Duncan and Kiki Dee's records. I don't see why I shouldn't. They sing on mine and we're all friends.

According to Madeline Bell, the best part was when 'they would come and hand her her six guineas in an envelope at the end of the session. She'd be going "Wow! and I even get paid!" '[4]

July brought a curiosity for the Dusty Springfield catalogue in the form of *Mademoiselle Dusty*, an EP containing French versions of 'Will You Love Me Tomorrow', 'Summer Is Over', 'Losing You' and 'Stay Awhile', with vocal backing by the Breakaways. Dusty had already proved that she was an accomplished singer in any number of foreign tongues – even if it was a matter of mimicry rather than of any genuine grasp of the language itself – but this kind of recording would soon be consigned to history as English became the international language of pop music.*

In August the pressure began to tell on Dusty once again, and she cancelled all engagements and flew to the Virgin Islands for a complete rest; but she was required to be back on duty in September for the release of her next single, 'Some Of Your Lovin' ', a Goffin-and-King song. This was Dusty's own favourite recording, principally on account of the 'ambient' sound she had achieved, and she accorded it the rare honour of playing the disc as soon as she received it – instead of putting it to one side for a while before venturing to listen to it.[5]

The B-side, 'I'll Love You For A While', another attractive song by Goffin and King, had originally been recorded by Jill Jackson, who became better-known as the 'Paula' of heartrending 'Paul and Paula' fame.

And then, in the same month, came Dusty's eagerly awaited second LP. Her record company spared no expense, and the sleeve of *Ev'rything's Coming Up Dusty* incorporated a large-format illustrated book. The packaging of *Sergeant Pepper's Lonely Hearts Club Band* (1967) may have taken its place in the history of twentieth-century art, but *Ev'rything's Coming Up Dusty* can still seem more satisfying and more

---

* *Mademoiselle Dusty* (Philips EP, 1965: BE 12579): Demain Tu Peux Changer · L'Été Est Fini · Je Ne Peux Pas T'En Vouloir · Reste Encore Un Instant.

Tracks 1 and 2 were included in the limited edition *Dusty: The Legend of Dusty Springfield* (1994); while tracks 3 and 4 were reissued on *Something Special* (1996). See Appendix.

Dusty made Italian versions of 'Every Day I Have To Cry' and 'Wishin' And Hopin' ', and she also recorded the latter song in German together with 'I Only Want To Be With You'. The Springfields had recorded no fewer than four songs in German – 'Settle Down', 'Island Of Dreams', 'Silver Threads And Golden Needles' and 'Where Have All The Flowers Gone' – and it would appear that the German market was still resisting a British invasion: even the Beatles were obliged to record – very much under protest – German versions of 'I Want To Hold Your Hand' and 'She Loves You'.

mature than its more celebrated successor. The record itself more than justifies this extravagance.*

The lively opening track, 'Won't Be Long', suggests that this new LP is taking over where *A Girl Called Dusty* left off, but it quickly becomes apparent that *Ev'rything's Coming Up Dusty* represents substantial progress – both musically and technically. In this collection all the major musical influences on Dusty's career so far – musical theatre, jazz, folk-song and soul – blend for the first time into a polished performance that confirms the promise of the first LP and puts beyond doubt Dusty's pre-eminence among British girl singers. No one else even comes close.

'Oh No! Not My Baby', written by Gerry Goffin and Carole King, is an attractive song and had created a lot of interest – although Dusty, of course, had discovered the song in America when she heard the original recording by Maxine Brown. Manfred Mann had enjoyed some success in Britain earlier in the year with a rather ragged version, and not even the usually reliable Shirelles were quite able to get to grips with the song. Impelled by gentle timpani and a rolling piano figure, Dusty's performance is assured and purposeful.

'Long After Tonight Is All Over' is a Bacharach-and-David song first recorded by Jimmy Radcliffe. The relaxed – and rather cute – opening soon develops into something more powerful.

* *Ev'rything's Coming Up Dusty* (Philips LP, 1965: mono RBL 1002; stereo SRBL 1002): Won't Be Long · Oh No! Not My Baby · Long After Tonight Is All Over · La Bamba · Who Can I Turn To (When Nobody Needs Me) · Doodlin' · If It Don't Work Out · That's How Heartaches Are Made · It Was Easier To Hurt Him · I've Been Wrong Before · I Can't Hear You · I Had A Talk With My Man · Packin' Up.

Ev'rything's Coming Up Dusty has been reissued once on vinyl (1990) and twice on CD (1990 and 1998). All three versions made a creditable attempt to reproduce the lavish presentation, but none matched the original.

When Philips launched tape cassettes in Britain in October 1966, *Ev'rything's Coming Up Dusty* was among the very first titles.

'Needle In A Haystack', originally a success for the Velvelettes, was also recorded by Dusty for the LP, but not actually released until 1996 when it was included on *Something Special*. See Appendix.

'La Bamba', a Mexican folk-song dating from the early years of the century, seems almost to be a piece of unfinished business from Dusty's days with the Springfields, but it justifies her defiant assertion that she could sing better on her own.* In complete contrast, 'Who Can I Turn To (When Nobody Needs Me)?' was a brand-new song by Leslie Bricusse and Anthony Newley from their show *The Roar of the Greasepaint, the Smell of the Crowd.*

Although Dusty's own interest in 'Doodlin' ' was probably first aroused by the Baby Washington recording, the song has its origins in 'vocalese' – a term coined by jazz critic Leonard Feather for 'the practice of jazz singing in which texts (newly invented) are set to recorded jazz improvisations'.[6] Perhaps more a phenomenon than a musical genre, vocalese reached its peak in New York in the late 1950s, but it continued to enjoy a life of sorts – particularly with groups such as Manhattan Transfer and the Swingle Singers – though it reached its nadir in 1973, when the use of Scott Joplin's music in the popular film *The Sting* managed to convince quite a few people that they possessed a talent for it, with unfortunate consequences. The foremost exponent of the art of vocalese is John Hendricks, described by *Time* magazine as 'the James Joyce of jive', and with 'Doodlin' ' he set words to Horace Silver's music.

> 'Doodlin' ' tells about the dubious bona fides of psychiatry as a form of healing people. You see, I don't believe psychiatry has ever cured anybody, so I constructed this little story. . . . It's really an exposé of psychiatry from a comical standpoint.[7]†

* Dusty's lingering interest in folk music may also be detected in her 'folksy-spiritual' recording, 'Standing In The Need Of Love' – a performance which seems to hark back to the self-conscious heartiness of skiffle and '6.5 Special'. The recording was eventually released in 1999 as an additional track on the reissue of an American LP, *Stay Awhile/I Only Want To Be With You.* See Appendix.

† In his own recording of 'Doodlin' ', Mark Murphy, who is a leading composer and performer of vocalese, and who appeared as a guest on one of Dusty's television shows, underlines the satire at one point by slipping into the guise of a Viennese psychoanalyst.

Dusty transforms this little piece of jazz whimsy into a solid piece of rhythm and blues, and gives one of the strongest performances in the collection. The influence of Baby Washington may be heard again later on 'That's How Heartaches Are Made'.

'If It Don't Work Out' was written by Rod Argent, the keyboard player with the Zombies, a group Dusty admired. Dusty makes the song sound more interesting than perhaps it is.

'It Was Easier To Hurt Him' is one of the big performances from Dusty that we were by now coming to take for granted, although this is one of the less impressive.

Although Dusty's musical relationships with Gerry Goffin and Carole King, and with Burt Bacharach and Hal David, are well known, her close association with the work of Randy Newman is easily overlooked. Newman is a remarkable writer whose talent ranges from blatantly commercial songs like 'Simon Smith And The Amazing Dancing Bear' to works that are so introspective and idiosyncratic that only the composer can sing them. 'I've Been Wrong Before' has a characteristically subtle and elusive melody, but Dusty has no problem in holding on to it.

'I Can't Hear You', another Goffin-and-King song, was first recorded by Betty Everett. Dusty gives a stronger performance, but her recording suffers from the lack of the feebly apologetic male refrain on the original version.

'I Had A Talk With My Man' is the outstanding track in the collection and a landmark in Dusty's career. A cover version of a recording by Mitty Collier, this haunting performance is the White Queen of Soul at her most intense, and demonstrates that Dusty had absorbed everything she had learned from the black American singers she admired so much and was now worthy to take her place alongside them. She confessed that she was 'thrilled when people tell me I sound coloured'; she had 'a definite and deep affinity with black musicians', but 'As long as I go on singing it will be only imitation. With them it's natural'. Nevertheless, 'I did actually sort of sound really daring for a white singer'.[8]

'Packin' Up' is more a burst of energy than a song but it provides a lively conclusion to the disc; Dusty used the number several times to close her television shows.

Sounding as fresh today as when it was first issued, *Ev'rything's Coming Up Dusty* is one of the outstanding collections of the decade.

In December 1965, Dusty found herself in the headlines for all the wrong reasons when she was brought to account for an error of judgement that could so easily have proved disastrous.

One rainy evening, while driving her expensive new sports-car – presumably the '130-mile-an-hour monster which I wanted more than anything in the world' – round Berkeley Square, she had struck a woman who was crossing the road.[9] Ida Judith Metzger, the 63-year-old owner of a Mayfair boutique, told the court: 'The car door was flung open and the driver dashed out and came over to me and flung herself over my face and said, "It was not your fault." I saw she wore dark glasses, was very pretty and very hysterical.' When the ambulance arrived for Miss Metzger, Dusty was taken to hospital, too, 'because she was so hysterical'.

Miss Metzger pursued a civil action for damages, and in court Dusty was ordered to pay £1900 and costs. Delivering his judgement, Mr Justice Phillimore said:

> I have no doubt that Miss Springfield was driving much too fast and I don't suppose her ability to keep a proper look-out was enhanced by wearing dark glasses. It seems an extraordinary thing to do when driving a car at night. It may well be why she did not see this elderly lady as she walked across dressed in a black coat and with an umbrella over her head.

To add to her problems, Dusty's insurance policy was found to be worthless because the company, Fire, Auto & Marine – whose chairman, Dr Emil Savundra, was one of the decade's more colourful crooks – had collapsed.

Even though Dusty was working in America at the time, and did not appear in court in person, she could not escape the attention of the press. When a celebrity who is already no stranger to controversy is found guilty of causing injury by careless driving, she can hardly expect the incident to go unnoticed; but Dusty's behaviour after the incident and her bizarre notion that dark glasses were appropriate for night driving revived speculation about her emotional stability.

'A pop singer should not hit an old lady,' Dusty reflected later, in a rather unattractive display of bravado. 'Particularly if the old lady used to be an ambulance driver in the war. And so suddenly I was this unstable person, this irresponsible, dirty *pop singer*. Nobody seemed interested in the damage the old lady's baked beans had done to the bonnet of my car.'[10]

Nevertheless, she had good reason to reflect on how close she had come to wrecking her career completely.*

Yet some difficult situations were beyond her control. Dusty had begun to experience one of the less welcome aspects of fame: the unwanted attentions of over-enthusiastic admirers. While she was rehearsing for *Ready Steady Go!* in April 1966 a monkey was delivered anonymously to the studio. 'Poor little devil. Heaven knows where he's come from, or why. . . . I don't know what I'm going to do with him.' The monkey was eventually adopted by a studio electrician.[11]

Shortly afterwards Dusty suffered some embarrassment when artist James Lawrence Isherwood included a half-length nude portrait of her ('from imagination') in an exhibition of his paintings at a Winchester hotel. At first the brewery that owned the hotel banned the painting, but relented when the artist offered to cover part of

---

* Although admitting that 'I'm not a very good driver. I'm short-sighted. I can't really see a thing without glasses' (*Daily Sketch*, 16 September 1966), Dusty drove an impressive selection of cars. In addition to the Italian sports-car she was driving on this occasion – 'I saw it at the Motor Show and it was so pretty. It's a sort of goldy colour' (*Sunday Times*, 7 June 1964) – there was the Cadillac in which Dusty took Martha Reeves sightseeing when she was in Britain in 1965; and later Dusty drove what she called her 'great brute of a Buick', in which, according to Frank Allen, she 'swanned around most elegantly'. In America in the seventies she drove a Jensen.

74

EVERYTHING'S COMING UP DUSTY

it discreetly with a duster. The painting was priced at 75 guineas and was reported to have been snapped up by Victor Rawlings, a 30-year-old pig-keeper. The painting's subsequent history is unknown, but we must hope that the work brought Mr Rawlings and his pigs much pleasure.*

None of this was allowed to interrupt her triumphant musical progress. Her first single of 1966 featured two more songs by Bea Verdi and Buddy Kaye. With its little rhythmic variations and the exhilarating lift in the chorus as Dusty lingers momentarily on the peak of 'bit *by* bit', 'Little By Little' is a superb production that demonstrates the growing musical understanding between Dusty and her backing singers, Madeline Bell and Lesley Duncan.

On the other hand, the B-side, 'If It Hadn't Been For You', is disappointing. Dusty never seems to be at ease with the rather aimless melody, and her voice soars and swoops with little sense of purpose.[†]

Dusty's next release, in March, was to prove a milestone in her career.

The record of 'Io Che Non Vivo . . . Senza Te' that she had brought back from San Remo was still in hiding under her couch; and around a year later, with no one else having taken any interest in the song in the meantime, she decided to do something with it. She handed the record – actually 'a scratchy old acetate' – to Vicki Wickham and asked her to provide an English lyric.

Vicki's friend Simon Napier-Bell was eager to break into the music business, and Vicki thought this commission might provide an opportunity. One evening at Vicki's flat, between returning from

---

* There are also known to have been portraits of Dusty by Norma Tanega and Caroline Coon.

[†] *Goin' Back* (1994) offers the last good transcription of 'Little By Little'. The track appears to have been remixed for subsequent reissues and is now merely a pale shadow of its former self.

dinner and leaving again for a club, they set about their task. Let us eavesdrop on the creative process:

> 'It's from Italy. The words have got to be romantic. It ought to start off "I love you".'
>
> Vicki shuddered at the thought. 'How about, "I don't love you"?' she suggested. I thought that was a bit extreme.
>
> 'No, it's going too far the other way. Why not: "You don't love *me*"?'
>
> That was more dramatic, more Italian, but a bit accusatory. So we softened it a little. '*You* don't *have* to love me.'
>
> But that didn't quite fit the melody, so we added two more words: 'YOU don't HAVE to SAY you love me.'
>
> Great. That was it. We could do the rest in the taxi.
>
> When we got to the Ad Lib club the song was all but finished, yet we only arrived ten minutes later than usual.

When Vicki and Simon presented their lyric to Dusty, 'Vicki told Dusty that we'd sweated through the night to get it just right'. But 'a great many songs are written in much the same way. It's just that most songwriters have the good sense not to tell people.'

The backing track had already been recorded, so the next night they went into the studio. Dusty was unhappy with the echo on her voice, and as the engineer ran down to the basement to make adjustments he noticed how good the echo was in the stairwell. Dusty needed no prompting; within minutes she was halfway down the stairs and singing into a microphone suspended in front of her – 'Sheer perfection from the first breath to the last'.

'You Don't Have To Say You Love Me' provided Dusty's only visit to the very top of the chart and has become the song most readily associated with her. 'It's a life-saver. . . . If everything else has gone wrong, when I get to that song I know it's going to be all right.'[12]

The same team tried their hand at writing lyrics for Dusty a second time. On this occasion they put words to a melody from Wagner's opera *Tannhäuser*.* There is, of course, a well-established tradition of borrowing (in both directions) between popular and classical music; but what distinguishes 'Don't Speak Of Love', which Dusty recorded in 1968, is the way in which it borrows not only Wagner's melody but also his orchestration.

The B-side, 'Every Ounce Of Strength', offers a complete contrast to the drama of 'You Don't Have To Say You Love Me'; it is a relaxed, gently swinging number on which Dusty is ably supported by the Echoes.

And there were still more riches in store. In July, Dusty's recording of Carole King's poignant ballad 'Goin' Back' was released. According to Dusty, Carole King 'was fiercely possessive of "Goin' Back". She wanted to do it herself, and she let me do it.' The recording session had an unpromising start when a thunderstorm affected all the equipment, but the recording that eventually emerged is Dusty at her very finest, a perfect blending of singer and song. Carole King is said to have wept when she first heard it.

For the B-side Dusty collaborated with Madeline Bell and Lesley Duncan. Dusty's career as a songwriter was very limited, but 'I'm Gonna Leave You' is a fine achievement.

In the middle of August, Dusty was able to broaden her career yet further when she began her first television series, *Dusty*, for the BBC. She would have a series every year for the next four years – three for the BBC and one for ATV. Her arranger and conductor for this first series, with a thirty-piece orchestra, was Johnny Pearson. Over the coming years the list of musical guests would be impressive – Dudley Moore, Mel Tormé, Jose Feliciano, Tom Jones, Scott Walker, Jimi Hendrix – and she sang duets with most of them. She was even reunited with her brother Tom. Few artists could have held their own in a live television performance with the likes of Mel Tormé – Mr Perfect Pitch himself – but Dusty was more than equal to the

* 'Don't Speak of Love' was eventually released in 1996 on *Something Special*. Dusty would expand her 'classical' repertoire even further in 1970 when she recorded 'Goodbye', for which Norma Tanega had set words to a melody by Bach.

challenge, and joined him to sing 'Let's Get Away From It All'. There were other guests, too: comedians, including Peter Cook and Woody Allen, and ventriloquists Señor Wences and Shari Lewis. For Dusty herself, the shows offered an opportunity to explore the full breadth of her repertoire – soul, rock, Motown, her own hits, music-hall (with Warren Mitchell and Danny La Rue) and occasional excursions into foreign languages – but most memorable were her exquisite performances of folk-songs such as 'Poor Wayfaring Stranger' and 'My Lagan Love', which served to underline just how *kinda* folksy the Springfields had been.[13]

Meanwhile her recording career went from strength to strength. September brought the release of 'All I See Is You', written by Clive Westlake and Ben Weisman, which is still one of Dusty's most popular recordings. Heralded by a fanfare of French horns, the song steadily builds into an expansive ballad reminiscent of 'You Don't Have To Say You Love Me'; and it comes as quite a surprise to find no Italian listed among the song's composers.

The B-side, 'Go Ahead On', is another impressive songwriting collaboration between Dusty and Madeline Bell.

There was to be no new collection in 1966. Instead, in October, Philips issued *Golden Hits*, a retrospective selection from Dusty's solo career so far.* With its striking cover photograph and fulsome sleeve-notes by Peter Jones, *Golden Hits* is a fitting tribute to 'this green-eyed blonde-haired explosion of vocal fire'.[†] However, Dusty, who was impatient to start work on her new collection, was worried that some people might 'make a big thing about it and treat it as the follow-up LP to *Ev'rything's Coming Up Dusty*'.[14]

---

* *Golden Hits* (Philips LP, 1966: mono BL 7737; stereo SBL 7737): I Only Want To Be With You · I Just Don't Know What To Do With Myself · In The Middle Of Nowhere · Losing You · All Cried Out · Some Of Your Lovin' · Wishin' And Hopin' · My Colouring Book · Little By Little · You Don't Have To Say You Love Me · Goin' Back · All I See Is You.

[†] Not to be outdone, the following year the anonymous author of the sleeve-notes to the American LP *The Look of Love* described Dusty as 'a singing, swinging, jet-setting, fun-begetting, 23-year-old, green-eyed, eight-stone chick'.

Golden Hits did indeed mark the beginning of a relentless recycling of a very narrow sample of Dusty's catalogue. *The Silver Collection*, released more than twenty years later, may be seen as merely a revised edition of *Golden Hits*. While this policy may have ensured that Dusty's hit records were always available in the shops, it also ignored Dusty's remarkable variety and versatility, and did much to confine her in a 'Swinging Sixties' straitjacket – and this became a cause for considerable resentment. Only recently have record companies begun to range more widely in their choice of material. But, at the time, *Golden Hits* was a handsome affirmation of her achievement; and in the following month Dusty flew to New York in pursuit of a fresh challenge. But, as things turned out, all she found was a fight.

She had been booked to appear at Basin Street East, one of the city's most prestigious jazz clubs where major artists such as Ella Fitzgerald, Duke Ellington, Tony Bennett and Peggy Lee performed regularly. Dusty had been engaged for a fortnight, giving two shows a night and three at weekends. For Dusty, who was ever eager to match herself with the best – 'You've got to prove something to people like that' – this was clearly an important step in her career. She confessed to being nervous: 'They're a tough audience', so 'I just have to make good'. Producer Tom Dowd sensed that Dusty 'looked up to people who were never popular in a certain way, and it disturbed her that she was popular for less'. But, in the event, the engagement would be memorable for all the wrong reasons.

In what was a strange pairing of talents, Dusty had been booked to share the platform with a band led by drummer Buddy Rich. Notoriously arrogant and short-tempered – on one famous occasion, he and the equally fiery Frank Sinatra had had to be pulled apart – and with a very high opinion of his own talents, Rich represented the older generation of popular music that had found itself overwhelmed at bewildering speed by young, highly successful performers for whom they could have no respect. They felt dispossessed by this brash, bright new musical phenomenon that was sweeping all before it. To add to the indignity, the main thrust of the attack had come from across the Atlantic, sidelining American musicians in their own country; and this probably explains why Rich 'appeared to have a chip on his shoulder about the British'. Now he was to share a stage with one of the most prominent representatives of this 'British invasion'.*

The collaboration began badly and grew relentlessly worse. 'He seemed to take an instant dislike to me,' Dusty recalled. 'He had me in tears for about a week.' In fact, Rich had reason to feel vulnerable, too. Earlier that year he had left the Harry James band and struck out on his own; and, with pop music in the ascendant, this was not a very promising time at which to launch a big band.

There was a dispute over who was top of the bill – Rich's manager asserting that 'Buddy's gotta top' and Vic Billings insisting that 'Dusty's supposed to be topping' – with a predictably silly compromise. Rich's name would have pride of place on the club's marquee for the first half of the week, and Dusty would be promoted to top spot for the second half.

Ever the perfectionist, and understandably apprehensive about such an important engagement, Dusty wanted plenty of time to work with the band, but she was denied the rehearsals she considered so essential. When she confronted Buddy Rich 'he had his legs up on the desk and he said, "You fucking broad! Who do you think you *are*, bitch?" My Irish temper got the better of me and I swiped him across the face.' This 'chorus-girl slap' dislodged his toupee. 'You've

---

* Jazz musicians in Britain had not been slow to appreciate the threat posed by the new teenage phenomenon. In his sublime autobiography *Owning-up* (1965), George Melly records the devastating impact of Tommy Steele on himself and his fellow musicians ('We've had it. In six months we'll all be in the bread line': p. 133). At this remove it is hard to imagine anyone being unnerved by 'Rock With The Cavemen' or 'Little White Bull', especially a man who claimed to have put a gang of thugs to flight by reciting dadaist poetry at them (p. 30), but such fears soon proved well founded.

Above: The O'Briens at home in Ealing. Mary still has her waist-length red corkscrews, while the plaster on her knee betrays yet another childhood scrape.

Inset: 'I decided I must change; that this person who was looking at me in the mirror was not going to make it.'

Above and Right: The young folk-singers: Mary and Dion in the 1950s.

Right: Rex Features

Above: The Lana Sisters: (left to right) Dusty, Riss Chantelle, Lynne Abrams

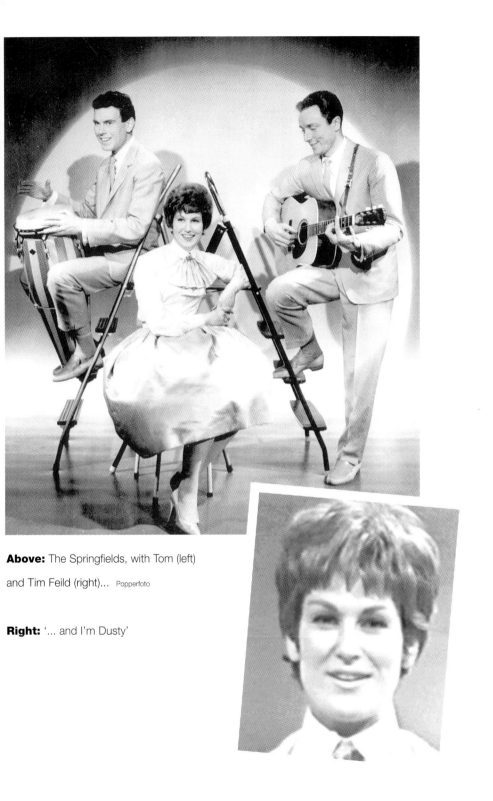

Above: The Springfields, with Tom (left) and Tim Feild (right)... Popperfoto

Right: '... and I'm Dusty'

Above: The new line-up, with the darkly handsome Mike Hurst.

Left: Going solo, 1963.

Hulton Deutsch

Right: Dusty and Eden Kane demonstrate their affection.

Below: 'We were a great team': Dusty with Johnny Franz.

Above: Dusty and the Echoes return to Heathrow from South Africa, December 1964. Her manager, Vic Billings, is behind her left shoulder. Hulton Getty

Left: Two weeks of hell with Buddy Rich at Basin Street East, New York, in November 1966.

Rex Features

Left: A reflective moment. Paul Howes

Below: An unwanted gift from a devoted fan. Hulton Getty

Above: Pet Shop Girl.

Retna

Right: Pet sanctuary girl:
Dusty at the Wildlife Way
Station. Mirror Syndication International

never seen anybody look so flabbergasted in your life . . . he threatened to sue me for assault.'*

Buddy Rich treated his own band in the same high-handed manner; and during rehearsals several musicians walked out, while those who remained came to side with Dusty in the test of wills that developed – 'Because Buddy's band weren't fond of him *either*'.

The incident may have allowed Dusty to vent her anger and show Buddy Rich that she was not easily to be pushed around, but it failed to gain her the rehearsals she wanted. Although she had sixteen numbers to prepare, she was only allowed to work with the band on the afternoon before opening night – and even then Buddy Rich devoted an hour of this precious rehearsal-time to setting up a special podium for himself and his drum kit.

His previous engagement, at the Chez Club in Hollywood, was recorded, so we are able to hear how the band sounded at this time. Both driven and restrained by Buddy Rich's commanding percussion, the performances are polished and tightly disciplined; no soloists take off on flights of melodic invention, and the arrangements tend to degenerate into a succession of unexciting riffs. Quite how Dusty was meant to fit into this musical picture is unclear.†

Life was no easier for Dusty once the show had actually opened on 3 November. Buddy Rich and the various supporting acts did their spots, the many celebrities in the audience were introduced, and Rich chatted to his cronies. This was clearly a working environment that Rich relished. Reviewing the Hollywood engagement, Leonard

---

* This is the account of the incident published at the time. A version of events subsequently emerged in which the confrontation took place after Dusty had climbed a ladder to change the billing on the marquee. This seems unlikely. Had Dusty ever climbed a ladder, she would surely have fallen off it.

† *Buddy Rich Swingin' New Big Band* (Pacific Jazz CD, 1995: 7243 8 35232 2 1). Of Count Basie, Dusty had remarked: 'I can't stand that kind of music. It's probably very good, but I have no appreciation of it whatsoever' (*Melody Maker*, 16 July 1966). If she was unable to appreciate Basie, then Buddy Rich stood no chance at all.

Feather noted that 'Night after night, the room was crammed with celebrities. . . . Standing ovations were a regular procedure.' Meanwhile, in her dressing-room, Dusty waited and waited – and suffered further indignities. Buddy Rich had perfected a line in spiteful putdowns of pop singers, and during the show he would treat the audience to such remarks as 'She's supposed to be a great singer, but I've seen better,' and 'Well, if you like that kind of garbage . . . then it's up to you'.

But Dusty was not without her own supporters. American friends such as Burt Bacharach and Dionne Warwick dropped in to see the show, as well as British friends who happened to be in town; and the reviewers, who had become aware of the poisonous atmosphere backstage, were friendly and complimentary.

The two weeks dragged past, and eventually the torment ended. Dusty had managed to survive Buddy Rich's systematic attempt to humiliate her, but the emotional cost must have been enormous. When she came to recall the experience more than twenty years later, it was clear that the pain and the resentment had not diminished with the passage of time. 'What a *bastard*! He was the arsehole of the world.' However, there had been one moment to enjoy:

> I've never been so happy as on the last night of my engagement when the little sax player, who had rooted for me all along the line, pushed his way forward and, grabbing the mike, said: 'Dear Dusty . . . she's a gas . . . and I just want to give her a little token of how the boys in the band feel about her.' With that he unwrapped a parcel and handed me a goodbye present – a pair of boxing gloves.

In the following year, when Dusty came to record her next LP, *Where Am I Going*, she included two numbers with a big band accompaniment: 'Sunny' and 'Come Back To Me'. Listening to Dusty's voice soar with ease above the brass, it is not too fanciful to hear in these tracks a determination to meet the likes of Buddy Rich on their own territory and her emphatic response to being dismissed as 'garbage' by such an oaf.[15]*

At the beginning of 1967, Dusty's career moved in a new direction when she recorded the theme songs for two films.

'The Corrupt Ones', written for an obscure film with the same title, although it was renamed *The Peking Medallion* for British release, is a typical written-to-order film-song of the period, played over the opening titles but making little sense when lifted off the soundtrack. The song's film origins are betrayed by the final expectant fanfare announcing – to quote Louis Armstrong from a different film entirely – 'end of song, beginning of story'; but Dusty does a fine job, and the track is perhaps undeserving of the obscurity into which it has been allowed to fall. 'The Corrupt Ones' was issued in February as the B-side to 'I'll Try Anything', a routine pop song which is raised above the commonplace by a fine brass accompaniment.†

In complete contrast, 'The Look Of Love', Dusty's other excursion into film music in 1967, quickly outgrew its brief outing on the soundtrack of *Casino Royale* where it accompanied Peter Sellers and Ursula Andress as they wafted in slow motion past a tank full of comatose tropical fish, as well as its relegation to the B-side of the lacklustre ballad 'Give Me Time', and became 'the song people seem to love me doing'.

Burt Bacharach had been commissioned to write the score for this James Bond spoof and invited Dusty to record the song he had included. Beset by problems – principally Peter Sellers – and passed

---

* Buddy Rich was dogged by heart disease for much of his career, but finally succumbed to a brain tumour in 1987. Asked by a nurse if there was anything to which he was allergic, he replied: 'Only country music.' For that alone the man deserves respect.

† 'I'll Try Anything' is notable for having inspired one curious promotional gimmick: a mini-skirt with the sheet music printed on it. Dusty did not model the garment herself; that was left to willowy model Karim Jensen. 'The skirt can be obtained by sending off 15s. with a voucher slipped into the record sleeve' (*Daily Mirror*, 11 March 1967). Have any of the skirts survived?

from one director to another, the film rapidly degenerated into an almighty shambles, and Burt Bacharach's score became its only redeeming feature. The music over the opening titles proved successful for Herb Alpert, while 'The Look Of Love' is one of Dusty's most memorable performances – although the version that was released on record is different from that on the soundtrack.*

Despite profound admiration on both sides, 'The Look Of Love' represents the only occasion on which Dusty and Burt Bacharach worked together in a recording studio. Burt is unstinting in his praise of Dusty's recording:

> I loved the way Dusty sang 'The Look Of Love'. It was just smoky; it was sexy; it was restrained. It was held in check, but underneath it was smouldering. It was just on fire. Just so much romance and passion and coolness to it.

But could this musical love-affair have survived a longer collaboration? With two such notorious perfectionists working together, there would surely have been blood on the studio floor before too long. As Burt acknowledged, 'We would probably have killed each other'.[16][†]

With her next single, 'What's It Gonna Be', Dusty had her first real taste of failure. The record made no impact whatsoever – at least, for the moment. Gradually, however, it was taken up in the clubs and in particular as part of the 'Northern soul' phenomenon, becoming

---

* For a more detailed account of the *Casino Royale* fiasco, with Peter Sellers cast in the role of demon king, see Roger Lewis, *The Life and Death of Peter Sellers* (1994).

† Directing the recording of 'Alfie' in London, Burt Bacharach pushed Cilla Black through one take after another until she was exhausted and past her peak. Eventually producer George Martin came to the rescue: ' "Burt, what exactly are you looking for?" . . . He said: "George, I'm looking for that little bit of magic." George came back and said: "Well, actually, Burt, I thought we had it in take three." Silence. Anyway, take three is what you got on the record' (Cilla Black interview, Channel Four television, 22 November 1997).

something of a cult recording. No doubt Dusty would have preferred it to have been a hit. Unfortunately, when 'What's It Gonna Be' sank swiftly from sight it took with it a delightful B-side, 'Small Town Girl', which had actually been recorded in 1965. 'I've Got A Good Thing', another fine track, which was probably recorded at the same session as 'What's It Gonna Be', was left to languish on a shelf for almost thirty years.*

Further disappointment came in November with the release of Dusty's next LP.† *Where Am I Going* did not live up to expectations, much to Dusty's regret. 'That's really upset me, because I'd worked hard on it.'[17] There are moments of brilliance, and a few tracks have taken their place amongst Dusty's finest work, but too many songs are remarkable only because it is Dusty singing them. The frantic but strangely unexciting 'Bring Him Back' is followed by an unappealing version of Aretha Franklin's 'Don't Let Me Lose This Dream'. 'I Can't Wait Until I See My Baby's Face' raises the tone a little, only to give way to 'Take Me For A Little While', which has Dusty working overtime in an attempt to make it work at all.

Ironically, after all the exertion of the previous tracks, the disc is finally brought to life by Dusty's relaxed and economical performance of an unassuming little song. 'Chained To A Memory' falls beautifully for her voice, and this track is still one of the best-kept secrets of the Dusty Springfield catalogue.

On 'Sunny', written and originally recorded by Bobby Hebb, Dusty breaks new ground by singing with a big band – as she does with

---

* For a full account of 'Northern soul', see Sheryl Garratt, *Adventures in Wonderland* (1998).

   'I've Got A Good Thing' was eventually released in 1996 on *Something Special*. See Appendix.

† *Where Am I Going* (Philips LP, 1967: mono BL 7820; stereo SBL 7820): Bring Him Back · Don't Let Me Lose This Dream · I Can't Wait Until I See My Baby's Face · Take Me For A Little While · Chained To A Memory · Sunny · (They Long To Be) Close To You · Welcome Home · Come Back To Me · If You Go Away · Broken Blossoms · Where Am I Going.

   Where Am I Going was reissued on CD in 1998 (Philips 846 050-2).

equal distinction on 'Come Back To Me', a song by Alan Jay Lerner and Burton Lane from the musical *On a Clear Day You Can See Forever* which quickly found favour as a reliable attention-getter for cabaret singers.

'(They Long To Be) Close To You', a Bacharach-and-David song, had been recorded in 1964 and intended as the follow-up to 'I Just Don't Know What To Do With Myself', but had been set aside in favour of 'Losing You'. The song is best-known for having launched the career of the Carpenters in 1970. We shall never know whether it would have been as successful for Dusty.

With 'Welcome Home' Dusty is again labouring to make something out of nothing; but with 'If You Go Away' we come to the outstanding performance in the collection. The song, by Jacques Brel, had been given an English lyric by Rod McKuen, but Dusty sings in both French and English. The song meant a great deal to her, and she gives a moving performance:

> You know, bringing out the emotion in a song is hard for me. They can't *all* be a cry from the heart. . . . But there is one song I can always perform with emotion and that's *If You Go Away*. It's about fear of rejection and abandonment and that's something a lot of people can identify with – especially me.[18]

'Broken Blossoms' brings a reunion with the songwriting talents of brother Tom. The song has an obvious affinity with 'Where Have All The Flowers Gone', which the Springfields had recorded for a German EP – a song with such unexceptionable pacifist sentiments that even an aged Hollywood legend like Marlene Dietrich could enjoy considerable success with it.

For someone as beset by uncertainties as Dusty, 'Where Am I Going' had particular significance.* Her moving performance of this

---

* 'Once I tried to escape. I had the weekend off and went down to Cornwall. I walked along the cliffs and thought: "What does it all mean? Where am I going? How long will it last?" And suddenly I was afraid' (*News of the World*, 16 August 1964).

song written by Dorothy Fields and Cy Coleman for the show *Sweet Charity* brings this rather uneven collection to a close. Dusty included another song from the same show, 'If My Friends Could See Me Now', in her television series that year but never recorded it.

After *Where Am I Going* Dusty released no further records for six months, although she kept herself before the public in the meantime with her television programmes. *It Must Be Dusty*, for which she had forsaken the BBC for ATV after two successful series of *Dusty*, began in May 1968. But the summer brought a flurry of activity, with cabaret, two new singles and an EP.

Released in June, 'I Close My Eyes And Count To Ten' has become one of the classic recordings of the decade, instantly recognisable from the opening notes of its piano introduction. It is not the piano *melody*, which has the same kind of false grandeur as Richard Addinsell's Warsaw Concerto, so much as the actual *tone* of the piano that captures the imagination; and Dusty's performance is superb, the light lilting chorus contrasting with the intensity of the verse. Dusty's manager, Vic Billings, realised that he had found something special the moment Clive Westlake, who was a staff composer for Carlin Music in Savile Row at the time, played it to him. The two men met often, and Vic took a particular interest in songs on which Clive was still working – and which, presumably, had not yet been promised to any other singer. Clive recalled that on one such occasion

> Vic says, 'You got anything you haven't finished yet?' and I says, 'Well, I'm working on this song at the moment called "I Close My Eyes And Count To Ten".' He said: 'Well, play me some.' So I played it on the piano . . . and when I got into the chorus . . . it's like a light comes on. Vic says: 'That's it! Finish that song and I'll get it done with Dusty.'[19]

Clive Westlake then made an astonishingly lavish demo recording, with a full orchestral accompaniment and with his own Welsh-chapel alto standing in for Dusty's voice. Dusty listened to the tape, fell in love with the song and recorded it herself – on this occasion at the end of a corridor.

For the B-side, Dusty turned to the work of her friend Norma Tanega. 'No Stranger Am I' is a beautifully unassuming song which Norma herself had included on her only sixties LP. For her own recording Dusty follows the original arrangement exactly, and her finely judged interpretation is complemented by some exquisite wood-wind.

Dusty spent the month of July in a return engagement in cabaret at the Talk of the Town where she had first appeared the previous year. The show, which was produced by Fred Perry, included Dusty's 'tribute' to Shirley Temple, with Dusty singing 'On The Good Ship Lollipop' while film footage of the child star was projected on to a screen behind her. More seriously, Dusty also performed a medley of Peggy Lee songs; and she would also include this selection in one of her television shows the following year.[20]

If You Go Away, issued in August, provided a second outing for three tracks from *Where Am I Going* together with one new recording, 'Magic Garden', which had been considered for release as a single.* Jimmy Webb, the song's composer, had been enjoying great success in Britain throughout the summer with another number, 'MacArthur Park', which actor Richard Harris had taken into the Top Ten – despite the record's inordinate length – and which was stubbornly refusing to go away. 'Magic Garden' is a similarly impressionistic piece of hippie dippiness. It had been recorded first by the 5th Dimension, and it is a further tribute to Dusty's talent for picking the right material that she was able to listen to what is a limp and listless perform-ance but still recognise the song's potential. She takes the song by the scruff of the neck and, assisted by a businesslike brass s e c t i o n a n d t h u n d e r o u s p e r c u s s i o n , d r i v e s i t a l o n g a t a f e r o c i o u s pace. ('MacArthur Park' had to wait until 1978, and the wondrous Donna

* *If You Go Away* (Philips EP, 1968: BE 12605): If You Go Away · Magic Garden · Sunny · Where Am I Going.
'Magic Garden' may now be found on *Songbook* (1990); see Appendix.

Summer, before it, too, could be stirred into life.) We shall never know how 'Magic Garden' would have fared as a single.

If You Go Away would be Dusty's last EP of the sixties. Indeed, the EP generally was an endangered species. Now no more than a historical curiosity, those delightful miniatures offered a halfway house between single and LP, and frequently provided a home for material that otherwise might never have seen the light of day.

September saw the release of 'I Will Come To You', which was to be Dusty's last collaboration with Clive Westlake. The composer had struck *hwyl* yet again; but, in spite of another fine performance from Dusty, splendid support from her backing singers, and a powerful arrangement that begins gently but develops into an enormous pop anthem, the new single enjoyed no success at all. Clive Westlake put much of the blame on Dusty herself: 'She played around and I think she missed the point. She wanted to do some soul on it, and that wasn't what I intended. She threw her voice around a bit.'[21] His disappointment is understandable – 'I Will Come To You' is a good record – but it is hard to see how the song could have been handled any other way.*

The B-side, 'The Colour Of Your Eyes', is a wistful number co-written by Norma Tanega.

Dusty's new LP, *Dusty . . . Definitely*, was released in November.[†] Dusty begins in her usual purposeful manner. 'Ain't No Sun Since You've Been Gone' is fast and powerful, and the mood is continued by the next track, 'Take Another Little Piece Of My Heart'. This is

---

* A prolific songwriter throughout the 1960s and 1970s, Clive Westlake eventually left London for Nashville, Tennessee, in 1980, and it was there that he died on 17 June 2000.

[†] *Dusty . . . Definitely* (Philips LP, 1968: SBL 7864): Ain't No Sun Since You've Been Gone · Take Another Little Piece Of My Heart · Another Night · Mr Dream Merchant · I Can't Give Back The Love I Feel For You · Love Power · This Girl's In Love With You · I Only Wanna Laugh · (Who) Will Take My Place · I Think It's Gonna Rain Today · Morning · Second Time Around.

Dusty . . . Definitely was reissued on CD in 1990 (Philips 846049) but is currently unavailable.

a cover of the recording by Erma Franklin, younger sister of Aretha, and Dusty's version matches the mood of the original. It was left to the astonishing Janis Joplin to push the song to another level of intensity. Dusty said she fought shy of the song because she was intimidated by all the high notes but, 'with the help of several cups of Philips tea', she eventually managed to record it.[22] Was Janis Joplin's recording similarly tea-assisted?

Three slight performances follow. 'Another Night' is an agitated shuffle from the less-interesting end of the Bacharach-and-David musical spectrum; 'Mr Dream Merchant' is an attractive, if insubstantial, number of the kind that used to be damned with the faint praise of being 'a good album track', meaning that it would not survive on its own; while the chirpy and inconsequential 'I Can't Give Back The Love I Feel For You' offers a foretaste of the musical cul-de-sac in which Dusty would find herself stranded in the early seventies.

Urged on by aggressive brass and percussion, Dusty's exultant performance on 'Love Power', which had been a success in America for the Sandpebbles (later C and the Shells!), puts the disc back on course. In the sleeve notes Dusty draws our attention to 'the unusual use of "soul-bells" ' – although the Sandpebbles had used them, too.

Bacharach and David's 'This Guy's In Love With You' had proved a great success for Herb Alpert during the summer; but after some appropriate changes to the lyric Dusty is able to make the song her own.*

'I Only Wanna Laugh', which follows, develops quickly from its wistful opening into a high-kicking cabaret number.

With 'Who (Will Take My Place)', a meditative samba composed by Charles Aznavour with an English lyric by Herbert Kretzmer, *Dusty ... Definitely* ascends to a higher level, and the last four tracks in the collection are pure gold.

* By a curious coincidence, in the summer of 1968, at the same time that Herb Alpert was enjoying success with the original recording of 'This Guy's In Love With You' his wife Lani Hall, lead singer with Sergio Mendes' Brazil '66, was also in the American Top Twenty with a cover version of 'The Look Of Love'.

With 'I Think It's Gonna Rain Today', Dusty renewed her acquaintance with the work of Randy Newman. This haunting performance has become an enduring favourite.

'Morning', a Brazilian song with an English lyric by Norma Tanega, is a piece of modern pastoral ('Come away!'), with Dusty's voice complemented by one of the string quartets that had been cropping up all over the place since George Martin put one behind Paul McCartney in 1965.

Dusty . . . Definitely closes with one of Dusty's rare excursions into the works of the twentieth century's great songwriters, on this occasion Sammy Cahn and Jimmy van Heusen. With its lush string arrangement, 'Second Time Around' enables Dusty to bring her new collection to an impressive conclusion.

But we have not quite finished. In what is obviously an allusion to her crockery-smashing days – although in this instance she seems to have used tin mugs rather than china cups – Dusty dispels the reflective mood she has established with the sound of an avalanche of scrap metal.

Dusty ends her sleeve notes with thanks 'in particular to Johnny Franz who has guided me through five years of recording and I hope will guide me through five more'. In fact, *Dusty . . . Definitely* would be their last major project together. Dusty had spent part of the summer recording in Memphis, and the first product of those sessions would provide her with a massive hit single over Christmas, with an LP to follow in the spring.

She had also decided to break with Vic Billings: 'we decided we'd done as much for each other as we could'. Vic had guided Dusty's career for the past five years. According to Madeline Bell, although he was not much older than Dusty, 'He could talk to her like nobody else could, and get away with it'. This was probably because he understood her. Dusty was

A sincere person. Honest, extremely feminine, but has a basic insecurity. . . . Temperamental, yes, but about the funniest things. A big thing won't bother her, but little things can drive her round the bend. She is like everyone: she wants to be liked. Possessive of people around her, but doesn't trust many people, unless she gets to know them. She's really a doll, like a little girl. [23]

With her attention focused increasingly on America, she had decided to draw a line under the last five years and search for fresh challenges. She had no way of knowing it at the time, but this break would mark the beginning of musical wanderings that would last for the rest of her life.

6

Memphis

WHILE IT MAY be true that there can be no gains without pains, it is unlikely that any of those who gathered at American Studios in Memphis in the summer of 1968 for Dusty's first recordings on the Atlantic label had any inkling of what agony lay ahead.

Producer Jerry Wexler may have begun to suspect that there were difficult times to come when he invited Dusty to his home on Long Island to choose songs. They sat for hours 'ass-deep in albums and acetates' as he offered her more than a hundred titles. She rejected all of them. Jerry was patient, reflecting that 'An artist of her fragile sensitivity had to be selective; to say yes to one song was seen as a lifetime commitment'.[1] This was no less than the truth: Dusty's remarkable success had been due in no small measure to her talent for picking songs that were right for her and meant something to her. At this turning-point in her career, when she was forsaking the people and the method of working that had brought her success so far in favour of a new team with their own approach to making records, the pressure on Dusty to find the right songs was particularly intense, so it is perhaps not surprising that Jerry Wexler's first attempt ended in failure. But he persevered – and, indeed, his dogged perseverance would prove vital in keeping the whole project on course – and after 'months of agonizing evaluations' a mutually acceptable selection of eleven songs emerged. Significantly, Dusty fell back on tried-and-tested musical relationships: the list included a song by Burt Bacharach and Hal David, two songs by Randy Newman, and no fewer than four songs by Gerry Goffin and Carole King.

Jerry Wexler likes to distinguish between what he calls the '*auteur* style' of record production –

the Phil Spector approach, where the principal ingredient is the producer himself and where the singer, the song, the studio, the background music, the musicians, the whole thing, are a confection of the producer; and the ingredients are all like little mosaic tiles or pieces in an intaglio

– and the style he prefers:

I call it serving the artist or serving the project, which is trying to discern what's germane or significant about the artist and working it best to bring that out, whatever it takes, to put him in the right musical setting. . . .

The producer's job is 'to know the potential of the singer and to push for it'. This is the approach that 'generates great artists'. With the *auteur* style, 'the artist would have no part in the creative process. I wanted the interplay of singer with rhythm section, with the musicians taking cues from the vocalist'. The *auteur* style 'doesn't develop artists at all of any durability. Nothing ever emerges. What is always remembered is a sound and a record.' This was the system within which Dusty had been working so far. Only her stubborn determination to pursue the effects she wanted – and, in the process, earning herself a reputation for being 'difficult' and hysterical – had brought her a measure of control. Now she was to work with a team dedicated to serving her talent and bringing out the best in her.[2]

Dusty's dissatisfaction with the American side of her recording career had been growing for some time. As early as 1966 she had made it known that, although she had no quarrel with the company in Britain, 'in the US they have done virtually nothing to promote me or my records. Most of the kids there seem to have no idea when I have a disc on release – in fact, they write telling me how badly I am being promoted in America!' She even went so far as to declare that 'I'm just not going to record again until something is done'.[3]* Ahmet Ertegun, co-founder and chairman of Atlantic Records, had heard 'Some Of Your Lovin' ' and liked the sound of Dusty's voice; so when he heard that Dusty had decided to change record companies in America he moved to sign her to Atlantic. Dusty insisted that Jerry Wexler be her producer, and Jerry in turn professed to be a 'big fan of hers'. His co-producers were equally enthusiastic. For Arif Mardin, Dusty was 'one of the important singers. Her voice contains the essence of soul. It's part of her instrument – it isn't foreign to her at all.' Tom Dowd recognised 'a jazz sense of timing and facility, and a sensitivity to pitch'. Learning that Dusty was coming to Atlantic, Tom 'went out and bought the four last Dusty albums that had come out on Mercury and I knew every key she sang in, I knew her intervals. . . . I knew where she could go or where she would come from. I was prepared.'[4]

It should have been the perfect combination; but the tensions that developed in the studio would test the commitment of all concerned and would push Dusty to the brink of vocal paralysis.

At the time Dusty painted a rosy picture of the experience. The Memphis sessions had been a challenge, but she had been equal to it. 'The sessions were all taken very easily,' she declared airily. 'I went to some sessions and didn't have to sing a note! I just sat around drinking tea and talking and getting to know people.' She had been a little intimidated at first because 'The Americans have a different approach to recording. They can take up to six hours to do the rhythm track and voice and then they add the extra instruments, brass, strings and things on later.' She was 'gassed' by the way things went. 'Being used to working in a different way, I felt very tight about it, almost entirely on my own and exposed all of a sudden'; but 'Working in this way forces you to be creative, to try to do something really good, because

---

* Dusty's recordings were repackaged for the American market. Her American LP releases at this point comprised *Stay Awhile/I Only Want to Be with You* (1964), *Dusty* (1964), *Oooooeeee!* (1965), *You Don't Have To Say You Love Me* (1966) and *The Look of Love* (1967). All have been reissued on compact disc; see Appendix.

it's like laying down a foundation, it has to be very strong'. And as for Jerry Wexler himself:

> He is not a temperamental producer in any way. He doesn't appear to be demanding. But as everything he produces is of a pretty high standard he knows that he has that standard to keep up and in that way I suppose he is demanding. But he is very patient and thoughtful; he doesn't mess around.

All in all, 'I sort of grew up as the album progressed. I became less inhibited, and I feel I can do much more now than I've ever done.'[5] Only later would she talk frankly about how difficult her time in Memphis had been. 'Without doubt, I think that's when Jerry went bald.'[6]

For the second time in her life, Dusty found herself a long way from home and having to adapt to a way of working that was completely alien to her – but on this occasion she did not have Tom and Mike with her, as she had in Nashville.

There was a clash of cultures from the very beginning. She arrived in Memphis with her hairdresser, John Adams, and, according to Tom Dowd, 'she'd have her hair blown, dried and cut every day. She had a Memphis beehive and looked like the queen of the Southern contingent.' And Jerry Wexler felt that 'She came on like she was grooming herself for court'. To Dusty, of course, this was her normal way of working – Neil Tennant, who worked with her twenty years later, remembered '*teams* of makeup artists' – but with her carefully tended hair and her flawless makeup the White Queen of Soul must indeed have cut an incongruous figure in the informal atmosphere of the notoriously rat-infested studio.

Dusty discovered that the Memphis way of working was the complete opposite of what she preferred. Instead of Dusty adding her voice last on top of orchestra and backing singers, she would be required to sing with only a rhythm track, and the rest of the arrangement would be added over the top of that.

I had never recorded with just a rhythm track – I've never done it since. I'm a shy singer, perhaps you might say a reluctant singer, at the best of times. . . . I like to hear more or less the whole thing . . . in my headphones. . . . But on *Memphis* I didn't have that luxury. . . .

To add to the pressure, she was constantly being made aware of the studio's illustrious history – 'That's where Aretha stood' and 'That's where Percy Sledge sang "When A Man Loves A Woman" ' – so that 'I became paralysed by the ghosts of the studio!' and 'I stayed frozen the entire time I was in Memphis'.[7]

Jerry Wexler has described Dusty as 'the most insecure singer in the world', 'all raw nerve ends and neuroses'. Dusty felt exposed and vulnerable; all her anxieties began to assail her, and she became reluctant to sing at all. She blamed 'very bad laryngitis', but in fact she had become *afraid* to sing. Never satisfied with anything less than excellence, she was worried that her performance would fail to live up to the high expectations of those around her, and she was afraid to utter a note. Those cosy little chats with musicians over a cup of tea were clearly Dusty's attempts to put off the moment when she would have to sing. Jerry Wexler had to plead with her to go to the microphone. Inside her head was 'a critical voice that tears down anything I do instantaneously', and

if there's one thing that inhibits good singing it's fear, or allowing the natural critic in me to criticise a note before it even left my throat, which destroys the flow of anything. I don't think they understood how intimidated I was.

Actually they did. Jerry Wexler recognised that 'when she did perform she was afraid to let it go because her standards were so high and it might not come out exactly right'; and Tom Dowd concluded that she was 'a tough, tough, tough taskmaster on her own vocals'. Burt Bacharach worked with Dusty only once but discovered that she was 'very hard on herself vocally'.[8]

Inevitably, the atmosphere in the studio became very tense, and there were occasional emotional outbursts. At one point Dusty aimed an ashtray at Jerry Wexler. She also managed to quarrel with the mild-mannered Tom Dowd, calling him a prima donna – an outburst that provoked an angry Jerry Wexler to point out that the only prima donna in the studio was Dusty herself.

Whether Dusty *could* not sing or *would* not sing, it became clear that no further progress could be made in Memphis, and work on the project continued in New York where Dusty said she felt 'more comfortable'. And so it was that the most famous record ever to be released with the name Memphis in the title was recorded for the most part in New York. But the move north appears to have improved the situation hardly at all. For Jerry Wexler, 'the sessions were hell. The emotional push and pull between me and Dusty was tricky', and recording Dusty's final vocals was 'the most excruciating experience I encountered'. Jerry liked to give singers the backing track at the lowest-possible volume, believing that the lower the volume in the headphones the harder the singer will project: 'it's a physiological fact'. Dusty, as we know, preferred the volume to be so high that it was physically painful. 'There was no way she could hear herself – it was like she was singing into a void, projecting an interior monologue'. Yet, almost miraculously, 'she sang perfectly in tune' and, 'despite everything, I finally got the performances I was after, and I still marvel at her vocals'. After all that he had been made to endure, Jerry Wexler's admiration for Dusty remained undiminished: 'Her pitch was miraculous', 'For intonation, there was not a better singer than Dusty, black or white', and 'I never heard her sing a bad note'.[9]

'I drove them crazy, a bit at a time,' Dusty reflected nonchalantly, 'but we got it.'

Anyone involved in the project who doubted whether all the agony was ultimately justified had only to listen to the record. The three producers were acutely aware that they had created something special. For Jerry Wexler, 'It stands out in my mind as one of my favourites of all times'; it was 'a masterful interweaving of voices and instruments' and 'like an intricate well-worn tweed'. To Tom Dowd it represented 'a strange fusion of artist and material and the concepts that Jerry, Arif and I had'. Arif Mardin reflected that 'Some products have an aura, like a blessing from above. Whatever it was, it worked.' He also believed that the enforced move from Memphis to New York had contributed to the distinctive character of the recording: 'we added the Memphis horns down South and up in New York I arranged the strings and woodwind. Somehow the combination worked. The strings and woodwind with the Memphis horns at the back gave a kind of echo, a wonderful lush, tough sound. . . . It had the essence of Memphis with a symphonic overlay.'[10] As for the lady herself, she would not listen to it for about a year – although this was not unusual for her – but eventually she acknowledged that 'there are about six tracks on there I'm really proud of . . . but six for me is pretty good!' It had 'the most peculiar atmosphere. It has an evenness to it that no other album I've ever done has.' She was unable to understand its status as a classic but conceded: 'It's a good record.'[11]

From the opening notes of of 'Just A Little Lovin' ', with the strings sounding almost like a rhythm section, to the closing fade of 'I Can't Make It Alone', *Dusty in Memphis* has a musical unity, an artistic wholeness, that is probably unique in popular music. It more than vindicates the Jerry Wexler philosophy of 'serving the artist' – though for much of the time Dusty must have doubted that she was being served at all – and confirms Arif Mardin's place among the very finest arrangers. In interviews, Mardin has invoked Ravel as his inspiration on *Dusty in Memphis*, and when we listen to his remarkable orchestration on one track after another this does not seem at all fanciful. But at the heart of it all is Dusty's voice, which emerges from what was undoubtedly a testing experience with a depth and an emotional intensity that are almost miraculous. It is as if Dusty needed to pile anxiety upon anxiety in order to achieve the performance she was seeking. Even old partnerships are made to sound fresh, with the work of Bacharach and David, and of Goffin and King, presented in a new light.

Although Dusty had chosen to turn once again to well-established musical relationships for much of her material, one song by John

99

Hurley and Ronnie Wilkins, a partnership new to Dusty, quickly outgrew the others, provided her with an enormous success when it was issued as a single ahead of the release of the LP, and remains a firm favourite to this day. 'Son Of A Preacher Man' is slow and sensuous – 'quite a gentle thing really' – and the blend of Dusty's smoky voice, the magisterial Memphis brass and the superb vocal backing made it an instant classic. The song had been offered to Aretha Franklin, who turned it down, so Jerry Wexler 'tried it on Dusty, the Ice Lady, the White Queen of Soul, and of course it came out just great, and the track is wonderful, and she did an incredible job with it'. A year later, Aretha recorded the song herself. She was the only singer who had the authority to cover Dusty's recording; any other singer would have made an almighty fool of herself. Inevitably perhaps, Dusty preferred Aretha's recording: 'She did it the way I wish *I'd* done it.' (Aretha had also given a cool reception to Paul McCartney's 'Let It Be', which he had offered to her; eventually he ran out of patience and recorded it himself. Aretha's version followed.)[12]

Released as a single towards the end of 1968, 'Son Of A Preacher Man' was given an early public outing on *The Ed Sullivan Show* on 24 November. Afterwards, in one of the touchingly inept 'interviews' that followed each performance, Sullivan raised the subject of Dusty's real name.

Dusty obligingly performed her party trick of reciting all her Christian names.

'You're an Irishman!' exclaimed Sullivan triumphantly.

'No,' said Dusty politely, 'an Irish *girl*, I *think*.'*

Dusty nominated 'I Don't Want To Hear It Anymore' as her favourite track – 'It just has a really good atmosphere to it' – and it is hard to fault her judgement. Dusty's poignant reading of this Randy Newman song is complemented by Arif Mardin's arrangement and

---

* Twenty-five years later, 'Son Of A Preacher Man' was featured in the film *Pulp Fiction*, and subsequent sales of the soundtrack CD earned Dusty a platinum disc – and 'I didn't have to do *anything*!'

by the final element in the Memphis magic, the backing singers, who are heard to best advantage on this number. Myrna Smith, Estelle Brown, Sylvia Shemwell and Cissy Houston (mother of Whitney) had been given their name, the Sweet Inspirations, by Jerry Wexler, a fervent admirer of these 'fabulous background singers' who 'instinctively understood harmonies' and could 'switch parts, and turn on a dime'. They repaid his trust; according to Cissy Houston, 'As soon as we started to achieve some success, everybody wanted us. But Jerry Wexler was so good to us, we thought we'd stick with him.' Although essentially backing singers – they had recorded with Aretha Franklin and Dionne Warwick (Cissy Houston's niece) as well as providing the backing for Elvis Presley's 'Suspicious Minds' – they had enjoyed success in their own right, most notably in 1968 with 'Sweet Inspiration', whose every note betrays the singers' gospel origins. Their contribution to *Dusty in Memphis* should not be underestimated.[13]*

Dusty had made an earlier recording of Goffin and King's 'Don't Forget About Me' in London in 1967, and a comparison of that version with the Memphis track highlights the full extent of the musical journey she had undertaken. On the London recording, with an arrangement by Arthur Greenslade, Dusty's performance has a bouncy exuberance. It is a good track and could have found a place on her next LP without any difficulty; but the Memphis recording is very different: the piano figure has been replaced by a rasping guitar, and Dusty's interpretation is more intense, more deeply felt, bringing an air of desperate pleading to the performance. They are obviously recordings of the same song, with the same singer, but the two performances are vastly different.†

---

* This 'Sweet Inspiration' should not be confused with the song of the same title (originally recorded by Johnny Johnson and the Bandwagon) that Dusty recorded for *See All Her Faces* but which was not ultimately included on that LP, finally surfacing in 1999 on the American CD *Dusty in London*. See Appendix.

† The London recording of 'Don't Forget About Me' was eventually released on *Something Special* (1996) and may also be found as an additional track on the reissue of *Where Am I Going* (1998). See Appendix.

'Breakfast In Bed' echoes the slinky sensuousness of 'Just A Little Lovin'', while with 'Just One Smile' Dusty gives a sensitive performance of yet another fine song from Randy Newman. 'Just One Smile' had proved successful for Gene Pitney, who had made an athletic recording of the song in 1967; but he generously acknowledged that 'the song was later done definitively by Dusty Springfield'.

'The Windmills Of Your Mind' brought a sharp difference of opinion between Dusty and Jerry Wexler: 'I didn't want to do that song. Jerry did, and so I went along.' To Dusty, 'it was such an odd thing to have on an album that I wanted to be more R & B based', but she acknowledged that Jerry 'knew something that I didn't'. The song, which had been composed by Michel Legrand with Alan and Marian Bergman for *The Thomas Crown Affair*, one of that year's big films, and had been nominated for an Academy Award, does indeed seem a strange choice; but it is a further tribute to Arif Mardin's talent as an arranger that he was able to make the song blend with the other material. According to Dusty, the song 'caused absolute mayhem in the studio trying to get the chords right', and she recalled that she slowed the whole thing down: 'Originally it was very much faster, and I think I slowed it down so that it would be more organised.' Arif remembers that they all took turns sleeping on the floor during the long sessions as everyone struggled to master 'such a complicated, inventive rhythm', and that he had to build half-notes into the arrangement 'so that Dusty could breathe'. Dusty handles the song beautifully; but, despite some promotional initiatives by Jerry Wexler, popular success with the song fell to Noel Harrison, son of the more famous Rex, whose recording enjoyed the advantage of being on the film soundtrack.[14]*

'In The Land Of Make Believe' – 'an obscure Bacharach song' as Arif Mardin calls it – has Dusty working so near the top of her range that it seems as if at any moment her voice must surely break up.

* In 1970, Dusty recorded the same composers' 'What Are You Doing The Rest Of Your Life', although this superb performance was destined to remain on a shelf until it was included on *Dusty: The Legend of Dusty Springfield* in 1994. See Appendix.

But it never does: the performance is perfectly controlled. 'I think the highest and most sure I've ever sung is some of the fades . . . on the Memphis songs. They're . . . stratospheric! I've never hit them again.' Dusty's etherial performance contrasts markedly with the rather operatic recording by the Drifters and moves the melody away from its characteristic Bacharach shuffle.[15]

The record ends with 'No Easy Way Down' and 'I Can't Make It Alone', two Goffin-and-King compositions in a similar mood. Dusty always had a particularly close affinity with such songs of regret and yearning, and on 'I Can't Make It Alone' her sensitive performance is complemented perfectly by a remarkable string arrangement by Arif Mardin at his most Ravelesque.

A further track, 'What Do You Do When Love Dies' by Mary Unobsky and Donna Weiss, was also recorded at the 1968 session but was omitted from the record when it was released. Here, again, we have two recordings: the version that was eventually issued, first in America and much later in Britain, and an earlier – and superior – mix that has Dusty singing with only the rhythm section and the backing singers. Dusty delivers a powerful performance, but an abrupt change of rhythm between verse and chorus is rarely quite the good idea it may have seemed at the time.

Dusty in Memphis was released in April 1969 to widespread acclaim – and poor sales. According to Jerry Wexler, 'Everybody loved it except the damn public.'[16] The commercial failure of *Dusty in Memphis* may have been due in large measure to bad timing. No one was in the mood for it. In April 1969 there was an unmistakable sense of things coming to an end, with no clear idea of where the future lay. Even the Beatles, the driving force behind the whole sixties phenomenon, were falling apart and could manage only the lazy and uninspired 'Get Back', which was followed by the self-pitying 'Ballad of John and Yoko'; while the dominant sound of the spring was Peter Sarstedt's 'Where Do You Go To, My Lovely?', which is the musical equivalent of the Chinese water torture. The girl singers, too, were stranded. Sandie Shaw had come to the end of the road with

'Monsieur Dupont'. Cilla Black was still hanging on; but she looked distinctly uncomfortable when she performed her latest offering, 'Surround Yourself With Sorrow', on *Top of the Pops* wearing the skimpiest of mini-skirts that already looked too young for her. Lulu, who had erupted on to the pop scene in 1964 with a cover version of the Isley Brothers' 'Shout', had recently been a joint winner of the Eurovision Song Contest with 'Boom Bang-a-Bang', which was certainly nothing to shout about.*

Everyone seemed to be waiting for fresh inspiration. Only Dusty thought to go in search of it. In spite of all the agony, she seemed eager to return to Memphis. 'I think I'll be more relaxed on future sessions,' she declared confidently. 'I'm looking forward to the next ones next year.'[17] In fact, the 1969 session was a more modest affair, with Dusty recording only three songs. Her spirited interpretation of Tony Joe White's 'Willie and Laura Mae Jones' contrasts starkly with the long and dreary recording by the song's composer; it highlights yet again Dusty's remarkable instinct for knowing exactly how to get the best out of a song, underlining Janis Ian's later claim that 'There aren't many singers you would beg to do your material, but Dusty was one of them,' and Neil Tennant's assertion that 'Dusty takes your song and makes it sound ten times better'.[18] 'That Old Sweet Roll (Hi-De-Ho)' is an engaging piece of nonsense from Gerry Goffin and Carole King. The third recording, of the Bee Gees' 'To Love Somebody', has been lost.

There were to be no further Memphis sessions. Plans were well under way for a second LP, but Dusty had decided to move on. 'Talks were amicable,' recalled Tom Dowd, 'but broke down. I figured we'd been dismissed.' Arif Mardin believed that Dusty had seriously underestimated the importance of *Dusty in Memphis* and 'Next time

---

* This was the year in which four entries tied for first place. Britain's 'Boom Bang-a-Bang' was joined by equally ghastly offerings from Spain and the Netherlands. The fourth winner, France's 'Un Jour, Un Enfant', performed by Frida Boccara, was actually a rather good song but (like most Eurovision winners) disappeared without trace – though not before Frida had sung it on Dusty's last series of television shows.

she didn't want to work with the same musicians in the same town'.[19] Although she cannot have known it at the time, *Dusty in Memphis* was to be her last sustained achievement. There were still wonderful things to come, of course, but they would be individual moments of brilliance. She had curtailed her partnership with Johnny Franz in favour of recording in Memphis; and now she had turned her back on the Memphis team, too.*

There is a rather curious tailpiece to the Memphis story. Dusty claimed that she was so elated by one of the sessions that she climbed a tree – 'something I have never done since I was a child' – but 'the branches were slippery from a shower' and 'I fell and ended up with a black eye and a cut head'. Bearing in mind her general mood during the Memphis sessions and the fact that she actually did most of her work in New York, this incident is hard to understand; and spontaneous tree-climbing hardly accords with the image of the immaculately groomed 'queen of the Southern contingent' that she presented. Her

---

* *Dusty in Memphis* (Philips LP, 1969: SBL 7889): Just A Little Lovin' · So Much Love · Son Of A Preacher Man · I Don't Want To Hear It Anymore · Don't Forget About Me · Breakfast In Bed · Just One Smile · The Windmills Of Your Mind · In The Land Of Make Believe · No Easy Way Down · I Can't Make It Alone.

'What Do You Do When Love Dies' was eventually released in America in 1971 as the B-side of 'What Good Is I Love You' but did not find its way across the Atlantic until 1980 when it appeared on *Dusty in Memphis Plus* (Mercury LP: 6381 023), a reissue of the original LP with four additional tracks. The other three newcomers ('I Wanna Be A Free Girl', 'I Believe In You' and 'Haunted') were all refugees from later sessions with Kenny Gamble and Leon Huff, and with Jeff Barry.

The original LP was transcribed on to CD in 1995 (Mercury 528 687-2); and on this occasion the three remaining tracks from the Memphis sessions – 'Willie And Laura Mae Jones', 'That Old Sweet Roll (Hi-De-Ho)' and 'What Do You Do When Love Dies' – were included. Curiously, the running order on the CD differs from that on the original LP. The American CD reissue of 1999 (Rhino R2 75580) retains the original order and includes the original mix of 'What Do You Do When Love Dies'.

A live BBC radio performance of 'To Love Somebody' from 1970 has survived and may be found on the privately produced collection *The BBC Sessions*. See Appendix.

later reference to 'that business in Memphis that nobody seems to believe' suggests that others also found the story hard to accept. At the end of the year, when she spent Christmas Day with her mother, she had a fall while 'larking around' in the back garden, and sustained further facial injuries; so she ended another eventful year with a collection of cuts and contusions.[20]

7

The Marriage Question

IN MARCH 1969, Paul McCartney married Linda Eastman. The wedding attracted great interest, of course, but there was not the hysteria and mass suicide that it might have provoked a few years earlier. The fine frenzy of the 'Swinging Sixties' had abated, and the time had come to settle down and consider the future. A few days later, John Lennon married Yoko Ono in a quiet ceremony in Gibraltar. She was his second wife. For both men, marriage served to underline the fact that their musical partnership was effectively over and influenced profoundly the direction each would take in the seventies.

Matrimony was in the air for the girl singers, too; Sandie Shaw, Cilla Black and Lulu would all enter the new decade as married women. But what of Dusty? Attractive, charming, talented, articulate and highly intelligent, she was surely the greatest prize of all?

Now, as a good Catholic girl, Dusty had no trouble extolling the virtues of marriage in general – 'Marriage is great. . . . [It] must be a great comfort to have someone close all of your own'[1] – but when she talked about her own case she was hesitant. 'Of course, like every other girl, I'd like to get married some day', but she was fickle and restless – and frightened of making a mistake. 'Divorce would be out of the question because I'm a Catholic. Anyway, I don't believe in divorce.'[2] And then there was her career: 'I want to get married of course. I don't want to be left on the shelf. Sometimes I feel, "Oh, Dusty, you'll have had it soon." But I don't think a career and marriage work too well together, and I want more from my career yet.'[3] Later she would offer yet another reason for her reluctance to marry:

her parents' unhappiness. 'I thought if I married I'd repeat their performance.'[4]

As for children, 'The urge to reproduce' – and the arm's-length vocabulary itself suggests a sniffy distaste for the whole business – 'is always there, of course, but then I think "what for?" '

> I probably wouldn't be a terribly good mother. It would be great spasmodic moods of affection which don't last and that wouldn't be very stable. I would like children psychologically and physically, there's something which stops me from just reproducing.[5]*

Anyway, she was not ready to settle in a 'little suburban house with a husband and kids', being 'still too restless even to *like* a nice suburban house for very long'.[6]

But, for all Dusty's eloquence on the subject, there was an obvious obstacle to any hopes of married bliss. There seemed to be no men in her life whatsoever.

Well, this is not entirely true. In February 1964, Dusty posed for a photograph with fellow singer Eden Kane. As they clutched each other in an awkward embrace, each apparently trying to avoid a collision with the other's lacquered hairdo, they spoke of their relationship. Eden would not use the word 'marriage' but declared that he and Dusty were 'more than just close friends. We see each other as much as we can. We enjoy being with each other. But our careers take us to different parts of the world – so it's difficult to be together.' Dusty, too, avoided any suggestion of marriage: 'My career must come first. I think he is a nice boy – the nicest I've met. And I've

---

* Fifteen years later, when motherhood was probably no longer an option, Dusty declared that she was 'glad I never had children' and, with a rather disturbing turn of phrase, explained: 'I've a very short fuse, and I was terrified that, if I had a child, I might love it to death one minute, and throw it at the wall the next' (The *Daily Express*, 9 August 1985). However, Anthony Husher, who was Dusty's neighbour when she was living in Taplow in the 1980s, recalls that she seemed to be fond of children and even – rarest of privileges! – sang to his own daughter, although 'I was never allowed to listen' (The *Maidenhead Advertiser*, 12 March 1999).

taken him home to meet my parents. But we have no definite plans. We just like being together.'[7]

Perhaps unnerved by how definite the relationship seemed when words and picture were eventually published, Dusty wasted little time in clarifying the situation: 'It's been hopelessly exaggerated. I'm fond of him as a friend, but neither of us has the time to see enough of each other for it to develop into a romance.'[8] A year later – and the man himself had emigrated to Australia in the meantime – she was still denying that there was anything between them: 'Some people think I'm in love with Eden Kane, the pop singer. It's all nonsense.'[9] And *more than three years* after that solitary self-conscious embrace, and when everyone had probably forgotten all about it, she once again felt it necessary to set the record straight: 'we've been friends. Nothing more than that. But because I was photographed giving him a hug once (when he'd been away some time) everyone thought we were going to be married!'[10] Not since the days of Elizabeth I had such a madrigal and pavane been made of the Marriage Question.*

There were also suggestions of a romance with Burt Bacharach, but Dusty was quick to squash such rumours. Their relationship was purely musical. In any case, it is difficult to imagine two such notorious perfectionists being able to live together under the same roof for very long.

Ring-spotting offered no real clues. Dusty liked to wear rings on both hands, and was aware of – perhaps even enjoyed – the confusion this could cause. 'I keep getting into trouble over the one on my left hand – people keep thinking it's an engagement ring, but it's not.'[11] She can be seen flaunting it on the sleeve of *Golden Hits.*

Dusty herself added to the speculation. Interviewed in April 1965, she declared that she was very much in love and hoped to announce her engagement soon. Nothing more was heard of this great romance. Later she revealed that in 1967 she had been 'pretty seriously in love'. On this occasion, however, not her career but her religion had proved

* Eden Kane eventually settled in California, where his subsequent career has included playing a Klingon in *Star Trek.*

a stumbling-block: the man was not a Catholic. For herself, she would have been willing to overlook the matter but she was reluctant to upset her parents, and so the relationship came to nothing.[12] Neither lover was identified. In the absence of any corroborative evidence, and in spite of Dusty's insistence that she would not invent a relationship simply to appease inquisitive journalists, it is difficult to regard these great love-affairs as anything other than imaginary.[13]

And still the question lingered. Why was there no man in her life? Dusty had no trouble providing an explanation. She frightened men off! Her shyness made her appear aloof and unapproachable. (Jerry Wexler christened her 'the Ice Lady'.) Fame, too, made relationships difficult: 'we couldn't exactly behave like other young couples and snog in a cinema. There'd be dozens of eyes watching us, saying: "Look, Eth, there's Dusty having a snog in the back row." '[14] ('Eth' seems to be a residual memory of Eth Glum from the 1950s radio series *Take It from Here*. If all eyes are on Dusty and her boyfriend in the back row of this imaginary cinema, then all the seats would appear to be facing the wrong way. Anyway, Dusty once claimed that she had stopped going to the cinema after a woman hit her for laughing at Jeanette MacDonald.) But she was also able to identify a more serious problem. Shyness, insecurity and her Catholic upbringing had conspired to deprive her of the ability to build relationships. In his autobiography, Frank Allen recalls an occasion in the early 1970s when Dusty, the worse for drink, suggested to him that they might have a baby together; time was running out, and her chances of ever becoming a mother were steadily dwindling. Mr Allen finds a particularly unattractive, 'laddish' way of describing the incident, and misses completely the sadness at the heart of it, but there is no reason to question the truth of the story. Such awkward blundering moments were inevitable for someone like Dusty who found so much of day-to-day human relationships difficult.[15]

Over the years this would bring her a great deal of unhappiness. In the early sixties she 'led a very sheltered life' and was 'almost living like a nun'. She developed formidable exterior defences to make herself – to use her own word – 'un-get-able', and claimed that when she consulted a hypnotherapist about her recurrent throat problems he was unable to hypnotise her because 'Apparently, I've got too suspicious a nature!' She distrusted compliments, and 'for a long time I couldn't stand kissing and cuddling because I had been told it wasn't right'.[16] There had been no boyfriends, no teenage crushes. Mick Jagger asked her out, but her nerve failed her and she turned him down.

> Men believed I must be so sexy with all this blonde hair, mini skirts and come-to-bed eyes. But it was all an act. That was Dusty Springfield pop star. Inside I was plain dumpy Mary O'Brien, good Catholic girl.[17]

The American singer Tony Orlando even asked her to send him a telegram when she lost her virginity. Consequently, 'I get letters from young fans asking me for advice on their problems, and I don't know what they're talking about.'[18] She wished for 'someone to knock me between the eyes and rough me up a bit. Even if it didn't work out, at least I'd be a more mature woman.' (Unfortunately, in time she would get her wish.) Her occasional self-conscious attempts to portray herself as a man-chaser – claiming to follow tennis avidly on account of 'all those dishy men in ankle-socks' or recommending Rome as 'a girl's city. Lots of good-looking men' – are unconvincing and sad.[19]

With such a conspicuous lack of *men* in her life, the predictable rumours began to circulate. Even Dusty's close friendship with Martha Reeves became the subject of gossip.[20]* She was hurt by such speculation:

> I have a certain pride in myself as a woman and it upsets my femininity. And because I don't float round from premiere to premiere I've been criticised. And it's no use saying anything: they say you're

---

* An artfully placed photograph of Dusty and Martha to accompany 'The Secret Life of Dusty Springfield', an article by Michelle Kort in the American gay magazine *The Advocate*, 27 April 1999, serves to revive this suggestion.

either a prostitute or a lesbian, so if you're neither where are you? You can't be in the middle, in people's minds. I've done nothing wrong. . . .[21]

Nevertheless, Dusty seemed to confirm the rumours in 1966 when she set up home with American singer Norma Tanega. The two women met when they appeared on the same television show. Dusty was due to sing her current hit, 'You Don't Have To Say You Love Me', while Norma was to perform 'Walking My Cat Named Dog', which was her only successful recording. During a tea-break at rehearsals Dusty introduced herself, and the two women took to each other. It was Dusty's most enduring relationship with another woman; they would remain close friends for the rest of Dusty's life. Norma had a distinctive, if rather limited, talent as a composer; and Dusty's tribute to 'a writer of immense talent and a fine recording artiste' on the sleeve of *Dusty . . . Definitely* (1968) was perhaps a *slight* exaggeration.*

Although Dusty insisted that she was not a part of the gay scene in the sixties, others have contradicted her.[22]

All Dusty's fine words on marriage and motherhood could be dismissed as an elaborate ploy to conceal the true nature of her sexuality – as perhaps her finest practical joke – but that would be unfair. There is no reason to believe that she was anything other than completely sincere. In the context of today's tyrannical gay politics, which tends to regard the slightest doubt or hesitation as a wilful refusal to face facts, Dusty's behaviour could be seen as wanton prevarication;

---

*Norma Tanega was co-author of a lyric, 'Dusty Springfield', which was set to music and recorded in 1970 by Blossom Dearie. This embarrassing, if well-intentioned, song demonstrates that, although 'Dusty Springfield' may be a musical name, it is not easy to *make music* out of it. The song's only rhyme for *Springfield* is *green field*. (It would all have been so much simpler if Dusty had been born in *Lingfield*.) And, while horses play *the dusty game*, we are urged to come to the *spring* and fill our cups. Blossom Dearie had earlier achieved greater success on *Sweet Blossom Dearie* (1967) with another tribute-song, 'Sweet Georgie Fame', an engaging jazz waltz. The same LP, recorded at Ronnie Scott's in London, included a performance of 'Sweet Lover No More', which Dusty would record in 1968.

but that, too, is unjust. After all, why should we expect a woman who was uncertain of every other aspect of her life to have been sure of her sexuality?

Dusty gave the first public glimpse of her inner turmoil during the summer of 1967 when she treated readers of the *News of the World* to a bizarre lecture on 'sickness' in show business. As we pick our way through oblique references to normality and abnormality, the sick-minded and the kinky, it is hard to decide whether Dusty is struggling to find expression for a subject she finds really difficult or whether she is being deliberately cryptic, but at the heart of the piece lies an incident that had clearly unsettled her. This is the story as Dusty tells it:

> I always feel a great compassion for anyone who is new to show business. One day I saw a young girl sitting all alone at a TV recording studio. She was a very new singer then. She had just had her first record released and I thought it was great. So I went up and told her so.
>
> Imagine how shattered I felt when this girl told a friend of mine that it was a bit odd of me to say so. Her sick little mind had obviously twisted my compliment into something else. Potty, isn't it?
>
> Ever since that incident I've been careful not to compliment any other girl.[23]

There are two obvious explanations: either Dusty had paid the girl a simple compliment and the girl, aware of Dusty's reputation, had panicked; or Dusty had made a pass at the girl but it had all gone horribly wrong. Whatever the truth of the matter, the incident highlights how difficult Dusty's position had become.

In September 1970 she decided to force the issue. In the course of a long interview with Ray Connolly she openly addressed the question of her sexuality for the first time. She was aware of the rumours and was upset by them: 'I've had this reputation for years, but I don't know how I got it.' She enjoyed 'walking down a street and having a guy who's digging the road giving me a whistle. . . . I love to be admired just for being a woman. . . . [Being] a woman is very precious to me'; but 'I'm as perfectly capable of being swayed by a girl as by a boy'.[24] She never elaborated on this elegantly vague statement – not even the formidable Jean Rook could bludgeon her into being more explicit[25] – and we may question whether she ever actually 'came out' in the accepted sense of the term.* But Dusty's sexuality was now in the public domain, and Dusty herself had put it there. That brief remark would dog her for the rest of her life. Many years later she reflected wearily: 'Is there a man in your life? Is there a woman in your life? Is there a horse in your life? People are always going to want to know.'[26]

(Asked much later how her parents had reacted to her admission, Dusty replied that to them 'it was just one of those things I used to say. I don't remember any reaction. Sexuality was never discussed in our house. It didn't exist.'[27])

Why did she do it? After all, she could have chosen to continue dancing around the subject, sidestepping awkward questions and refusing to commit herself at all; others have done so. A possible explanation is to be found by taking a broader view of her position at this time. As we have seen, Dusty found herself having to make decisions about her future: the sixties party was winding down, record sales had dipped, and for almost all of the decade's brightest stars there were tough questions to be answered. By this time Dusty had concluded that her future lay in America – a new life, a new career, new friends. Emboldened perhaps by this fresh bright prospect opening up for her, she decided to set the record straight, to draw a line under the old life before embarking on the new. It is tempting to try to cast Dusty in the role of a Pilgrim Mother leaving the oppression and hypocrisy of her native land for a new life of freedom in America, but this would be wide of the mark. At this time Dusty's career was still the dominant factor in her life; and, while it may be true that she

* 'I'm not going to commit myself to being homosexual or heterosexual because people are going to write what they want about me – they always have' (*Gay News*, 24 February 1978).

found a kind of sexual liberation in California, she left Britain for purely professional reasons.

The Ray Connolly interview brought another big surprise. The girl who claimed that she spent much of the sixties 'almost living like a nun', rarely went to parties and liked to spend her evenings listening to records with a few friends now boasted of being 'promiscuous' and even declared that she could handle 'a lot more action', although she qualified her admission immediately:

> I suppose to say I'm promiscuous is a bit of bravado on my part. I think it's more in thought than in action. I've been that way ever since I discovered the meaning of the word.

Earlier in her career she had revealed, rather touchingly, 'I'm one of those people whose minds have done everything, but who have never had real experiences', adding later: 'I'm all talk and no action'.[28] At what point she 'went from nothing to over-indulgence almost overnight' is unclear – as is precisely what she meant by 'over-indulgence'.[29] Time and again over the years, even after she had embraced Californian hedonism with enthusiasm, her revelations about her private life are accompanied by slight hints that what she has told us might not be literally true – 'just one of those things I used to say'. A Catholic urge to confess had encouraged her at an early age to make things up, 'just to make sure I was cleansed'; and always, as we listen to her 'confessions', loitering nearby is the suspicion that much of her outrageous sex life existed more in thought than in deed. And she devised an ingenious closing strategy to curtail any discussion of the subject: 'If you want to know the truth – ask the people who go to bed with me.'[30] Naturally, she had no intention of providing a list. She never identified any of her lovers.

8

Am I the Same Girl?

AFTER ALL THE EXCITEMENT of 1968, Dusty may have felt that the question posed in the title of her next single, 'Am I The Same Girl', released in September 1969, seemed particularly apt, and Dusty may have felt that the title of her final release of the decade, 'Brand New Me', answered that question. If so, she would have been disappointed. Finding a record good enough to follow the remarkable 'Son Of A Preacher Man' was always going to be difficult, and neither single had any real impact, hovering at the very bottom of the Top Forty. In spite of an attractive brass figure, 'Am I The Same Girl' is only a slight performance; and on the B-side, 'Earthbound Gypsy', a jazz-influenced song by Norma Tanega, Dusty attempts an intimate caba-ret style of performance – with only moderate success. 'Brand New Me' offered a foretaste of the forthcoming successor to *Dusty in Memphis*. It was certainly different.

Dusty began the new decade in some confusion. Her first single was the gentle ballad 'Morning Please Don't Come', on which she sang with brother Tom once again and which inevitably revived memories of the Springfields; but in the same month her new LP, *From Dusty . . . with Love*, was released, and it marked yet another drastic change of direction.

Having abandoned the Memphis team, but still under contract to Atlantic, for her next musical alliance Dusty chose to go to Philadel-phia and work with Kenny Gamble and Leon Huff at Sigma Sound Studios. Once again she was entrusting herself to a production team she knew only by reputation; and at this stage Gamble and Huff, who would soon become a dominant force in black American music in the 1970s, working with the likes of Harold Melvin and the Blue Notes, the O'Jays, Billy Paul, and the Three Degrees, were still developing their talents. Dusty's commitment to this young team was all the greater because Gamble and Huff were also writing the songs for the LP. Dusty had already recorded a Leon Huff song, the uplifting 'Live It Up', for her *Dusty in New York* EP, but by 1969 his musical style had changed completely.

Once again, Dusty had to adjust to a new way of working. After the deliberation and the painstaking attention to the smallest detail in Memphis, she found that in Philadelphia everything moved more swiftly. She had difficulty in adapting to *this* style, too.

> I like to live with songs for a while. One never gets enough time to do that. I like to sort of roll it around for a month – not actually sing it, but just have it around. And Gamble and Huff didn't work like that. They might well have written a song the night before.[1]

Listening to *From Dusty . . . with Love*, released in February 1970, we might well reach the same conclusion.* It is a very slight performance; nothing lingers in the memory. The arrangements seem to be little more than promiscuous twangs and thumps that distract attention from Dusty's performance rather than enhance it. (On 'Silly, Silly Fool' the orchestra appears to slip into Percy Faith's 'A Summer Place'.) 'Brand New Me', released as a single in November 1969, is the only number to have achieved a life of its own, yet even this track is fortunate to have found a place alongside Dusty's big successes. 'Lost' and the inappropriately jaunty 'Bad Case Of The Blues' sound as if they would probably have done well in the Eurovision Song Contest; while 'Joe', the big ballad in the collection, fails to live up to

---

* *From Dusty . . . with Love* (Philips LP, 1970: SBL 7927): Lost · Bad Case Of The Blues · Never Love Again · Let Me Get In Your Way · Let's Get Together Soon · Brand New Me · Joe · Silly, Silly Fool · The Star Of My Show · Let's Talk It Over.
   From Dusty . . . with Love was reissued on CD in 1990 (Philips 846 251-2). At the time of writing there are plans to reissue it again some time in 2001.

the grand orchestral introduction. 'Let Me Get In Your Way' allows Dusty to give one of her delicately wistful performances, but this is really the only moment of musical respectability. There is little else of any interest.

Dusty made other recordings with Gamble and Huff, but only 'I Wana Be A Free Girl' saw the light of day, released in 1970. The others, 'Cherished' and 'Goodbye', sat on a shelf for thirty years.

That Dusty was now pursuing parallel careers on either side of the Atlantic is underlined by the fact that in 1970 she actually recorded two different songs with the title 'Goodbye', one American and one British. With its distinctive lilting rhythm, the American 'Goodbye' is the best work Dusty did with Gamble and Huff; while, for the British 'Goodbye', Norma Tanega set some words to a melody by Bach. This track, too, was locked away.*

Once again, Dusty chose not to repeat the experience; so that when she went into the studio to make her third LP for Atlantic it was in New York and with yet another producer – Jeff Barry. The sessions yielded two American singles, 'Haunted' (with 'Nothing Is Forever') and 'I Believe In You' (with 'Someone Who Cares'). Neither record made any impact; and, disenchanted, Dusty decided to leave Atlantic and sign for ABC/Dunhill. The remaining Atlantic tracks were left on the shelf, although all have subsequently become available.†￼ The quality of the recordings is uneven. 'I Believe In You' and 'Nothing Is Forever' are Dusty's worst performances on record: the former

* 'I Wanna Be A Free Girl' may be found as an additional track on the American reissue of *From Dusty . . . with Love* under its American title of *A Brand New Me* (1992); while 'Cherished' and the Gamble-and-Huff 'Goodbye' were released as additional tracks on the American reissue of *Dusty in Memphis* (1999). The British 'Goodbye' may be found on *The Dusty Springfield Anthology* (1997). See Appendix.

† If it had eventually appeared, Dusty's projected third LP for Atlantic would have comprised: Haunted · Someone Who Cares · I Believe In You · You've Got A Friend · Make It With You · Love Shine Down · All The King's Horses · Have A Good Life Baby · I'll Be Faithful · Live Here With You · Natchez Trace · I Found My Way. Anyone who wishes to re-create Dusty's 'lost' LP will find all the numbers included as additional tracks on the reissues of *A Brand New Me* (1992) and *Dusty in Memphis* (1999). See Appendix.

is simply a dreadful song; while on the latter Dusty seems to have trouble holding on to the big chorus, with her voice wandering all over the place. But there are some delights amongst the other tracks: 'Make It With You' is a fine cover of a David Gates song; 'Live Here With You' is a charming folk-influenced number, with the piano taking the guitar part; and 'I Found My Way' is a glorious gospel-influenced performance that echoes happier times. Dusty even chose to turn her back on 'You've Got A Friend', a splendid Carole King song that would bring great success to James Taylor.

In September 1970, Dusty achieved modest chart success with 'How Can I Be Sure', a powerful and uplifting number that also brought success to David Cassidy and Helen Reddy. Dusty herself had doubted the record's chances of success: 'That comes from a backlog of doubts in myself because the last few records have gone wrong.'[2] It would be Dusty's last successful record in Britain for nine years.

Continuing Dusty's practice of burying wonderful things on B-sides, 'Spooky' is another hidden delight, offering an intimate jazz-influenced contrast to the grandeur of 'How Can I Be Sure'. The song had given Classics IV a hit record in the late sixties, and there had also been a meandering version by Andy Williams, but Dusty's light and witty performance finally does it justice.

There would be no further releases until May 1972 when two tracks from Dusty's next LP were issued as a single. By this time the full horror of the seventies was upon us, dominated for the moment by T. Rex's 'Debora' (which turned out to rhyme with 'zebora'), although Tom Jones was managing to hang on with the truly awful 'The Young New Mexican Puppeteer'. Quite how Dusty's sublime recordings of 'Yesterday When I Was Young' and 'I Start Counting' were meant to survive in such a climate is a mystery.

In November the LP itself appeared. What are we to make of *See All Her Faces*? Initially, it marks a welcome reunion of Dusty with Johnny Franz, and brings Dusty together with such fine British arrangers as Peter Knight and Wally Stott, while for the first time Dusty is given credit as co-producer. Side 1 represents a remarkable recovery after the banality of *From Dusty . . . with Love*. The bouncy confidence of the opening track, 'Mixed Up Girl', gives way to the rugged 'Crumbs Off The Table', with Dusty sounding relaxed and back on top form. The gently lilting 'Let Me Down Easy' is followed by Jobim's 'Come For A Dream', the first of two sambas in the collection. The record falters slightly with 'Girls Can't Do What The Guys Do', but then we are treated to a reappearance of 'I Start Counting' and 'Yesterday When I Was Young'.

But when we turn the record over the collection begins to fall apart. Although there are two further Franz–Springfield tracks, notably the wistful samba 'See All Her Faces', the remainder of side 2 is devoted to a mixture of old tracks from sessions with Jeff Barry, Jerry Wexler, Ellie Greenwich and Mike Rashkow. 'That Old Sweet Roll' and 'Willie and Laura Mae Jones' were left over from the Memphis sessions and were here made available in Britain for the first time, as were two Jeff Barry productions and a stray Greenwich–Rashkow production, 'What Good Is I Love You'. The two Barry tracks are the weakest on the record: 'Someone Who Cares' switches from a wistful verse to a thunderous and rather laboured chorus, but the change is too drastic and not entirely pleasing; and the unfortunate 'Nothing Is Forever' should have been left to rest in peace.*

The curious composition of side 2 has become even more difficult to understand now that we are able to hear the Franz–Springfield tracks that were set aside to make way for the odd assortment of

* *See All Her Faces* (Philips LP, 1972: 6308 117): Mixed Up Girl · Crumbs Off The Table · Let Me Down Easy · Come For A Dream · Girls Can't Do What The Guys Do · I Start Counting · Yesterday When I Was Young · Girls It Ain't Easy · What Good Is I Love You · Willie And Laura Mae Jones · Someone Who Cares · Nothing Is Forever · See All Her Faces · That Old Sweet Roll (Hi-De-Ho).

See All Her Faces has never been reissued in its entirety, but most of the Franz–Springfield tracks were included on the American CD *Dusty in London* (1999) along with 'Wasn't Born To Follow', 'A Song For You' and 'Sweet Inspiration'. See Appendix.

A prolific arranger, Wally Stott had also been musical director for *Hancock's Half Hour* and the Goons in the 1950s – an association that must have delighted Dusty. In the early seventies he underwent a sex-change operation and was henceforth Angela Morley, who went on to enjoy considerable success composing film scores.

material from the archives. Finally released in 1999, 'A Song For You', 'Wasn't Born To Follow' and 'Sweet Inspiration' should have been given their chance on the original LP. *See All Her Faces* remains an enigma.

By the end of 1972, Dusty was permanently located in Los Angeles. She had finally turned her back on Atlantic and signed for ABC/Dunhill. Her first project for her new record company, *Cameo*, was released in April 1973.*

Once again Dusty had entrusted herself to an untried team and, as in Philadelphia, had also relied on them for material: no fewer than five songs in the collection are by Dennis Lambert and Brian Potter, who also co-produced the record with Steve Barri. The dreadful sleeve design does not inspire confidence – although British record-buyers were spared the lurid orange gatefold – and the collection is disappointing. The arrangements are often banal, with a heavy dependence on electric piano, and only four tracks have any lingering appeal. Alan O'Day's 'Easy Evil' provides Dusty with the opportunity for a slinky performance reminiscent of 'Spooky'; 'The Other Side of Life' is another haunting David Gates composition; and 'Tupelo Honey' offers a powerful performance of a Van Morrison song; but the wistful 'Of All The Things', by Lambert and Potter, is the outstanding track and could perhaps take its place alongside Dusty's finest work.

Dusty sounds bright and confident on *Cameo*, but this is deceptive; and, in the circumstances, we may marvel that the record is as good as it is. Dusty was in trouble. According to Steve Barri, 'We could tell she was emotionally unstable, but it was hard to say why. She was having breakdowns in the studio, crying and carrying on, and having trouble keeping her pitch. . . . We wound up punching in so

---

* *Cameo* (Philips LP, 1973: 6308 152): Who Gets Your Love · Breakin' Up A Happy Home · Easy Evil · Mama's Little Girl · The Other Side of Life · Comin' And Goin' · I Just Wanna Be There · Who Could Be Loving You Other Than Me · Tupelo Honey · Of All The Things · Learn To Say Goodbye.

Cameo has never been reissued in its entirety, but some of the tracks have found their way on to subsequent compilations.

much, little details that destroyed the feel of the performance.' It was 'a tough experience' and left him feeling 'Thank God it's over'. According to his co-producer, Dennis Lambert, Dusty 'could never accept that her vocal, cold, was fabulous. She had to satisfy a need to be hard on herself – she was in search of perfection.'

Dusty remembered it rather differently. 'I'd never worked in a system where the artist comes in and the basic tracks are already laid. On some of those things they didn't even ask me what key I wanted to sing in.' This is hard to believe. While it may not be unknown for session singers to find that they are expected to work in keys that are difficult for them, it is surely inconceivable that a record company would invest a large amount of money in new recordings by a major singer without anyone whatsoever bothering to enquire as to the artist's vocal range. We have only to recall the preparations Tom Dowd made for Dusty's Memphis recordings.[3]

Something was obviously wrong, and when Dusty went into the studio in New York in 1974 to record her second LP for ABC/Dunhill, to be produced by Brooks Arthur, and provisionally entitled 'Longing', her problems reached a crisis. If work on *Cameo* had been difficult, the 'Longing' sessions were hellish, with Dusty collapsing into tears and tantrums – until, finally, she mutilated herself by cutting her wrists. Brooks Arthur took her to hospital, where she was admitted under the name of Mary O'Brien; but, unfortunately, a British nurse working at the hospital recognised her and the news leaked out. Work on 'Longing' was abandoned; only four tracks have emerged.* And so Dusty Springfield the perfectionist was left clinging to the wreckage of her career and of her life. How had everything gone so wrong and so quickly?

---

* 'I Am Your Child' may be found on *Something Special* (1996);while 'Home To Myself', 'Exclusively For Me' and a superb recording of Janis Ian's 'In The Winter' were included on *Simply Dusty* (2000). See Appendix.

9

The Descent into Hell

AS WE KNOW, Dusty's love-affair with America had begun in her early teens when she sat in Ealing cinemas and absorbed the sights and sounds of the Hollywood musicals. Success with the Springfields eventually took her to America, where she discovered an exciting new world of music that suddenly gave her career a sense of purpose and offered her a way out of the limited and unadventurous musical environment in which she had become trapped. She started to work and record in America very early in her solo career, crossing the Atlantic frequently and establishing important musical relationships. In 1966 she declared that there were still 'a few things I want to do in the States yet', and by the end of the decade she was in effect pursuing parallel careers on either side of the Atlantic.[1]

The commercial failure of *Dusty in Memphis* and her lack of success with any of her single releases after 'Son Of A Preacher Man' served only to confirm her opinion that the sixties party was over and that she had to give serious thought to her future. 'I remember thinking there was nothing left to do.'[2]

She became convinced that her future lay in America, and Los Angeles in particular was 'the place I wanted to be'. With no alternative career opportunities available to her, she knew that if she stayed in Britain she would be condemning herself to a dreary round of clubs, cabaret and summer season. 'I could see the future clearly. I would end up doing second-rate clubs, just wearing myself down, wearing myself out.' After all, this was where she had begun her career with the Springfields, and no doubt she felt that after all her hard work and success she deserved better than having to use a toilet as a dressing-room and make her grand entrance through a kitchen. And she had always loathed summer season, stuck at the end of a pier for twelve weeks. 'I had to leave for my own sanity.'³

In fact, working the Northern club circuit was hardly a thankless task: the people always wanted to see her. For example, at the Greasbrough Working Men's Club 'I finished my forty-minute act, left the stage and started to change my clothes. They started banging on tin trays like a prison riot. I had to get dressed again and go back on stage.' And Dusty could be quite sentimental about it, recalling a young Greasbrough mother 'with her scampi and chips': 'I could tell she was enjoying my songs so much. Overworked as she was, swollen ankles and all, I was her big night out. That's why I used to go out and do it.'⁴*

Apart from the sheer drudgery of taking herself round the country night after night – the sheer effort of having to do it – what Dusty really disliked about clubs and cabaret was the *intimacy* of the performance: 'I don't like being that close to people. I like concerts, where you have to work, to reach out.' And she spoke of her fear of being 'defeated into accepting that type of existence' if she stayed in Britain.⁵

By the early seventies Dusty's visits to America were growing longer and were now for social as much as for professional purposes. Returning to London at the beginning of 1971 after a three-month absence, she confessed to having been a 'drop-out', doing nothing at all but meet old friends and take tennis lessons.⁶ At this point she had still not plucked up the courage to settle in California permanently: 'I find I can take it for two or three months, but then I have to come home again.' And she assured her fans: 'I don't intend to

---

* For Labour politician Joe Ashton the Greasbrough evening was memorable for the manner in which the club chairman introduced Dusty: 'Before the show starts, I 'ave an important announcement: would the gentleman who urinated against the front wall pack it in. Now, 'ere's Dusty Springwell.' Dusty laughed so much she was unable to sing – until the chairman uttered the magic words: 'Get on with it, luv, or I'll cut your fee' (The *Mail on Sunday*, 6 August 2000).

take out American citizenship.'[7] Nevertheless, the lure of America was becoming irresistible: 'I was seduced by the great American Dream. I thought it would re-kindle the challenge'.[8]

Dusty had even revived her dream of a career as an actress. She never entirely abandoned this ambition – even as late as 1995 she confessed that 'I would have liked to act, but no one asked me' – but towards the end of the sixties, as her thoughts focused increasingly on a future in America, the dream of Hollywood stardom became more intense.

By this time she had outgrown her earlier suggestion of 'a Doris Day kind of part in a comedy' and had her sights set on a 'serious' film; but 'I haven't got the courage to be kitchen sink so I would have to play someone totally neurotic'. She felt sure that with the right director ('that's so important'), who could 'spark off something from me', she could do a good job. 'It wouldn't have to be a director I got on with particularly as long as there was a reaction.' She later claimed that in the seventies 'two acting coaches of great stature' who saw her performance at a charity concert offered to give her lessons, although there was no suggestion that they were so overwhelmed by her potential that they were prepared to offer this service for nothing. But there was the problem of public acceptance, because 'it's hard to get people to see past the image; they don't see me as anything other than Dusty Springfield, pop singer' – which seems an extraordinary remark when we consider the pains she had taken to create the image and to ensure that no one ever *did* get past it. Dusty Springfield herself was a character played by Mary O'Brien, and for any dream of a film career to become a reality Mary would have had to be allowed to re-emerge and dismantle Dusty Springfield so that she could assume other roles. And, when we think of the agonising sessions in the recording studio and the strain imposed on all those around her, we cannot even begin to imagine the havoc her quest for perfection would have wreaked on a film set. Would there ever have been enough film in the camera to cope with the number of takes she would have demanded before she was satisfied with her performance? ('You're stuck with it, you know.')

But Dusty knew that it was all merely an idle dream. She lacked the commitment and the application – and, to be frank, she was too *lazy* – to turn her back on her singing career and study a new craft: 'I am not so dedicated that I would go away and train as an actress'.

It was probably all for the best. This was hardly a promising time at which to embark on a film career. The best she could have expected would have been to scream prettily as she was rescued from the clutches of guerrillas – or even gorillas – by Richard Burton or Lee Marvin.[9]*

Eventually she took the plunge and by late 1972 had settled permanently in Los Angeles. She bought a house in Laurel Canyon with 'a fantastic view, a big pool' – even though she could not swim – and 'all the gadgets' and was 'determined to be as Californian as possible'. She slipped into the Beverly Hills routine – shopping, the hairdresser's, the beauty parlour, lunch – and in her publicity photographs at this time she sported sun-bleached shoulder-length tresses.

She even learned to cook. 'I would spend ages shopping for these enormously complicated recipes and cooking them very successfully and getting very fat.' And this was the woman who once boasted of being thoroughly undomesticated and who, on one occasion, had rashers of bacon delivered to her London home by taxi when she fancied a sandwich in the middle of the night.

But behind this sun-kissed façade all was far from well. For someone as shy as Dusty, the task of building a new life for herself and taking her place in a new social circle must have been daunting; and in order to conquer her inhibitions she began to drink more heavily. Soon she was also taking tranquillisers.

In the sixties Dusty had admitted to smoking marijuana twice. 'It just made me hungry or sleepy. I used to roll them up for other people. And I didn't inhale. Whatever I did was amateurish in that respect.' The police had raided her home on one occasion but found nothing; and Dusty was convinced that they were acting on false

---

* Twenty years later, pop videos were to offer Dusty a belated opportunity to play the movie queen. See below, Chapter 11.

information from 'a rather hysterical lady who was upset because I didn't fancy her'. As for the more exotic concoctions like LSD, 'I think it's a bit foolish to take things like that'. Nevertheless, when required, Dusty could spout the sixties party line as well as anyone:

British pop stars have been totally persecuted for smoking marijuana. . . . I know it sounds corny, but pot is less harmful than alcohol, and soft drugs do not lead to harder drugs. It is usually environment that drives a person to them.[10]

Here, too, California changed everything. Dusty found herself in a cultural environment in which drug-taking of one kind or another was the accepted way of life. 'People offered them to me at first and then I got them from crooked doctors.' And 'I didn't see the downward slide'.[11]

To make matters worse, the bright new career that had seemed to be opening up for her was already in trouble. Having turned her back on the British clubs-and-cabaret circuit and put herself in the hands of new management, Dusty now found herself trapped in exactly the same kind of drudgery in America. According to Vicki Wickham, 'Management did not understand Dusty. . . . [I]nstead of talking to her, working out what she could and couldn't do, they put her into the hotel circuit . . . but working hotel rooms night after night . . . she hated it'. To Dusty, 'It was like Blackpool all over again', 'Same things night after night'.

After two or three years on the American circuit, I was a *complete nutcase*. I didn't like that world at *all*. I couldn't deal with it. I had agents who would book me into clubs that were completely wrong for me. . . . It was *not* a happy time. *Cursing* it every time I found myself in yet another bloody club.

'I felt I'd lost control over my career.' In her desperation, she even reverted to smashing crockery: 'That was all I could do to ease the tension – smash some plates against a wall.'[12]

A return engagement at the Talk of the Town in London towards the end of 1972 only added to her misery. It was a disaster. Dusty collapsed with flu on opening night, and a doctor advised her not to go on. She was reported to have been suffering from bronchitis. The audience, who had been kept waiting for three-quarters of an hour, were now impatient and began a slow handclap and also to tap their coffee-cups with their spoons. Elton John, who was in the audience, offered to stand in for Dusty, but eventually the lady herself decided to go ahead with the show. Coughing heavily, she announced: 'There are many songs I would like to sing but I can't because they would be an embarrassment to you and to me.' She managed to get through some kind of act and seems to have won her audience over, but before she was able to recover sufficiently to return to work she received a letter informing her that her contract had been terminated. Bruce Forsyth took over, and Dusty's triumphant return ended up in the hands of the lawyers.[13]

Dusty's unhappiness inevitably began to affect her recording career. 'I wasn't proud of the sounds coming from my throat, and I didn't think I could tell what the good songs were any more.'[14] As we have seen, Dusty broke down repeatedly during the *Cameo* sessions, and she finally reached the end of the line in New York in 1974 while struggling to record her next LP for ABC/Dunhill. The sessions ended prematurely with Dusty in a hospital bed after she had slashed her wrists. 'I hit the biggest depression you've ever imagined. I hated life. I hated singing. I hated everyone and everything.'[15] Worst of all, she hated herself.

Dusty's response to this crisis was simply to stop singing. 'I just couldn't hack it.'[16] With the exception of some work as a backing singer for Elton John and Anne Murray, Dusty would remain silent for three years. This precipitated another crisis. Having mislaid the need to sing that had driven her since her early teens, Dusty was left with nothing.

And the landscape of her dreams had begun to lose its charm. 'I staggered around the house for a while trying to convince myself that I belonged. But every time I looked at the burnt-up hillside I felt

terribly alien.' Los Angeles was now 'sick' and 'vapid', and Dusty
was unable to adapt to the social round of the ladies who lunch. She
even felt uncomfortable in her own home: 'it was sort of nouveau
riche. The trouble was I was not very nouvelle and not at all riche.'[17]

Her drinking lurched out of control. She became a drunk – and an
unpleasant drunk, too: 'bad-tempered, rude, truly obnoxious'.[18] On
one occasion she even suffered the classic humiliation of having a
waiter ask her: 'Haven't you had enough, Lady?' The alcohol was
supplemented by a growing reliance on drugs – 'I just wanted to stop
the noise of frustration inside my head' – and Dusty slid ever faster
towards self-destruction. 'I lost nearly all the Seventies in a haze of
booze and pills.'[19] The woman who had once devoted every waking
moment to keeping herself 'rigidly together' had now lost control of
her life.

The sexual promiscuity – real or imaginary – of which she had
boasted in 1970 became 'extreme promiscuity'; 'I lost my judgement'.
At the beginning of the decade Dusty had attached herself to the
women's tennis circuit, which included a very strong lesbian element.
Dusty had now embraced an exclusively gay lifestyle and, according
to Rosemary Casals, had 'many lovers' – although, quite remark-
ably, in public Dusty never wavered in her refusal to commit herself
to a firm and unambiguous declaration of her sexuality, and at one
point even managed to produce a boyfriend. 'His name is Howard. I
won't tell you his surname because it won't mean anything to you
and it might offend him.' Howard worked in the music business but
was not terribly successful, and as Dusty, too, was 'professionally in-
active' at the time 'There was an edginess and moodiness between
us, and no fulfilment'. The affair lasted about a year. 'Looking back,
it was an interesting experience. We did have our moments of great
happiness together and, though the end was inevitable, I have no
regrets or remorse. I couldn't have handled it any differently from
the way I did.' Although 'For the first time in my life I felt myself
rejected', 'the whole episode was marvellous for me. It made me
much more at ease with men.' As we have seen, back in the sixties
Dusty had been quite capable of inventing boyfriends when she felt

it necessary, and as we listen to her accounts of this curious alliance, all delivered in a style reminiscent of the worst excesses of Mills & Boon, we may doubt whether the affair ever existed. Apparently Howard found someone else. 'I go to the same health club as she does' – a nice touch – 'and there's no friction.'[20]

It seems likely that the confidence that such belated sexual liberation gave her contributed greatly to Dusty's view of California as the Promised Land. However, as the drugs and alcohol took over her life, and her career fell apart, Dusty began to keep less wholesome company. Relationships gave way to casual affairs which in turn degenerated into one-night stands. 'I became a lot less selective about my partners', and 'Some of them were genuinely rotten people'. Her addiction to Mandrax in particular made her 'very naughty' and inclined to 'say yes to everyone'. There was even a report of Dusty having participated in a gay 'wedding'. The other blushing 'bride' was 'a flamboyant singer-actress'. The partnership 'turned sour and even threatening'. Dusty was now little more than the star attraction in a gay freak show.[21]

And always at her shoulder, tormenting her and adding immeasurably to her misery, were the Catholic values instilled in her from the cradle. In the early sixties her religion had been 'the most steadying influence in my haphazard life'; but, as her career developed, pressure of work made regular church-going impossible. In 1970 such lapses worried her:

It's about six years since I made my Easter Duties. My mother's going to love this. I still think that because I don't go I'm going to go to hell. I'll be very lucky to go to purgatory. But I don't want to go to hell because I haven't really done anything evil. I'm just lazy and self-indulgent.[22]

By the late seventies she was dismissing her Christian faith as 'stupidity':

Okay, it works for some people – and that's great. My mother, for instance, was a very good Catholic and it worked for her. But it doesn't work for people who constantly question it, because there are no answers. And I can't accept that. I want answers.[23]

And, having rejected such 'stupidity', where did she find the answers she was seeking? In *Star Wars*. 'I believe there's a force of some kind. And that works for me.'* But, of course, no amount of drugs, alcohol, casual sex and strip-cartoon theology can eradicate values and attitudes so deeply ingrained. Dusty retained a strong belief in the possibility of damnation; and, as she continued her frantic pursuit of a lifestyle which everything she had ever been taught told her was wrong, the pressure of this inner conflict became unbearable.

She began to mutilate herself. Eventually she attempted suicide – although she insisted later that she did not really want to die.

I wanted to go to sleep for a very long time. . . . I wanted peace and quiet but I never wanted to do myself in. I suppose all those Catholic whatevers come at you when your mind begins to enter those murky waters. You go to hell, you know, if you kill yourself.[24]

Dusty claimed that the final stage in her decline, and what finally convinced her that she had to start putting her life back together, was her introduction to cocaine: 'It was not a drug that suited me; it just scrambled my life.' Cocaine 'brought me to my knees quicker than anything. In seven months I was a wreck. And it was that which made me change my life.' She was also broke. According to Vicki Wickham, although Dusty 'hated work of any sort', singing 'was the only thing she could think of to make any money, so she had to sing'. After three years of 'being idle and doing it very badly', Dusty embarked on the road to recovery.[25] The journey would be long, with many setbacks, and after such a spectacular decline there was little in her life to which she could turn for support.

* Dusty also underwent 'regression therapy' with her friend Lee Everett Alkin and came to believe that in a former life she had been a Cree Indian. (Why is it always an Indian? Why can it never be an actuary from Godalming?)

131

But help was at hand. It had four paws, a tail and whiskers. Apart from a brief period as the owner of a dog named Mo, Dusty had been a cat-lover since the early sixties. Her first cat was called Boots. She had even committed the unpardonable sin of giving kittens as presents. In the late seventies cats – and later animal welfare generally – would become a focal point in her life; and if occasionally she presented the image of a dotty spinster with a house full of straggly moggies, then that was a small price to pay for their undoubted importance in her struggle to rescue herself from the hell into which she had descended – and, indeed, to hold on to her sanity. The therapeutic value of cats in helping to reduce stress and anxiety is well known. Cats have access to levels of serenity and self-possession that are denied to all but the most fortunate human beings. Even though the mortgage may be in arrears and creditors are knocking at the door, cats maintain a lofty indifference to all man's petty tribulations; and, for those able to respond to it, such equanimity serves to put everything in perspective.

Dusty's cats appear to have been mostly strays she had adopted, and at one time she had as many as a dozen. Few people can have found salvation in a litter tray, but as Dusty strove to put her life back together the daily routine of caring for her cats became a significant stabilising factor in her life. 'Whenever everything's in chaos, you know you have to open a can to feed them or clear up a litter tray. That's structure.' Whenever she found herself becoming 'really agitated' she would clean out the cat tray. 'That brings me back down to earth. It is my favourite form of relaxation!'

My cats mean everything to me. They are like real people to me, and I can't stand to be away from them even for a day. They are my true friends and a great comfort to me when I get lonely. I love to speak with them on the phone to make sure they are all right. I know they understand me. When I am away from home I miss them awfully.

When Dusty began to return to Britain to work in the late seventies and early eighties, the quarantine restrictions meant that the cats had to stay at home, although on one occasion some friends lent her a couple of kittens while she was in London. But the cats sometimes accompanied her on shorter trips. 'If I feel things mounting up I pack my bag, pick up one of my cats' – what happened to the others? – 'and go to the nearest hotel for a couple of days. There I drop out with a load of fashion magazines.' She was attracted to cats because 'their lives are totally devoted to pleasure. They love luxury and will do anything to get it' and – because, after all, they were Californian cats – they are 'very mysterious and psychic' and have 'hidden powers'.

For T. S. Eliot, the naming of cats had been a difficult matter, but for Dusty it seems to have been a holiday game: over the years she shared her home with – among others – Edward-Bear, Moomin, Sister Mary Catherine, Fortnum and his brother Mason, Malaysia, and Nicholas Nicholaivitch, 'so called because he has a false glamour about him – he looks very grand, very Russian', although he was also 'a total gangster, attacking smaller cats'. Nicholas would be with Dusty to the end.

Later Dusty became associated with the Wildlife Way Station, an animal sanctuary that specialised in caring for exotic animals bought as status symbols or fashion statements by the rich and stupid, and discarded when caring for them became too much of an effort or when they were overtaken by a fresh gimmick. This, too, became an important element in her struggle towards recovery.

Yet even the cat population fluctuated over the years, and it is a melancholy thought that perhaps the longest emotional relationship in Dusty's life was with her teddy bear, Einstein, acquired in the early sixties when she saw him pinned by the ear in an Oxford Street shop window. 'He looked so forlorn I just had to rescue him.' But Einstein was never allowed to accompany Dusty on tour; although there would have been no problems with quarantine, Dusty had 'this "thing" about him not having enough room to breathe in my suitcase'.[26]

By sheer effort of will Dusty managed to stop drinking, give up drugs and rediscover her voice, and in 1977 she signed a contract with United Artists to record an LP with Roy Thomas Baker. In the circumstances, this was a remarkable achievement.

10

Beginning Again

THE DUSTY SPRINGFIELD who casts her cool gaze upon us from the sleeve of *It Begins Again* exudes a calm confidence suggesting that even if she has not actually slain her demons she does at least have them firmly under control. And the record itself reflects this: it is a confident performance with no obvious signs that she had been away from the studio for such a long time. Dusty worked well with producer Roy Thomas Baker; and, though the project went seriously over budget, they were both pleased with the result.*

Dusty told *Rolling Stone*:

> I've lost some of the aggression, but that's just the way I'm going to have to be. I've had to smooth out because I'd abused my voice rather badly. But I don't think I've ever liked my singing better than now. . . . [It's] the first time my voice has given me chills.[1]

The first track, 'Turn Me Around', opens confidently with Dusty singing at the top of her range – although the song itself is of little interest. 'Checkmate' is no better, and we might begin to have our doubts about the collection as a whole, but with 'I'd Rather Leave

---

* *It Begins Again* (Mercury LP: 9109 607): Turn Me Around · Checkmate · I'd Rather Leave While I'm In Love · A Love Like Yours · Love Me By Name · Sandra · I Found Love With You · Hollywood Movie Girls · That's The Kind Of Love I've Got For You.

  It Begins Again has never been reissued in its entirety, but several tracks have found their way on to various compilations.

While I'm In Love' we reach the heart of the record and some of the best work Dusty ever did. 'A Love Like Yours' was originally a gentle B-side by Martha and the Vandellas, but Dusty's powerful perform-ance owes more to the version by Tina Turner.

The next three songs offer a wry commentary on the lifestyle Dusty had adopted in California. 'Love Me By Name', co-written by Lesley Gore, who had been one of America's top girl singers when Dusty embarked on her solo career, explores the futility of casual sex; while 'Hollywood Movie Girls', describing the lives of young hope-fuls doing the rounds of auditions and screen tests, is a song that was certain to appeal to Dusty, for whom the dream of Hollywood star-dom lingered in her imagination for most of her life.

Between them is 'Sandra', which is little short of miraculous. Writ-ten by Barry Manilow, this tale of a bored American suburban house-wife who first seeks solace in the bottle and then slashes her wrists was potentially disastrous: in the hands of a less sensitive singer it would have been mawkish and embarrassing. But Dusty finds the quiet desperation at the heart of the song, tells the story simply – almost *talking* the lyric at times – and hangs on to the elusive melody. 'It's about people who get trapped. ... I have sympathy for her.' She acknowledged that 'Love Me By Name' and 'Sandra' were 'acting performances' – 'just wait till you hear me do them live'.[2]

Another forgettable track follows, and then an electronic fanfare announces that with 'That's The Kind Of Love I've Got For You' Dusty has moved into the world of disco. She would stay there for the next decade; but, ironically, this first attempt would turn out to be one of her better efforts in that genre.

Despite massive promotion by the record company, *It Begins Again* failed to make it all begin again for Dusty, leaving Roy Thomas Baker to reflect that ultimately 'the end product didn't warrant the money that was spent on it'. Nevertheless, just as *Cameo*, for all its limitations, gave no obvious hints that Dusty's career was about to fall apart, so *It Begins Again* is not obviously the work of a singer struggling to pull herself together. Both collections are bright and confident, and we can only regret the tortured silence that fell between them.

By the time she came to record her second collection for United Artists, the soft image she had managed to maintain for *It Begins Again* had come unravelled, she was fighting her demons once again, and the sessions for *Living Without Your Love* with producer David Wolfert were not so creative.* The sleeve photograph shows a much harder Dusty in a spangled purple jacket.

> I did try to ditch the thick make-up for a scrubbed, tanned look, but to hell with that – I reminded myself of those suntanned women in Miami who look like old handbags. I did dye my hair magenta, but I spent half the night in the bath with Persil to get it out.[3]

Now she had assumed the role of 'disco diva' entirely. Following the success of *Saturday Night Fever* in 1977, disco mania had run through pop music with all the ferocity of the Ebola virus; and *Living Without Your Love* is simply one disco soundtrack among hundreds of others. With banal arrangements and the oppressive bass-line characteristic of disco music, the record moves from one repetitious chorus to the next. 'I Just Fall In Love Again' and 'I'm Coming Home Again' offer Dusty an opportunity for vocal respectability, but even on these two tracks she is working well within her capabilities. Dusty described the record as 'unstunning', and it is difficult to disagree.

Once again Dusty fell victim to the vagaries of the record business. United Artists was bought shortly before *Living Without Your Love* was due to be released, the record was not promoted at all and passed unnoticed. Twenty years later it is still too easy to pass it by.

However, *Living Without Your Love* demonstrates Dusty's determination to re-enter the mainstream of pop music as a *current* artist and not as a historical curiosity for the nostalgia market. In Britain her

---

* *Living Without Your Love* (Mercury LP: 9109 617): You've Really Got A Hold On Me · You Can Do It · Be Somebody · Closet Man · Living Without Your Love · Save Me, Save Me · Get Yourself To Love · I Just Fall In Love Again · Dream On · I'm Coming Home Again.

Living Without Your Love has never been reissued in its entirety, though a couple of tracks have found their way on to subsequent compilations.

record company had continued to reissue her sixties successes at regular intervals, but Dusty had no interest in revisiting past glories. Even though such offers came, and she probably needed the money, 'I couldn't do it, because I knew I'd blow my bloody brains out; I knew that I didn't have the emotional capacity to always be looking back. It's not enough.'[4]

Becoming a visible presence on the music scene again, giving interviews to promote her new records, meant that Dusty had to handle questions about her private life once more. While still managing to avoid a firm declaration about her own sexuality, she became more open about the close affinity she felt with the gay community: 'I've always come off as being rather dramatic and temperamental, and I think the sensitivity of gays can tune in to some sadness that I'm singing about.'[5] In an interview with Keith Howes for *Gay News* she was fulsome in her tributes to gay people:

> I have an enormously strong gay following and I'm grateful for it. I love gay people. I'm comfortable with them. I respect gay people. That doesn't make me one and that doesn't not make me one. I'm me.[6]

That final qualification was significant. Not even for her new gay chums would she move beyond the position she had adopted in 1970. In the burgeoning world of gay politics in the late seventies Dusty would have been a major deity to add to the gay pantheon, and she knew it. Of the *Gay News* interview she remarked:

> They were a bit militant. They wanted me to take a stance on the subject, but I couldn't because I don't have any stance. People are people. It doesn't make any difference to me what their sexual habits are. It's not a major issue in my life.[7]

Later she was even more forthright: 'I don't want to be owned by anyone, by any movement', and 'I'm only militant about animals'.[8]

She must also have known that, loyal and understanding as her gay constituency might be, it alone could not restore her fortunes.

Listening to Dusty's relentless litany of praise for the gay community, we might reasonably expect that she would be more at ease in interviews for gay publications, but this proves not to be the case. Gay journalists were accorded no special privileges, their interviews being restricted to the usual tour of Dusty's career so far and whatever brief glimpses of her private life she was in the mood to offer. Keith Howes confesses to having a hard time, and as we read his interview we can almost hear the awkward silences.

The gay following had an opportunity to show their loyalty in the spring of 1979 when, to coincide with the release of *Living Without Your Love*, Dusty returned to Britain for a series of shows. There were to be three shows at the Theatre Royal, Drury Lane, and ten shows outside London. She had not sung on stage for five years. 'At the moment my whole life is dominated by thoughts of what it is going to be like, what am I going to wear and will anybody come to see me.'[9] She received a blunt answer to the last question when the provincial shows had to be cancelled for lack of interest. 'I guess I've been away too long,' she reflected.

> I've got a badly dented ego, but I really feel sorry for the people who have bought tickets. It's strange that the sales have done well in London and not in the provinces. It proves that people don't like you going away. My appeal to the bloke in the street was strong while I was selling records. During the time I have been away I have developed a cult following. It seems most of the cult are in London. The project is still worthwhile. It has not gone totally down the drain. I've just learned a few lessons. The real disappointment has not sunk in yet.[10]

With the 'cult following' out in force, the Theatre Royal was packed every night. 'Give a butch roar or a girlish shriek. I don't mind who does what. Sort it out for yourselves,' Dusty roared defiantly. Buoyed up by the enthusiasm of the audience, she performed as if she had never been away. Every night she made a bold – or rash – attempt at a routine on roller skates, and every night (of course) she fell over. What did it matter if she could only see a few inches in front of her face and had never been on roller skates before? The provinces never knew what they were missing.

'Baby Blue', released in September of that year, found Dusty the disco queen still dancing round her handbag. The record was a modest success and also gave Dusty her introduction to the wonderful world of the 12-inch remix. Just as a stretch limousine can only be achieved by means of a long, boring section in between the two interesting bits, so the extended version of 'Baby Blue' has an uninteresting interlude that gives Dusty enough time to go to the hairdresser's before she has to be back at the microphone.*

In December, Dusty topped the bill at a charity concert at the Royal Albert Hall in aid of the Invalid Children's Aid Association. The guest of honour was Princess Margaret. 'It's nice to see that the royalty isn't confined to the box,' quipped Dusty mischievously with a glance at the queens in the audience. The princess did not appreciate the joke, and when the stars lined up after the show for the ritual shaking of the royal paw she snubbed Dusty. Furthermore she sent Dusty a typewritten apology for insulting the queen, which Dusty had to sign and return. In the interview she gave to *Gay News* in 1978, Dusty had boasted jokingly: 'I'm having a three-way with Princess Anne and one of her horses.' Perhaps this lapse of good taste had also been brought to Princess Margaret's attention.

The saddest aspect of the whole affair is that while the princess was busy taking offence in the royal box she probably failed to appreciate a classic performance from Dusty on stage. When Dusty sang 'Quiet Please, There's A Lady Onstage' she dedicated the song to the

---

* There were to be 12-inch versions of most of Dusty's subsequent singles, but this book will take no account of them. It is worth considering that if the public had heard the self-indulgent 12-inch versions of 'What Have I Done To Deserve This' before the 7-inch version, then the final phase of Dusty's career would probably have been rather different.

memory of Judy Garland: 'This is a song for all women who've been legends in their time. Sometimes the ladies involved give too much of themselves, sometimes not enough. This song is for all those women, no matter where they are.' The song was written by Carole Bayer Sager and Peter Allen, who is Judy Garland's son-in-law; and, although Dusty had rejected such a suggestion in the 1960s, a direct comparison of the self-destructive element in the two singers now seemed more tempting than ever.*

At the end of the show a woman managed to climb on the stage and throw herself into Dusty's arms.[11]

Dusty's triumph at the Royal Albert Hall was all the more remarkable in the light of the personal loss she had suffered only a few days earlier. Her father had been found dead at his home in Rottingdean. He had died alone, with only the milk-bottles accumulating on the doorstep to alert neighbours to the fact that something was wrong. Dusty suffered the feelings of guilt and regret that are inevitable at such a time, and which were intensified by the circumstances in which her father had passed away.

In 1980, Dusty signed to 20th Century Records. She recorded two singles – 'Your Love Still Brings Me To My Knees', which is bouncy and purposeful, if more a chant than a song, and 'It Goes Like It Goes', the theme song from the film *Norma Rae* – before her record company was once again taken over, and she now found herself recording for Casablanca.

When she came to record *White Heat*, which she co-produced with Howard Steele – 'I had to fire the original producer because he had put half the budget up his nose'[12] – she was at a particularly low point in her life: she was still battling drink and drugs, had suffered several breakdowns, and had recently emerged from a relationship

---

* This performance was made available on *Simply Dusty* (2000); see Appendix. Another performance she gave on a Tom Jones television show is available on *Tom Jones & Friends*, Vol. 2, *The Red Album* (Bellevue Entertainment CD, 1999: 30017-2). Dusty also joins Tom on a performance of 'Upside Down', which had been a hit for Diana Ross in 1980.

in which she had been physically abused and which had drained her self-confidence.

> There were circumstances I should never have been in but that women get themselves into. I've been in that trap that I've seen other women in, and you get so frightened that you are ashamed to tell anyone what's going on, you retreat. I did get myself out in the end – it had been a very destructive relationship.

Her later revelation that 'I've been punched many times in my life' appears to suggest this was not the first such incident; but it is unclear how literally we are to take this remark.[13] There is an unsubstantiated story that she was photographed for the sleeve of *White Heat* wearing a crash helmet because her face was bruised.

But once again work gave her the focus she needed, and the record that emerged is remarkable.* With its rough edges and with inconsistencies of sound-balance – Dusty's voice sounding remote on one track and almost in our faces on the next – *White Heat* has an uncompromising attitude that defies us to like it. At times Dusty's voice seems to have become a snarl – as if, after all her recent vain attempts to please the public and the record industry, she has now decided to please only herself. The disco sound has been toughened by a blend with hard rock; and, consequently, *White Heat* is far from easy listening. The first three tracks, 'Donnez-Moi (Give It To Me)', 'I Don't Think We Could Ever Be Friends' (co-written by Sting) and 'Blind Sheep', make a fierce onslaught on the listener until the last two tracks on side 1 bring Dusty back on to more familiar territory: 'Don't Call It Love' is an attractive number that might have found favour as a single; while on 'Time And Time Again' Dusty plays her old game of pushing her voice to the very top of its range and almost daring us to believe it is going to crack.

* *White Heat* (USA only, 1982: Casablanca LP NBLP 7271): Donnez-Moi (Give It To Me) · I Don't Think We Could Ever Be Friends · Blind Sheep · Don't Call It Love · Time And Time Again · I Am Curious · Sooner Or Later · Losing You · Gotta Get Used To You · Soft Core.

But this relief is short-lived. Emerging from a jangle of discordant guitars and driven by a rasping bass drone, 'I Am Curious' is *White Heat* at its most challenging. The song was written by Kevan Staples and Carole Pope of the Canadian band Rough Trade; they were managed at the time by Vicki Wickham, who introduced them to Dusty. 'Sooner Or Later' begins as an aggressive rock number but mellows into a surprisingly tuneful chorus. 'Losing You' is little more than a rugged treatment of an uninteresting Elvis Costello song; while the frenetic and repetitious 'Gotta Get Used To You' harks back to 'That's The Kind Of Love I've Got For You', the track on *It Begins Again* with which Dusty had launched herself into the disco arena.

At this point we might feel that the project has finally run out of ideas; but then something wonderful happens.

Performed with only a piano and some brief basic percussion – which seems a bold act in itself when we recall how, in the sixties, Dusty had preferred to add her voice last of all over the massive arrangements, and how unnerved she had been when required to sing against only a basic rhythm track in Memphis – 'Soft Core' demonstrates how, when she found a song that meant something to her, she could still leave all other singers standing. Tired and deeply unhappy, her voice sounding ragged and neglected – and the effect is intensified by the lyric's disjointed rhyme-scheme – Dusty somehow manages to reach inside herself to produce a performance that can still knock the listener back on his heels. 'Sick of being submissive when I really want to scream': all the mechanical triviality of Dusty the disco diva fades into insignificance beside the raw heartfelt desperation she brings out in this song by Carole Pope and Kevan Staples. So many influences and comparisons spring to mind – Lotte Lenya in a Brecht–Weill *Songspiel* perhaps, or Marlene Dietrich, or Peggy Lee, or the later recordings of Billie Holiday – but 'Soft Core' is really the culmination of a twenty-year exploration of the art and craft of singing; it is the direct descendant of a line stretching from 'My Colouring Book' to 'Goin' Back', 'I Think It's Gonna Rain Today', 'I Don't Want To Hear It Anymore' and 'Sandra'. 'Soft Core' is Dusty Springfield's last great performance – and probably the finest of them all.

What followed must by now have seemed almost inevitable. Although *White Heat* received critical acclaim, it was not a commercial success. It has never been released in Britain. Once again Dusty returned to Los Angeles and to doing nothing very much – until, in 1984, she was lured out of retirement once again to embark on a highly speculative venture.

Dusty's brief and inglorious association with nightclub-owner Peter Stringfellow's new record label was launched with an extravagant press conference at the Hippodrome near London's Leicester Square. Wearing a silver suit that was variously described as 'something left over from a NASA space probe' and making her look like 'a minicab driver in Bacofoil', Dusty emerged from a confusion of dry ice and flashing lights. Peter Stringfellow was delighted at having signed Dusty to his label and was brimming with enthusiasm. To him Dusty was the 'epitome of glamour', 'a real superstar', 'charismatic and outrageous', and he promised 'a new, modern Dusty'.[14] But behind the glitter all was far from harmonious.

For all Peter's enthusiasm, the endeavour lacked experience and expertise. The original plan had been for Dusty to work with Steve Jolley and Tony Swain, who had proved so decisive in the career of Alison Moyet, a singer Dusty particularly admired – 'Christ, what a voice. I'd love to duet with her!'[15] – but the two men were still working with Bananarama, and Dusty had to continue without them.* According to Simon Bell, Dusty's backing singer and a close friend, 'She was surrounded by total amateurs, people who were playing at making a record. There was no one in charge.'[16] There was no guiding hand at the controls: everyone took a turn at mixing and remixing. Recording sessions degenerated into squabbles. The squabbles became ugly rows. Dusty, whose self-confidence had been sapped by all

---

* Dusty was almost granted her wish in June 1995 when Alison Moyet was one of her backing singers on a television performance of 'Where Is A Woman To Go'.

the disappointments of the previous few years and who could surely feel this latest opportunity collapsing around her, screamed and shouted at Peter Stringfellow. Unimpressed, Peter gave as good as he got. 'I'm not the sort of person who's going to take all that sort of nonsense from anybody.'[17]

Dusty's manager, Vicki Wickham, was otherwise engaged, and Dusty was reunited temporarily with her former manager, Vic Billings, who found himself acting as mediator and struggling to wrest something from the chaos. 'The whole thing was a disaster. . . . It was dreadful.'[18]

Almost miraculously, six tracks were recorded. Then a new battle began. Which track should be released first? Dusty and Vic thought they should begin with one of the upbeat tracks; but Peter Stringfellow favoured a slower number called 'Sometimes Like Butterflies', and his view prevailed. According to Dusty:

> We had long and fierce battles because I wanted to come back with a funky, hit-you-between-the-eyes number, but Peter had fallen in love with 'Butterflies' and from then on there was nothing I could do. It was his personal crusade – there was no listening to anything else. . . . [T]his is the first time I've ever come across an absolutely adamant attitude from a record company. It wasn't out of bloody-mindedness. Peter was convinced it was the right thing. . . . I lost the battle and Jolley and Swain went down with the ship.[19]

It was probably at this point that Dusty began to withdraw from the project. 'I couldn't get any enthusiasm out of her whatsoever,' Peter later complained.[20] But Dusty knew that the record – and consequently her latest chance for a comeback – was heading for disaster: 'I may be as near-sighted as a bat, but I can always see the writing on the wall.'[21] Ironically, as Peter Stringfellow pointed out, Dusty had found the song herself. Slow, long and uninteresting, with the sort of backing track that sounds as if it is sold by the yard, 'Sometimes Like Butterflies' might have survived as an LP track or on the back of something stronger; but in the fiercely competitive world of eighties pop music, with so much new material vying for attention, it would disappear without trace. And that is what happened. It was 'a risky record', Dusty recognised, 'because it's such a slow developer'.[22] Fifteen years later, 'Sometimes Like Butterflies' is still developing.

After a handful of television appearances Dusty declined to play any further part in promoting the record. This was no help to Peter Stringfellow, who was left considerably out of pocket, but in the circumstances there was really little else that Dusty could do. 'I've been very patient with Hippodrome, under some very trying circumstances.'[23] Why should she set herself up to be humiliated yet again? So she took the only sensible course: she went home to her cats.

None of the remaining tracks, which included one song with the intriguing title 'My Love Life Is A Disaster', was ever released. Dusty's quarrel with Peter Stringfellow became public, with both sides making charges and counter-charges in the press. For Dusty, the root of the problem was that 'Peter knew fuck all about the record business'. Peter Stringfellow readily conceded as much, adding: 'that naivety cost me a great deal of money. . . . But I never made her suffer financially.'[24] Reflecting on the episode many years later, he said: 'She was difficult. I was warned, but I thought that my charm could win her over. It didn't quite do that.'[25]

Success may change us, but failure turns us back upon ourselves, forcing us to re-examine our life. By nature introspective, as Dusty reflected on the premature end to yet another dream and, beyond that, the succession of failures and dashed hopes over almost a decade – and without even the compensation of some happiness in her personal life – she must have undertaken the kind of painful inner journey that few people ever have to make. Time and again she had managed to pull herself together and make yet one more effort, only to face rejection once more and to see some of her best work fall by the wayside. Now she must have wondered whether this was finally the end of everything. 'Dear God, how many times can you do a comeback?'[26]

Fortunately, she was to be granted one last chance.

11

Pet Shop Girl

ACCORDING TO DUSTY – and the story varied slightly with each telling – she received a telephone call from her manager, Vicki Wickham, in New York. Vicki had been approached by the Pet Shop Boys, who wanted Dusty to sing on one of their records, and they needed a quick decision. Was Dusty interested? 'Luckily I had heard of them, because I had nearly had a car accident when I heard "West End Girls", because I thought it was such a great sound' and 'I made my mind up in five minutes'.[1]

In fact, as accounts by Neil Tennant and Peter Stringfellow make clear, the pattern of events was rather different: Dusty turned down the proposal at first and took quite some time to change her mind.[2] There is nothing to criticise here. After such a grim period of relentless disappointment, it was natural that she should wish to romanticise the moment at which her fortunes changed so decisively. And, as we have seen, Dusty liked to identify turning-points in her life.

In late 1984, Neil Tennant and Chris Lowe, who were about to erupt into the public consciousness – after a hesitant beginning – as the Pet Shop Boys with 'West End Girls', collaborated with American writer Allee Willis on a song called 'What Have I Done To Deserve This'. The following year they began work on their first LP, and planned to include the song; but they had a problem. The song also required a female singer. 'We wanted a woman with a voice suggesting both experience and vulnerability, warmth but also a tough take-it-or-leave-it attitude.' None of the singers who came to mind

147

was really suitable; but then their manager's assistant suggested Dusty Springfield. After all, 'I thought she was your favourite singer'.

Initial enthusiasm for this suggestion was tempered by doubts about whether it was even worth approaching Dusty: 'Rumour had it that she was a recluse in Los Angeles, surrounded by cats, impossible to work with.' However, they decided to take a chance. 'It seemed to take ages to track her down, but nobody else would do.'[3] They sent a demo tape to Dusty's manager, Vicki Wickham. Several weeks later they received a reply: Dusty was not interested. The Pet Shop Boys' first LP eventually appeared without the song.

Several months later their manager received a telephone call from Vicki Wickham. Dusty wanted to make the record after all. Did they still want her? They did. Shortly before Christmas 1986, Dusty flew to London from Los Angeles.

Peter Stringfellow had his own explanation for Dusty's sudden change of heart. When the Pet Shop Boys first approached Dusty she was still under contract to Hippodrome, and she rejected their offer because she had no desire to work with Peter Stringfellow again. As soon as she was free of Hippodrome, she reconsidered her decision and was able to sign with Parlophone, the Pet Shop Boys' record label. 'It doesn't particularly seem fair to me,' Peter Stringfellow complained later.[4]*

Whatever the politics of the situation, Dusty's decision – whenever she took it – was to change her life completely.

'What Have I Done To Deserve This' was not her first collaboration with other artists. In 1984 she had joined sixties veteran Spencer Davis on a pointless revival of the old Judy Clay and William Bell hit, 'Private Number'; the record sent out all the wrong messages, and it came as no surprise to find references to 'pop dinosaurs' in the press. More recently Richard Carpenter, who was striving to re-define his own career after the death of his sister Karen, had invited

* According to Chris Lowe, there was some resistance from Parlophone at first: 'When the record company heard that we were going to do this song with Dusty, they freaked out. They tried to dissuade us from working with her' (*Today*, 8 December 1986).

148

Dusty to work with him. 'Something In Your Eyes' is actually a rather good record, with Dusty singing solo until the final chorus when Richard Carpenter swoops in with the lush vocal backing he once provided for his sister. Richard Carpenter later described it as one of the best records he had ever made; but, again, it would not put Dusty back into the pop mainstream where she wanted to be. (Although Dusty takes the whole of the vocal, and we might reasonably consider it to be *her* record, when 'Something In Your Eyes' was released her name was not even on the label – an understandable cause for resentment.)

The Pet Shop Boys were different. They were at the peak of their success. They could not only give Dusty a hit record; they could also put her back at the heart of the current music scene.

The Dusty who arrived in London was very different from the mellow and philosophical woman of a decade earlier. The setbacks and disappointments that had followed the early promise of *It Begins Again* had caused Dusty to retreat behind her mask. As Jean Rook put it, with characteristic delicacy:

> At first startling glance, she looks like a terrorist with a built-in hood. Or an Ancient Greek death mask. Her mouth is a blood red gash. Her make-up looks bullet-proof. She has two terrible black eyes. Or else she's wearing dark glasses with no sides or bridge to keep them on her thin, ivory nose. For a living legend, Dusty Springfield . . . has a deathly impact.[5]

Her obsession with her appearance was now out of all proportion. She would keep people waiting, quite literally, for hours as she prepared to make her grand entrance. Neil Tennant recalled her being 'out of bounds in her dressing-room for hours with two make-up artists and three hairdressers'. On one celebrated occasion, after having kept an interviewer in suspense for a very long time, she emerged suddenly from the hotel bedroom, pecked her record company's representative on the cheek – and promptly disappeared 'with a muffled squeak' into the walk-in wardrobe. 'I caught my nose on Murray's cheek. Now I'll have to check my make-up all over again.' When she eventually reappeared she was hiding her face behind 'a trellis of fingers', and it was a while longer before she felt confident enough to lower her hand. Journalist Alan Jackson, who was also given the treatment, concluded that 'She came across as mad as a hatter, but so sweet. Really kind.'[6]

This disturbing lack of self-confidence was apparent when she arrived at the studio to begin work with the Pet Shop Boys. She seemed to have no real idea of why they wanted her there. 'I went in and said, "What is it you want?" And they said, "The sound of your voice." And all these years, I've always thought that . . . it's never enough for me, so I assume it's never enough for anyone else.'[7] She sang her part – 'Breathy, warm, thrilling', in Neil Tennant's words – and then asked: 'Is that the sort of thing you want?' It was exactly the sort of thing they wanted.

> I have a tendency to . . . complicate matters, because I don't think my voice is enough; therefore I have to invent this kind of vocal decoration . . . and really you can't do that to a Pet Shop Boys song. They write songs that are meant to be sung rather plainly.[8]

Perhaps self-conscious about being overweight, Dusty refused to do any interviews or pictures to promote the new record. Having done her bit, she returned to Los Angeles.

Released in August 1987, 'What Have I Done To Deserve This' was an enormous success around the world, and gave Dusty her second-biggest hit. She was back where she belonged. 'I didn't have to sing it all, just the bit in the middle, which was an ideal way to re-enter the fray.'[9] And it is indeed ironic that after all her endeavours of the previous ten years she should finally be restored to prominence by contributing an effortless chorus to someone else's record. But, then, 'I always take the scenic route towards anything'.[10]

Philips, too, was making an effort. At the beginning of 1988 the company issued *The Silver Collection*, bringing together Dusty's most popular recordings from the sixties and early seventies. It was a huge success; and, for once, Dusty was happy to see her sixties catalogue being exploited. And there was also an appearance in a television commercial for BritVic to confirm that she was back at last.

In 1988, Dusty finally left Los Angeles for good. She settled in Amsterdam, which was the closest she could get to Britain without having to put her cats into quarantine. In April of that year she gave an interview to the *News of the World* which she regretted immediately. Perhaps a sense that at last things were going well for her and she was getting her life in order gave her the courage to speak so openly, or perhaps she simply failed to appreciate quite how much the popular press had degenerated since she gave her interview to the *Evening Standard* in 1970. Whatever the reason – and Dusty later claimed that she did it for 'some quick money' – it was a huge blunder. At the very time that her career had taken off again, and she should have concentrated on maintaining the momentum, she chose to rekindle interest in her private life.

She began calmly enough, declaring that she now chose to be celibate and was talking openly about her sexuality because 'I'm sick of being asked about it, so perhaps by talking I'll shut people up'. As with drink and drugs, so with sex: 'I went from nothing to overindulgence almost overnight. . . . I tried everything at once.' By now she was warming to her theme, and the *News of the World*'s readers learned of casual sex with men and women, three-in-a-bed sex romps, together with a cryptic reference to Dobermanns – and all of this conducted in a drug-induced haze. Assuming that all this is true, promiscuity seemed to have tipped over into depravity. The whole piece was accompanied by pictures of an overweight Dusty posing on pieces of exercise equipment at a health farm, apparently struggling to remedy the effects of a lifestyle reminiscent of the last days of the Roman Empire. The *News of the World* could hardly complain about not getting its money's worth. Giving that interview was 'truly dumb', Dusty acknowledged later. 'Truly, unadulteratedly stupid. . . . Didn't I know? Didn't it occur to me?'[11]

She stayed in Amsterdam three years, making regular trips to London to buy cat food: one visitor to her hotel room saw an enormous

quantity of a turkey-and-chicken variety not available in the Nether-
lands. Finally she took the big decision to place her beloved cats,
Malaysia and Nicholas Nicholaivitch, in quarantine and return to
Britain.

She bought a house in Taplow, Buckinghamshire; but soon after
she settled there Malaysia was run over by a car. Anthony Husher, a
Taplow neighbour, remembered her surviving cat, Nicholas, as 'one
of the stupidest cats I've ever met but also one of the most endear-
ing'. Dusty was devoted to Nicholas and would not go to bed until he
was safely indoors; and she was often to be seen going round the
garden with a torch and calling his name. Like any cat-lover she
would stop to pass the time of day with any cat she encountered;
and, at Christmas, Mr Husher's cat received Harrods pet stockings
from Dusty's cat.[12]*

The return to Britain also brought a comic reunion with another
female – and equally short-sighted – pop star of the 1960s. Dusty
was now a near neighbour of Sandie Shaw, but neither woman was
aware of this until one day when Sandie was out collecting signatures for a petition to protest at local traffic problems. She knocked
on Dusty's door, and the two women chatted for several minutes
without recognising each other before Sandie suddenly stopped,
peered through her spectacles and said: 'Is that you, Dusty?' Dusty
squinted back at her. 'Sandie?'[13]

There had been no immediate attempt to build on Dusty's success
with 'What Have I Done To Deserve This', but a year later Neil
Tennant and Chris Lowe were commissioned to write the theme song
for *Scandal*, a film about the Profumo affair of 1963. 'Dusty was around
then, and yet she was around in the late eighties as well, so it seemed
very resonant to get her to do it.' Released in February 1989, 'Nothing Has Been Proved' gave Dusty her first major solo success since
the early seventies. 'That was such an incredible song, it really was a
gem. There's a lyric that, to half its audience, nobody understood a

---

* There is no point in even trying to explain such behaviour to any reader who is
not a cat-lover.

word of, but it didn't matter because it had a sound.'[14] During this recording session she felt confident enough to reveal: 'I'm getting my power back.' According to Neil Tennant, 'suddenly she realised it wasn't all over, that she could be back, and she really took that very very seriously'.[15]

The session also came as a revelation to Neil Tennant, who is perhaps the most perceptive observer of Dusty at work, 'standing by the microphone with a cigarette and a cup of coffee, and the lyric-sheet in front of her with lots of pencil marks on it'.

> She records very very slowly. . . . She likes to record something a word at a time, even sometimes a *syllable* at a time. . . . [T]he first line [of 'Nothing Has Been Proved'] is 'Mandy's in the papers 'cause she tried to go to Spain'; and the track started a great introduction, and she goes 'Ma–'. Stops. And I just looked at the lyric-sheet. There are so many words in this song. And I wanted her to double-track quite a lot of it, too!

Nevertheless, 'I learned an awful lot about singing just from listening and watching her recording'. 'Incredibly intelligent at phrasing', as Dusty slowly recorded the song 'she vocally arranged it', so that 'every verse and chorus sounded different from each other, painstakingly building up to a thrilling climax', and 'the last chorus would suddenly go through the roof'. He found a word for this creative process: 'She takes your song and dustifies it.'[16]

As for the smoking, Dusty claimed to have taken it up as a substitute for alcohol, although 'I'm not very good at it. It makes me cough.'[17]

In April, Dusty was able to face her fiftieth birthday with confidence – though she resisted the notion that her renewed success was actually a comeback. ('It's always called a "comeback", even if you only went to Woolworth's.'[18])

> The word 'comeback' implies *desperation*. It suggests that you're *desperate* to get back what you had. But I *don't* want to get back what

I had, thank you. I was a wreck. So why should I want *that* back? Working at the pace I used to, eaten up by it all, nothing but sleepless nights, getting completely screwed up by it all . . . I don't *ever* want *that* person again. So this is *not* a comeback.[19]

She also disliked being described as a 'survivor': 'It sort of implies something in the Antarctic.'[20]

In November 1989 the Pet Shop Boys gave her 'In Private'. According to Neil Tennant, as soon as Chris Lowe had played him the melody he decided: 'This is a Dusty song.' This was her third successful record in a row.

She was by now at work on an LP for Parlophone.* *Reputation* was the work of two production teams. Side 1 was produced by Dan Hartmann, partly in London and partly at his studio in Connecticut. The title track, 'Reputation', was released as a single in May 1990 and gave Dusty yet another success; while 'Arrested By You' was issued in November of that year and failed to have any impact at all. Quite why anyone believed that 'Arrested By You' stood a chance of maintaining Dusty's run of success remains a mystery: a tedious dirge, it makes even 'Sometimes Like Butterflies' sound vibrant and businesslike in comparison. As for the rest of side 1, it is little more than upmarket disco music.

Side 2 was produced by Neil Tennant, Chris Lowe and Julian Mendelsohn. As well as giving 'In Private' and 'Nothing Has Been Proved' another outing, it included three new recordings.

Tennant and Lowe's 'Daydreaming', a fine example of comfortable white middle-class rap, is definitely *not* a Dusty song. Dusty sounds as if she is producing a cover version of a Pet Shop Boys record: even as she sings we can hear Neil Tennant's voice in our mind.

On the final track, 'Occupy Your Mind', Dusty sounds like a session singer brought in to add some vocal touches to a lot of elec-

---

* *Reputation* (Parlophone: LP on PCSD 111; CD on CDPCSD 111): Reputation · Send It To Me · Arrested By You · Time Waits For No One · Born This Way · In Private · Daydreaming · Nothing Has Been Proved · I Want To Stay Here · Occupy Your Mind.

tronic self-indulgence; and by the time Dusty's voice finally arrives, after a long and tedious introduction, we have already lost interest. 'Occupy Your Mind' demonstrates that Dusty had gone as far as she could down this electronic avenue – and perhaps too far at that.

'I Want To Stay Here', a cover version of a Steve Lawrence and Eydie Gorme record from the early sixties, offers a brief jaunty interlude, and it seems entirely appropriate that Dusty should celebrate her return to the music scene by renewing her musical association with the song's composers, Gerry Goffin and Carole King.

There was a delay over the selection of a photograph for the sleeve – and we may wonder whether the final choice, with Dusty looking emaciated and ill, was worth the wait – but *Reputation* was eventually released in June 1990. Malaysia's passing is commemorated in the sleeve notes.

Reputation was Dusty's most successful LP since the sixties, but there would be no return engagement. She never worked with the Pet Shop Boys or Dan Hartmann again. Perhaps she had had enough of singing along to musical computers. Indeed, as we listen again to *Reputation* a decade later, we may wonder at times to what extent it is really a Dusty Springfield record at all. We may be forgiven if, now and again, we have an uneasy feeling that Dusty is merely one small element in a larger picture, that her voice has been appropriated for someone else's purpose.

This was all a world away from her long collaboration with Johnny Franz and Ivor Raymonde, who understood her voice and allowed her to follow her own musical instincts. Twenty years later, the arranger had been replaced by the computer programmer, and the man with the baton had made way for the man with the screwdriver. Dusty embraced this new electronic age enthusiastically – but she must also have been aware that her struggles with musicians and with inadequate recording equipment were a key element in the development of her vocal style and of her remarkable success and status in popular music. Individual musicians are able to respond to direction, to modify their performance to suit the particular musical moment; while human ingenuity can often compensate for the deficiencies of studio equipment. An electronic synthesiser will reliably emit the same phrase or the same pulse – flawless but characterless – until there is a power cut; but the *musical* possibilities are very limited. Neil Tennant has successfully developed his own distinctive form of *Sprechgesang*, the 'talking singing' already made famous in our own time by Rex Harrison in *My Fair Lady*, and it forms the perfect complement to the electronic inventions of Chris Lowe; but, for all her enthusiasm, it is unlikely that an artist as sensitive as Dusty could have remained patient with such a restrictive musical environment for very long. As we have seen, when Dusty came to record *Reputation* she often worked on only a word, or even a syllable, at a time – an approach to her work that had also made life difficult for the producers of *Cameo* in the previous decade. It was almost as if she had lost confidence in the musical phrase, or in her own ability to sustain it, and was having to feel her way uncertainly, constructing her performance a note at a time. Anyway, the passion that had once led her to harass, cajole and harangue resentful musicians to produce the elusive sounds she was seeking was inappropriate in this new environment. Scowling at a musical calculator achieves nothing whatsoever. She was only one sound effect among a lot of others.

None the less, Dusty was well aware of how much she owed to the Pet Shop Boys:

> Gratitude is a new feeling to me. I was always accused of being a very ungrateful child. . . . I'm really grateful to the Pet Shop Boys, and I feel embarrassed to say that. It sticks in my craw to be grateful. I am, because they had the faith in me that I didn't have. They saw something in me that I was about to lose.[21]

The Pet Shop Boys, too, had reason to be grateful. The association with Dusty Springfield did them no harm at all, and brought them to a much wider audience. It is even possible that, when their own career is eventually assessed, they will be remembered best for having given Dusty Springfield back to us.

Dusty's return to the mainstream of pop music brought with it an introduction to a new phenomenon: the promotional video. Exciting new art form or colossal waste of time and money, depending on your point of view, the pop video is now firmly established as a vital aspect of the contemporary music scene. In the video for 'What Have I Done To Deserve This' Dusty looks plump and unprepared, but by the time she came to work on the videos for 'In Private' and 'Reputation' she had regained her characteristic wit and elegance. She had always known how to sell a song and how to work to camera, and she seized the opportunities that video offered. It is also clear that in pop videos she found at last a chance to play the movie queen. Sean O'Hagan, who directed the video for 'Roll Away' in Ireland in 1995, recalls:

> Dusty made her daily entrance on set around midday. That is, she left the hotel and made her way over to the 40ft silver Winnebago we had hired at her insistence (making considerable inroads into the budget) from a Neil Jordan film shoot further down the coast. . . . Our schedule went rapidly out of the window.[22]

After *Reputation* Dusty seemed to be in no hurry to record again. She would wait three years before going back into the studio, and then it would involve yet another dramatic change of direction and lead her to retrace a journey she had made more than thirty years earlier. But, for the moment, she was quite happy to stay at home with her cat.

12

Time and the River

In March 1991, Dusty's rural idyll was rudely interrupted when she found herself forced to revisit past unhappiness. Comedian Bobby Davro portrayed her as a drunk in his television show, and she felt obliged to sue the company, TVS, for damages. While she 'could stand being mimicked', she said, 'this particular portrayal went to the heart of my personality and was deeply hurtful'. In court her counsel stated that Dusty had not touched alcohol for eight years. The judgement went in Dusty's favour, and she was awarded damages of around £75,000.[1]

Aside from this ugly interlude, she was happy to potter around at home in the country, alone with her cat, with no great desire to go back into the recording studio again. The only lingering ambition to which she confessed at this time was to open a high-class boarding cattery.

Then, in 1993, she contributed to a recording to celebrate her friend Cilla Black's thirty years in show business. When Cilla's singing career had finally run out of steam at the end of the sixties, she had made a smooth transition to television. Although Dusty, too, had had tough decisions to take about her future, such an option had not been available for her: 'Cilla has the magic common touch, which I lack. I'm more aloof, based on my shyness. . . . I want separation from the audience – the curtain to go up and down.'[2] Besides, for Dusty singing was everything.

Cilla chose to celebrate her thirtieth anniversary with a record. She sang duets with Barry Manilow and Cliff Richard – and with

Dusty. 'Heart And Soul' is an effortless piece of unashamed nostalgia for the golden days of the early sixties when the world was at their feet. The track was also released as a single. The record is charming enough, and the two friends obviously had fun making it, but it was never going to take the charts by storm.*

In July of that year Columbia Records in London acquired a new managing director, Kip Krones. On his very first day in the office he called Vicki Wickham and told her that he wanted Dusty to record for Columbia. The following year would see the twenty-fifth anniversary of the release of *Dusty in Memphis*, and he wanted to produce a companion-piece, provisionally entitled 'Dusty in Nashville'. Vicki was enthusiastic, Dusty agreed, and the deal was struck. For Dusty it meant retracing a journey of more than thirty years ago – a journey that had changed everything for her. 'And it was right that I went back there.'[3]

Unfortunately, the experience was not to be as happy as Dusty had hoped it would be. She was in poor health, and would tire easily, so producer Tom Shapiro could only record her for short periods – sometimes for merely a line or two. She also had problems with her voice for which a specialist could find no explanation. Ever the perfectionist, the awareness that her voice was often far short of its best only added to her discomfort.

None of this pain was apparent in an interview she gave to Andrew Duncan for *Radio Times* in early April, while still in Nashville. The article was intended as a preview to a major BBC documentary, *Dusty: Full Circle*, in which Dusty talked at length of her life and career. Unfortunately, the programme was marred by colossally unfunny interruptions by Dawn French and Jennifer Saunders that must have tested the loyalty of even their most devoted admirers. (To add to the embarrassment, Dusty made a pointless guest appearance on their show shortly afterwards.) Dusty emerged from Andrew Duncan's interview as very relaxed and philosophical, suggesting

* The track may be found on Cilla Black's *Through the Years* (Columbia LP, 1993: 474650 1).

strongly that at last she had found a kind of happiness. She had also grown closer to brother Tom; their relationship had never been easy, but now 'we're much better friends. We have late-night conversations about the cost of decorators and the price of string beans.'[4] As for the future: 'I haven't a clue. That's one of the wonderful things. Imagine how awful it would be to know the ending.' Within a matter of weeks she would receive a stark intimation of just what that ending would be.

Dusty first realised that she had a problem when she embarked on one of her diets after returning home from Nashville, where she had 'eaten like a hog'. As the weight fell away she noticed an indentation in one of her breasts. Within three days she knew the worst. She consulted a GP, who referred her to the Royal Marsden Hospital straight away. As the specialist examined the results of a biopsy, she chatted to Dusty about her cat. The doctor's cat, Dusty recalled, was called Moses. (It is a peculiarity of cat-lovers that they can remember the name of every cat to have come into their life.) Then came the verdict: 'I'm afraid it's a tumour, and it's one we just don't want.' Dusty's mother had died from lung cancer in the seventies, and the memory of a visit to the Hove nursing home to see her was vividly present in Dusty's mind. 'She looked like one of those horror masks, all sunken. Her eyes were glassy from the drugs, but suddenly they focused and she just reached up this claw and tweaked my nose. I don't remember her ever doing that to me before. And then she passed out again.' Dusty had to return to America the next day, but before she went she called the nursing home to ask how her mother was. 'Oh, she passed away,' she was told matter-of-factly. 'I did come unglued then. I handled it very badly. Partly guilt.'[5]

The diagnosis, which also explained Dusty's lassitude during the Nashville sessions, was followed by six months of treatment: chemotherapy ('wonderful junk'), surgery and radiotherapy. Dusty coped well with the treatment, although there were moments when the harsh reality of her situation was brought home to her forcefully. She recalled one occasion when she caught sight of her cat, Nicholas, lying asleep and suddenly thought: 'Who's going to look after you?' Then 'It was like somebody had run a train through me. I wept and wept and wept. Because then I realised: it is you. Yes, this might kill you.'[6] And there was also an understandable rage at the unfairness of it all: 'I had brought a lot of stuff on myself in my life, for which I was responsible. This was the first time I had to face illness I didn't bring on myself.'[7]*

Dusty's condition was diagnosed on the very day that work began on mixing the Nashville recording in London, and she had to break the news to the record company. Columbia agreed to postpone the release date for a year. Her treatment ended just before Christmas; she felt fine, if rather tired, and the new record – now called *A Very Fine Love* – was eventually issued in June 1995.[†] According to Dusty:

> It was just a question of finding songs I was comfortable with, songs appropriate to who I am at this point in my life. I could have done that whole rent-a-diva thing again, but what would be the point? There's no substance to it, and if I'm going to go out there before the public and promote a record, it might as well be one that is honest and sincere.[8]

Although the overall quality of the tracks is uneven, drifting from the raw energy of 'Roll Away' and 'Wherever Would I Be' to the rather sluggish 'Go Easy On Me' – the track Dusty favoured when she went out to promote the record – and then to the powerful 'Where Is A Woman To Go', which is a female slant on the Frank Sinatra classic 'One For My Baby' and the highlight of the collection, *A Very*

---

* According to Lee Everett Alkin, one of Dusty's last wishes was that Nicholas might be 'married' to Lee's own cat, Purdey: 'It might sound odd but she was terrified that Nicholas would be lonely after she was gone and it would give her a kick to know that he was bonded to Purdey' (The *Mail on Sunday*, 25 April 1999).

† *A Very Fine Love* (Columbia: LP on 478508 1; CD on 478508 2): Roll Away · Very Fine Love · Wherever Would I Be [with Daryl Hall] · Go Easy On Me · You Are The Storm · I Can't Help The Way I Don't Feel · All I Have To Offer You Is Love · Lovin' Proof · Old Habits Die Hard · Where Is A Woman To Go.

Fine Love has a *humanity* that was lacking from the production-line work of Dusty the disco diva, a sense of Dusty exploring songs that meant something to her and responding to living musicians rather than to mere electronic pulses.

'Wherever Would I Be', on which she sang a duet with Daryl Hall, was also released as a single around the same time but made no impact. This is a pity; it is a powerful track and undeniably superior to all her recordings with the Pet Shop Boys which had brought her such success. While recording the song, Dusty had come to feel that it needed a second voice; several singers were considered, but eventually Daryl Hall's name emerged. Duets have a hard time in the market-place: they require the public to like both artists and to like them both together. Dusty did record a solo version, a remarkable performance for a woman in her fifties, but it is impossible to say if that recording would have fared any better.

In October 1995 a second track, 'Roll Away', was released as a single. It was to be her last. She had a fraught and tearful time in Ireland filming a promotional video with Sean O'Hagan and Seamus Mcgarvey. 'We shambled along on the verge of panic, shooting what we could where we could,' O'Hagan recalled. At the end of a particularly frustrating day Dusty apologised: 'I haven't been well, and it all catches up with me from time to time.'[9] And then, in the summer of 1996, Dusty realised that the cancer had returned.

She seemed to respond well to the fresh round of treatment, and at the beginning of 1997 was even able to consider working again; but later that year her condition deteriorated, and in February 1998 she had to cancel a guest appearance at the BRIT awards because she was too ill to attend. Her health declined steadily after that. In April of that year, Linda McCartney lost her own battle against breast cancer. The two women had become close friends, and Linda's death affected Dusty deeply.*

For the last year of her life her friend and backing singer Simon

---

* In 1997 that fine singer Carly Simon was also diagnosed as having breast cancer but, mercifully, she has emerged from the battle victorious.

Bell moved in with Dusty to take care of her. 'Her way of coping was to fight it. She would have the latest information sent to her by the Cancer Institute in America and go to the doctors armed with it.' She stayed at home and received few visitors; but she refused to take to her bed – as if that would be an admission of defeat – and slept on a large couch in the living-room. Always a night owl, she now stayed awake most of the night, reading or watching television. In the spring of 1998 she sold the rights of 275 recordings to Prudential Insurance for an estimated £6.25 million. During the summer, when the World Cup dominated the television schedules, she discovered a passion for football and became an ardent fan of Brazil. Mail-order catalogues enabled her to continue to indulge her love of shopping, and on one occasion she managed to persuade an ambulance-driver to pull over while she went to buy a draining-board. With perhaps a wry backward glance at the image she had so pains-takingly created, she even had her silver hair coloured, declaring: 'I'm going out blonde.' Determined to remain clear-headed for as long as possible, she refused morphine until at last the pain became unbearable.

It was a time for reconciliation. She was reunited with the Catholic faith she had mislaid in the seventies, and she was able at last to make peace between Mary and Dusty. Dusty Springfield had provided the means for shy and frumpy Mary O'Brien to escape from her unhap-piness and fulfil her dreams of international stardom, but Mary had had to be suppressed – or 'smashed down', as Dusty herself had expressed it with remarkable violence – and at times the strain of having to maintain her glamorous, confident new identity had proved too much; at times the escape-tunnel had itself become a prison.

Dusty's achievements received belated official acknowledgement in the New Year's Honours of 1999 when she was awarded an OBE. She felt 'deeply and genuinely honoured', but by this time she was too weak to receive the award in person from the queen. By special arrangement her manager, Vicki Wickham, collected the OBE from St James's Palace – 'they were so disappointed that she hadn't come herself, because they'd all brought their albums to be signed' – and took it, in a Fortnum & Mason carrier-bag kindly provided by a member of the palace staff, to Dusty's bedside in the Royal Marsden. 'What a tacky ribbon!' was Dusty's immediate response.

Having grown weary of the attentions of the press and her fans, she had moved to a large secluded house near Henley. And it was there that she died on the evening of Tuesday, 2 March 1999. She died as Mary O'Brien. Dusty Springfield had served her purpose.[10]

Songwriter Clive Westlake spoke for many: 'A lot of my life died that day. . . . It's a loneliness somehow, which I can't explain.'[11]

Epilogue

THE FUNERAL of Dusty Springfield on Friday, 12 March 1999 brought the centre of Henley-on-Thames to a standstill. The crowds that lined the streets in the rain as two black horses drew the hearse to the Church of St Mary the Virgin were their own moving tribute to a woman who could never quite understand why people liked her so much. The service, which was relayed to those outside the church by loudspeaker, was a blend of the sacred and the secular, Charles Wesley's 'Love Divine, All Loves Excelling' taking its place alongside Larry Henley and Jeff Silbar's 'The Wind Beneath My Wings' sung by Dusty's close friend and former backing singer Simon Bell. There were tributes from Lulu, Elvis Costello and Neil Tennant, and the whole service was framed by the sound of Dusty's voice.

Dusty's remains were later cremated. Part of her ashes were buried in the churchyard, and her brother Tom later travelled alone to the west of Ireland to scatter the remainder at a favourite spot, the Cliffs of Moher in County Clare.

In her last television interview, Dusty was asked what she thought she would have done if she had not become a singer. 'I'd like to retouch photographs, because I think people, including myself, are so insecure about the way they look in photos. Imagine sitting there and . . . making everybody happy.' Whether or not her reply was entirely serious, it did reveal that, more than forty years after those moments of teenage despair in front of her bedroom mirror, she was still obsessed with the image she presented to the world, still haunted by the thought that Mary O'Brien in herself was not good enough.

165

The transformation of Mary into Dusty was a subtle, complex and painful process, and it is unlikely that any of us will ever understand it fully. The portrait offered here will certainly prove to be inaccurate in some respects. Other attempts will undoubtedly follow; and they, too, will be wrong, to a greater or lesser extent. But always, as we contemplate the various images of Dusty that are presented to us, and consider the different accounts of her triumphs and disasters, we will return to the sound of her voice. That is where the truth is to be found.

'I'm not saying I'm Goody Two Shoes but I wasn't quite the chaotic person they made me out to be. They can call me loopy. They can call me a mad old crone. They can say I'm fat and fucking *useless* if they *really* want to. It's taken me a bloody long time but I realise now that none of that matters. Because I was meant to *sing*. So the only way they can ever hurt me is by saying my *singing* is no good. And even *then* I wouldn't believe them. . . .'

DUSTY SPRINGFIELD

Appendix

The Recordings

ANYONE who wishes to undertake the daunting task of collecting copies of all the original recordings by Dusty Springfield will require the discography compiled by John McElroy and Paul Howes and printed in Lucy O'Brien's *Dusty*, 3rd edn (2000). He will also need patience, persistence and a lot of money. Yet even the reader with more modest ambitions may be bewildered by the confusing array of discs that have come on to the market in recent years and by the manner in which Dusty's catalogue has been fragmented. For example, simply to acquire all Dusty's sixties singles, together with their respective B-sides, would involve obtaining a large number of items from the following list – and, with many of Dusty's most popular recordings being included in almost all of the selections, substantial duplication of tracks would be unavoidable.

What follows is offered as a guide to the more significant selections, large and small, that have been issued on compact disc. It includes several American titles, but these should be readily available through British record shops. There are also two important discs produced only for subscribers to the *Dusty Springfield Bulletin* (PO Box 203, Cobham, Surrey KT11 2UG).

Two more titles are promised for the year 2001: a boxed set from Reader's Digest and a collection of transcriptions of Dusty's television performances to be issued for subscribers to the *Dusty Springfield Bulletin*. Provisional details of the latter project have been included here. No information about the Reader's Digest set was available at the time of writing. There are also projected reissues, with additional tracks, of *Dusty . . . Definitely*, *From Dusty . . . with Love* and *It Begins Again*, together with the first British release – eighteen years late – of *White Heat*; but, again, firm information about these releases was not available.

The Lana Sisters

Only one Lana Sisters recording is currently available; see item 30.

The Springfields

1. *Over the Hills and Far Away* (1997) (Philips 2CD set: 534 930-2)

DISC 1: Dear John · I Done What They Told Me · Breakaway · Good News · Wimoweh Mambo · The Black Hills Of Dakota · Row, Row, Row · The Green Leaves Of Summer · Silver Dollar · Allentown Jail · Lonesome Traveller · Dear Hearts And Gentle People · They Took John Away · Eso Es El Amor · Two Brothers · Tzena, Tzena, Tzena · Bambino · Goodnight Irene · Far Away Places · Silver Threads And Golden Needles · Aunt Rhody · Swahili Papa · Gotta Travel On DISC 2: Island of Dreams · The Johnson Boys · Settle Down · There's A Big Wheel · Greenback Dollar · Midnight Special · Wabash Cannonball · Alone With You · Cottonfields · Foggy Mountain Top · Little By Little · Maggie · Darling Allalee · Mountain Boy · My Baby's Gone · Waf Woof · Say I Won't Be There · Little Boat · Come On Home · Pit-A-Pat · If I Was Down And Out · Maracabamba · No Sad Songs For Me · Where Have All The Flowers Gone? (Sag Mir, Wo Die Blumen Sind)

This set contains almost the entire Springfields output, including all the tracks from both *Kinda Folksy* (1961) and *Folk Songs from the Hills* (1963).

2. *The Very Best of the Springfields* (USA, 1998) (Taragon CD: TARCD-1047)

Dear John · Breakaway · Bambino · Star Of Hope · Goodnight Irene · Far Away Places · The Green Leaves Of Summer · Dear Hearts And Gentle People · Silver Threads And Golden Needles · Swahili Papa · Island Of Dreams · Little By Little · Settle Down · Cottonfields · Say I Won't Be There · Little Boat · Come On Home · Allentown Jail (Alternate Version) · No Sad Songs For Me · Alles Gold Und Alles Silber (Silver Threads And Golden Needles) (German version)

With its alternate versions of 'Allentown Jail' and 'Silver Threads And Golden Needles', this American selection is a valuable supplement to *Over the Hills and Far Away*.

Dusty Springfield

3. *The Silver Collection* (1988) (Philips CD: 834 128-2)

I Only Want To Be With You · Stay Awhile · I Just Don't Know What To Do With Myself · Wishin' And Hopin' · Losing You · Give Me Time · Twenty-Four Hours from Tulsa · If You Go Away · Just One Smile · Son Of A Preacher Man · All I See Is You · You Don't Have To Say You Love Me · I Close My Eyes And Count To Ten · Some Of Your Lovin' · In The Middle of Nowhere · Little By Little · How Can I Be Sure · The Look Of Love · My Colouring Book · Brand New Me · I'll Try Anything · Anyone Who Had A Heart · Am I The Same Girl · Goin' Back

4. *Songbook* (1990) (Pickwick CD: PWKS 580)

I Close My Eyes And Count To Ten · I Start Counting · Summer Is Over · Your Hurtin' Kinda Love · Who Gets Your Love · Where Am I Going · Son Of A Preacher Man · Am I The Same Girl · What's It Gonna Be · Morning

Please Don't Come · Yesterday When I Was Young · Breakfast In Bed · Magic Garden · Give Me Time · Spooky · I Will Come To You · Brand New Me · I'll Try Anything · The Colour Of Your Eyes · Learn To Say Goodbye

One of the more satisfying of the shorter selections, this should not be confused with item 18.

5. *A Brand New Me* (USA, 1992) (Rhino CD: R2 71036)

Lost · Bad Case Of The Blues · Never Love Again · Let Me Get In Your Way · Let's Get Together Soon · Brand New Me · Joe · Silly, Silly Fool · The Star Of My Show · Let's Talk It Over · I Wanna Be A Free Girl · What Good Is I Love You · What Do You Do When Love Dies · Haunted · Nothing Is Forever · Someone Who Cares · I Believe In You · I'll Be Faithful · I Can't Give Back The Love

This is a reissue of an American LP (1970) with nine additional tracks. *A Brand New Me* was released in Britain as *From Dusty ... with Love*, which is currently out of the catalogue.

6. *Blue for You* (1993) (Spectrum CD: 5500052)

I Just Don't Know What To Do With Myself · Your Hurtin' Kinda Love · Will You Love Me Tomorrow · Every Day I Have To Cry · Some Of Your Lovin' · No Easy Way Down · If You Go Away · Goin' Back · Morning Please Don't Come · How Can I Be Sure · What Do You Do When Love Dies · I Can't Make It Alone · My Colouring Book · Yesterday When I Was Young

7. *Dusty: The Legend of Dusty Springfield* (1994) (Philips 4CD set: 522-254-2)

DISC 1. *Hits and Bits:* How Can I Be Sure? · Stay Awhile · I Just Don't Know

THE RECORDINGS

What To Do With Myself · Son Of A Preacher Man · All Cried Out · I Will Come To You · Some Of Your Lovin' · Give Me Time · I'm Coming Home Again · What's It Gonna Be? · Losing You · Nothing Has Been Proved · Yesterday When I Was Young · Your Hurtin' Kinda Love · I Only Want To Be With You · All I See Is You · I'll Try Anything · I Close My Eyes And Count To Ten · Brand New Me · Your Love Still Brings Me To My Knees · Magic Garden · What Good Is I Love You? · You Don't Have To Say You Love Me

DISC 2. *Pearls and Rarities:* Baby Don't You Know · Stupido Stupido · The Corrupt Ones · Tanto So Che Poi Mi Passa · Learn to Say Goodbye · L'Eté Est Fini · Where Am I Going? · Something In Your Eyes · I Only Wanna Laugh · Sweet Lover No More · Meditation · Come For A Dream · Once Upon A Time · Demain Tu Peux Changer · Goodbye · Lose Again (live) · I Want To Be A Free Girl · Don't Say It Baby · Heartbeat · He's Got Something · What Do You Do When Love Dies · Time After Time · Soft Core · When The Midnight Choo Choo Leaves For Alabam/Breaking Glass And Other Bits

DISC 3. *Downright Dusty:* La Bamba · A Love Like Yours · Go Ahead On · What Have I Done To Deserve This? · In The Middle Of Nowhere · Another Night · Little By Little · That's The Kinda Love I've Got For You · In Private · I Just Wanna Be There · Mama's Little Girl · I Can't Give Back The Love I Feel For You · Oh No! Not My Baby · Donnez Moi · Reputation · Mockingbird · Am I The Same Girl? · When The Lovelight Starts Shining Thru His Eyes · Take Me For A Little While · Bring Him Back · Every Ounce Of Strength · Blind Sheep

DISC 4. *The Look of Love:* Goin' Back · I Think It's Gonna Rain Today · Tupelo Honey · Chained To A Memory · Who Can I Turn To (When Nobody Needs Me)? · If You Go Away · What Are You Doing The Rest Of Your Life? · Love Me By Name · No Easy Way Down · Never Love Again · I Just Fall In Love Again · That's How Heartaches Are Made · I Don't Want To Hear It Anymore · I Wish I'd Never Loved You · Just A Little Lovin' · Who Will Take My Place? · I'd Rather Leave While I'm In Love · Sandra · I've Been Wrong Before · If It Hadn't Been For You · I Had a Talk With My Man Last Night · Second Time Around · They Long To Be Close To You · The Look Of Love

Released as a limited edition, this set is now a collector's rarity and is perhaps best-regarded as unobtainable.

8. *Goin' Back: The Very Best of Dusty Springfield* (1994) (Philips CD: 848 789-2)

Wishin' And Hopin' · Little By Little · All Cried Out · Losing You · Son Of A Preacher Man · All I See Is You · In The Middle Of Nowhere · What Have I Done To Deserve This [with the Pet Shop Boys]· Goin' Back · Island Of Dreams · I'll Try Anything · Reputation · Stay Awhile · In Private · Time And Time Again · I Just Don't Know What To Do With Myself · I Only Want To Be With You · Windmills Of Your Mind · Silver Threads And Golden Needles · Say I Won't Be There · Some Of Your Lovin' · The Look Of Love · I Close My Eyes And Count To Ten · Nothing Has Been Proved · You Don't Have To Say You Love Me

This generous selection covers most of Dusty's career; but, unfortunately, it is marred by the incomprehensible arrangement of the tracks, which has Springfields numbers mingled with much later recordings.

9. *Dusty in Memphis* (1995) (Mercury CD: 528 687-2)

Just A Little Lovin' · So Much Love · Son Of A Preacher Man · In The Land Of Make Believe · Don't Forget About Me · Breakfast In Bed · Just One Smile · The Windmills Of Your Mind · I Don't Want To Hear It Anymore · No Easy Way Down · I Can't Make It Alone · Willie And Laura Mae Jones · That Old Sweet Roll (Hi-De-Ho) · What Do You Do When Love Dies?

The British reissue of *Dusty in Memphis* (1969) with three additional tracks. See also item 25, the American reissue, which has an alternative version of 'What Do You Do When Love Dies'.

10. *A Very Fine Love* (1995) (Columbia CD: 478508 2)

Roll Away · Very Fine Love · Wherever Would I Be [with Daryl Hall] · Go Easy On Me · You Are The Storm · I Can't Help The Way I Don't Feel · All I Have

To Offer You Is Love · Lovin' Proof · Old Habits Die Hard · Where Is A
Woman To Go

Dusty's solo recording of 'Wherever Would I Be' can be found on
item 20.

11. *Am I The Same Girl* (1996) (Spectrum CD: 552 093-2)

Son Of A Preacher Man · I Close My Eyes And Count To Ten · Take Another
Little Piece Of My Heart · All I See Is You · Stay Awhile · This Girl's In Love
With You · Don't Let Me Lose This Dream · Welcome Home · Give Me Time ·
Sunny · Spooky · Second Time Around · Just One Smile · Breakfast In Bed ·
(They Long To Be) Close To You · The Windmills Of Your Mind · Haunted ·
Am I The Same Girl

12. *Something Special* (1996) (Mercury 2CD set: 528 818-2)

Disc 1: Something Special · Reste Encore Un Instant · Je Ne Peux Pas
T'En Vouloir · I'll Love You For A While · Needle In A Haystack · Tu Che Ne
Sai · Di Fronte All'Amore · I Will Always Want You · I'm Gonna Leave
You · Small Town Girl · I've Got A Good Thing · Don't Forget About Me ·
No Stranger Am I · Don't Speak Of Love · Earthbound Gypsy · Wasn't
Born To Follow · A Song For You · Haunted · I Am Your Child · You Set
My Dreams To Music · Give Me The Night · Baby Blue (12" version) ·
Your Love Still Brings Me To My Knees · It Goes Like It Goes (Theme from
Norma Rae)
Disc 2: Just One Smile · Something In Your Eyes · I'd Rather Leave While I'm
In Love · Let Me Love You Once Before You Go · Tupelo Honey · I Just
Fall In Love Again · What Are You Doing The Rest Of Your Life? · Who
(Will Take My Place)? · Who Can I Turn To (When Nobody Needs Me)? ·
Joe · Who Could Be Lovin' You Other Than Me? · I've Been Wrong Before · I
Can't Make It Alone · (They Long To Be) Close To You · My Colouring
Book · If You Go Away · Sandra · No Easy Way Down · Breakfast In Bed ·

Long After Tonight Is All Over · This Girl's In Love With You · I Think It's Gonna Rain Today · Love Me By Name · The Look Of Love

13. *We Wish You a Merry Christmas* (Zone CD: X001); exclusive to subscribers to the *Dusty Springfield Bulletin*

O Holy Child · Jingle Bells · Bambino · Star Of Hope · The Twelve Days Of Christmas · Mary's Boy Child · Away In A Manger · We Wish You A Merry Christmas

This disc contains all the Christmas recordings by Dusty and the Springfields.

14. *The Dusty Springfield Anthology* (USA, 1997) (Mercury 3CD set: 314 553 501-2)

DISC 1: Silver Threads And Golden Needles · Island Of Dreams · I Only Want To Be With You · Stay Awhile · Wishin' And Hopin' · Anyone Who Had A Heart · Do Re Mi · I Just Don't Know What To Do With My -self · All Cried Out · Guess Who? · Live It Up · He's Got Something · Losing You · Your Hurtin' Kinda Love · Now That You're My Baby · In The Middle Of Nowhere · Some Of Your Lovin' · Oh No! Not My Baby · It Was Easier To Hurt Him · I've Been Wrong Before · Needle In A Haystack · I Had A Talk With My Man · Who Can I Turn To? (When Nobody Needs Me) · Little By Little · You Don't Have To Say You Love Me · Goin' Back · All I See Is You · I'll Try Anything · The Corrupt Ones
DISC 2: The Look of Love · Give Me Time · What's It Gonna Be · Chained To A Memory · If You Go Away · Don't Let Me Lose This Dream · I Close My Eyes And Count To Ten · Sweet Ride · Magic Garden · I Think It's Gonna Rain Today · Son Of A Preacher Man · Just One Smile · Don't Forget About Me · Breakfast In Bed · The Windmills Of Your Mind · Willie And Laura Mae Jones · Am I The Same Girl? · In The Land Of Make

Believe · Brand New Me · Goodbye · Silly, Silly Fool · I Wanna Be A Free Girl · How Can I Be Sure? · Spooky · What Good Is I Love You? · Haunted · Yesterday When I Was Young

DISC 3: Who Gets Your Love · Tupelo Honey · Mama's Little Girl · The Other Side Of Life · Let Me Love You Once Before You Go · You Set My Dreams To Music · Give Me The Night · Sandra · A Love Like Yours · I'd Rather Leave While I'm In Love · Living Without Your Love · You've Really Got A Hold On Me · It Goes like It Goes · Bits And Pieces · Don't Call It Love · Soft Core · Time And Time Again · What Have I Done To Deserve This [with the Pet Shop Boys] · Nothing Has Been Proved · In Private · Where Is A Woman To Go

A comprehensive survey of the whole of Dusty's career, and including tracks from the LPs *Cameo* (1973), *It Begins Again* (1978), *Living without Your Love* (1979) and *White Heat* (1982), which are all currently out of the catalogue, this generous American selection represents the best individual investment at the time of writing.

15. *A Girl Called Dusty* (1997) (Mercury CD: 534 520-2)

Mama Said · You Don't Own Me · Do Re Mi · When The Lovelight Starts Shining Thru His Eyes · My Colouring Book · Mockingbird · Twenty-Four Hours From Tulsa · Nothing · Anyone Who Had a Heart · Will You Love Me Tomorrow · Wishin' And Hopin' · Don't You Know · I Only Want To Be With You (alternate mix) · He's Got Something · Every Day I Have To Cry · Can I Get A Witness · All Cried Out · I Wish I'd Never Loved You · Once Upon A Time · Summer Is Over

A reissue of *A Girl Called Dusty* (1964) with eight additional tracks. Unfortunately, the indifferent quality of the transcription makes this disc hard to recommend. The 1990 reissue (Philips CD: 842 699-2) may still be found on the secondhand market, and better versions of almost all the additional tracks are available elsewhere.

16. *Hits Collection* (1997) (Spectrum CD: 537 549-2)

The Look Of Love · How Can I Be Sure · Stay Awhile · I Just Don't Know What To Do With Myself · Son Of A Preacher Man · All Cried Out · I Will Come To You' · Some Of Your Lovin' · Give Me Time · I'm Coming Home Again · The Windmills Of Your Mind · Losing You · I Can't Make It Alone · Yesterday When I Was Young · Your Hurtin' Kinda Love · I Only Want To Be With You · All I See Is You · I'll Try Anything · I Close My Eyes And Count To Ten · You Don't Have To Say You Love Me · What Good Is I Love You

17. *Reputation and Rarities* (1997) (EMI CD: 7243 8 59882 2 6)

Reputation · Send It To Me · Arrested By You · Time Waits For No One · Born This Way · In Private · Daydreaming · Nothing Has Been Proved · I Want To Stay Here · Occupy Your Mind · Any Other Fool · When Love Turns Blue · Getting It Right · In Private (12" version)

A reissue of *Reputation* (1990) with four additional tracks

18. *Songbooks* (1997) (Philips CD: 552 863-2)

(They Long To Be) Close To You · In The Land Of Make Believe · Another Night · Wishin' And Hopin' · Long After Tonight Is All Over · The Look Of Love · This Girl's In Love With You · I Just Don't Know What To Do With Myself · Twenty-Four Hours From Tulsa · Anyone Who Had A Heart · Goin' Back · Will You Love Me Tomorrow? · I Can't Make It Alone · Oh No! Not My Baby · Some Of Your Lovin' · Don't Forget About Me · So Much Love · No Easy Way Down · I Can't Hear You No More · That Old Sweet Roll (Hi De Ho) · Wasn't Born To Follow · I'll Love You For A While

A reissue of *Dusty Springfield Sings Burt Bacharach and Carole King* (1975) with two additional tracks

19. *Ev'rything's Coming Up Dusty* (1998) (Philips CD: 536 852-2)

Won't Be Long · Oh No! Not My Baby · Long After Tonight Is All Over · La Bamba · Who Can I Turn To (When Nobody Needs Me)? · Doodlin' · If It Don't Work Out · That's How Heartaches Are Made · It Was Easier To Hurt Him · I've Been Wrong Before · I Can't Hear You · I Had A Talk With My Man Last Night · Packin' Up · Live It Up · I Wanna Make You Happy · I Want Your Love Tonight · Now That You're My Baby · Guess Who? · If Wishes Could Be Kisses · Don't Say It Baby · Here She Comes

A reissue of *Ev'rything's Coming Up Dusty* (1965) with eight additional tracks

20. *Dusty: The Very Best Of Dusty Springfield* (1998) (Philips CD: 538 345-2)

I Only Want To Be With You · In Private · I Just Don't Know What To Do With Myself · Give Me Time · Some Of Your Lovin' · Goin' Back · You Don't Have To Say You Love Me · What Have I Done To Deserve This? [with the Pet Shop Boys] · I Close My Eyes And Count To Ten · Wishin' And Hopin' · Little By Little · Stay Awhile · All I See Is You · Nothing Has Been Proved · Losing You · Twenty Four Hours From Tulsa · In The Middle Of Nowhere · Son Of A Preacher Man · Anyone Who Had A Heart · If You Go Away · I'll Try Anything · How Can I Be Sure? · Wherever Would I Be [solo] · The Look Of Love

It includes Dusty's solo recording of 'Wherever Would I Be'.

21. *Where Am I Going* (1998) (Philips CD: 536 962-2)

Bring Him Back · Don't Let Me Lose This Dream · I Can't Wait Until I See My Baby's Face · Take Me For A Little While · Chained To A Memory · Sunny · (They Long To Be) Close To You · Welcome Home · Come Back To

Me · If You Go Away · Broken Blossoms · Where Am I Going? · I've Got A
Good Thing · Don't Forget About Me · Time After Time

A reissue of *Where Am I Going* (1967) with three additional tracks,
including the London recording of 'Don't Forget About Me', a song
which she would later record again for *Dusty in Memphis*.

22. *Dusty* (USA, 1999) (Mercury CD: 314 538 909-2)

All Cried Out · I Wish I'd Never Loved You · Can I Get A Witness? · Summer
Is Over · Don't Say It Baby · Guess Who? · Live It Up · My Colouring
Book · Nothing · Do Re Mi · Don't You Know · I Just Don't Know What
To Do With Myself · Every Ounce Of Strength · I'm Gonna Leave You ·
Heartbeat

A reissue of an American LP (1964) with three additional tracks

23. *Dusty in London* (USA, 1999) (Rhino CD: R2 75581)

Take Another Little Piece Of My Heart · This Girl's In Love With You · How
Can I Be Sure · Mixed Up Girl · I Will Come To You · I Only Wanna Laugh ·
A Song For You · Crumbs Off The Table · Let Me Down Easy · Who (Will
Take My Place) · Ain't No Sun Since You've Been Gone · Yesterday When I
Was Young · I Start Counting · See All Her Faces · Wasn't Born To Follow ·
What Are You Doing The Rest Of Your Life? · Love Power · I Think It's
Gonna Rain Today · Morning · Girls It Ain't Easy · Another Night · Come
For A Dream · Sweet Inspiration · The Second Time Around

This valuable American selection makes available a generous selection of tracks from the LPs *Dusty . . . Definitely* (1968) and *See All
Her Faces* (1972), which are both currently out of the catalogue.

24. *The Look of Love* (USA, 1999) (Mercury CD: 314 538 912-2)

The Look Of Love · Give Me Time · They Long To Be Close To You · If You
Go Away · Sunny · Come Back To Me · What's It Gonna Be? · Welcome
Home · Small Town Girl · Take Me For A Little While · Chained To A
Memory · I've Got A Good Thing · I Can't Wait Until I See My Baby's Face ·
I'll Try Anything · It's Over

A reissue of an American LP (1967) with three additional tracks

25. *Dusty in Memphis* (USA, 1999) (Rhino CD: R2 75580)

Just A Little Lovin' · So Much Love · Son Of A Preacher Man · I Don't
Want To Hear It Anymore · Don't Forget About Me · Breakfast In Bed ·
Just One Smile · The Windmills Of Your Mind · In the Land of Make
Believe · No Easy Way Down · I Can't Make It Alone · What Do You
Do When Love Dies · Willie And Laura Mae Jones · That Old Sweet
Roll (Hi-De-Ho) · Cherished · Goodbye · Make It With You · Love Shine
Down · Live Here With You · Natchez Trace · All The King's Horses · I'll
Be Faithful · Have A Good Life Baby · You've Got A Friend · I Found My
Way

The American reissue of *Dusty in Memphis* (1969) with no fewer than
fourteen additional tracks. The version of 'What Do You Do When
Love Dies' included here differs from that on the British reissue
(item 9).

26. *Oooooooweeee!!!* (USA, 1999) (Mercury CD: 314 538910-2)

Losing You · Here She Comes · Once Upon A Time · He's Got Something ·
You Don't Own Me · Now That You're My Baby · If Wishes Could Be Kisses ·
I'll Love You For A While · I Wanna Make You Happy · Your Hurtin' Kinda
Love · When The Lovelight Starts Shining Thru His Eyes · I Want Your

Love Tonight · Go Ahead On · I Will Always Want You · Don't Let Me Lose This Dream

A reissue of an American LP (1965) with three additional tracks.

27. *You Don't Have to Say You Love Me* (USA, 1999) (Mercury CD: 314 538 911-2)

You Don't Have To Say You Love Me · Won't Be Long · Oh No! Not My Baby · Long After Tonight Is All Over · La Bamba · Who Can I Turn To (When Nobody Needs Me)? · Little By Little · If It Don't Work Out · It Was Easier To Hurt Him · I've Been Wrong Before · I Can't Hear You · I Had A Talk With My Man · Doodlin' · That's How Heartaches Are Made · Packin' Up

A reissue of an American LP (1966) with three additional tracks.

28. *Stay Awhile/I Only Want To Be With You* (USA, 1999) (Mercury CD: 314 538 902-2)

I Only Want To Be With You · Stay Awhile · Twenty-Four Hours From Tulsa · Mama Said · Anyone Who Had A Heart · When The Lovelight Starts Shining Thru His Eyes · Wishin' And Hopin' · Mockingbird · Will You Love Me Tomorrow · You Don't Own Me · Something Special · Every Day I Have To Cry · Baby Don't You Know · Standing In The Need of Love · If It Hadn't Been For You

A reissue of an American LP (1964) with three additional tracks

29. *The BBC Sessions* (Zone CD: X002); exclusive to subscribers to the *Dusty Springfield Bulletin*

I Can't Hear You · Wishin' And Hopin' · Losing You · I Can't Hear You ·

In The Middle Of Nowhere · Mockingbird · Little By Little · Up Tight (Every
thing's Alright) · Chained To A Memory · We're Doing Fine · Every Ounce Of
Strength · You Don't Have To Say You Love Me · Good Loving · To Love
Somebody · Son Of A Preacher Man · Higher And Higher (Your Love
Keeps Lifting Me)

This valuable collection makes available radio performances from
Saturday Club and *Top Gear*, interspersed with interviews.

30. *Simply Dusty: The Definitive Dusty Springfield Collection* (2000) (Mercury 4CD set: 546 730-2):

DISC 1: Dusty Springfield [Blossom Dearie] · Ragtime Selection: I Love A Piano,
Pretty Baby, When The Midnight Choo Choo Leaves For Alabam [Mary and
Dion] · (Seven Little Girls) Sitting On The Back Seat [The Lana Sisters] · Far
Away Places [The Springfields] · Island Of Dreams [The Springfields] · Say I
Won't Be There [The Springfields] · No Sad Songs For Me [The Springfields] ·
I Only Want To Be With You · Once Upon A Time · Stay Awhile · Will You Love
Me Tomorrow · Wishin' And Hopin' · I Just Don't Know What To Do With
Myself · All Cried Out · Losing You · Summer Is Over · I Will Always Want You ·
Your Hurtin' Kinda Love · I Wanna Make You Happy · In The Middle Of
Nowhere (remix) · Baby Don't You Know (remix) · Some Of Your Lovin' · Who
Can I Turn To (When Nobody Needs Me)? · Doodlin' · I've Been Wrong Before ·
Little By Little · If It Hadn't Been For You (remix) · You Don't Have To
Say You Love Me · Every Ounce of Strength (remix)
DISC 2: Goin' Back · Poor Wayfaring Stranger (live) · All I See Is You · Go Ahead
On (remix) · I'll Try Anything (remix) · Give Me Time · The Look Of Love ·
What's It Gonna Be (remix) · Chained To A Memory · Welcome Home · Broken
Blossoms · If You Go Away · Where Am I Going? · It's Over · Magic Garden
(remix) · I Close My Eyes And Count To Ten · I Will Come To You (remix) ·
Sweet Lover No More · Another Night (remix) · I Can't Give Back The Love I
Feel For You (remix) · I Think It's Gonna To Rain Today · Son Of A Preacher
Man · The Windmills Of Your Mind · No Easy Way Down · Am I The
Same Girl?

THE RECORDINGS

Disc 3: Let Me Get In Your Way · Brand New Me · The Star Of My Show · Someone Who Cares · Live Here With You · Make It With You · You've Got A Friend · Morning Please Don't Come [with Tom Springfield] · How Can I Be Sure? · What Are You Doing The Rest of Your Life · Mixed Up Girl · Crumbs Off The Table · Yesterday When I Was Young · See All Her Faces · Easy Evil · Of All The Things · Learn To Say Goodbye · Sea And Sky · In The Winter · Home To Myself · Exclusively For Me · I'd Rather Leave While I'm In Love · Turn Me Around · Love Me By Name · Hollywood Movie Girls
Disc 4: That's The Kind of Love I've Got For You [US DJ Disco Extended Mix] · Closet Man · I Just Fall In Love Again · I Wish That Love Would Last · (But It's A) Nice Dream · I Don't Think We Could Ever Be Friends · Blind Sheep · Losing You (Just A Memory) · You'll Be Loving Me [alternate take of Sooner Or Later] · What Have I Done To Deserve This [with the Pet Shop Boys] · Nothing Has Been Proved · In Private · Daydreaming · Something In Your Eyes · Go Easy On Me · I Can't Help The Way I Don't Feel · Wherever Would I Be? [solo] · Quiet Please, There's A Lady Onstage [live] · Someone To Watch Over Me

Attractively presented and rather expensive, but not as 'definitive' as its title suggests, this selection covers Dusty's entire career from the recordings made at home with her brother when she was in her early teens to her last recording, 'Someone To Watch Over Me', and makes several tracks available for the first time. However, the omission of 'Soft Core' is astonishing, and the extensive remixing of which the set boasts can hardly be said to have done Dusty any favours.

31. *Good Times* (forthcoming 2001) (2CD Zone set); exclusive to subscribers to the *Dusty Springfield Bulletin*:

The Real Thing · Some Of Your Lovin' · Bring Him Back · Poor Wayfaring Stranger · The Mood I'm In · Twenty-Four Hours From Tulsa · Call Me Irresponsible · Tell The World About You · I Don't Want To Go On Without You · I'll Never Stop Loving You · You Lost The Sweetest Boy · To Love And Be Loved · Anna (El Baion) · Gonna Build A Mountain · Losing You · Live It Up · I'll Try

THE RECORDINGS

Anything · The Water Is Wide · Everybody Needs Somebody · Get Ready · The Beautiful Land · All I See Is You · Do Re Mi, Soulville · Don't Let Me Lose This Dream · Peel Me A Grape · You Can Have Him · By Myself · Two Brothers · Time After Time · You'd Better Run · Good Times · If My Friends Could See Me Now · I Wish You Love · It Was Easier To Hurt Him · (Love Is Like A) Heatwave · Nowhere To Run · My Lagan Love · The Mood I'm In · You Don't Have To Say You Love Me · Knowing When To Leave · Up On The Roof · Movie Star · On The Good Ship Lollipop · What Did She Know About Railways? · Manha De Carnival · People Get Ready · I Am Woman · Since I Fell For You · Stepping Out With My Baby · I Close My Eyes And Count To Ten · I'm Coming Home Again

This is a provisional track listing for what promises to be a most valuable set, making available transcriptions of live BBC television performances.

Notes

'... if you set out to create ...': Gay News, 24 February 1978.

Chapter 1. 'Sing Up, Mary!'

1 Dusty Springfield interviews: *New Musical Express*, 15 July 1966; *Des O'Connor Tonight*, Carlton television, 1995.

2 *Today*, 11 April 1964; *The People*, 7 July 1968; *The Daily Express*, 9 August 1985; *Radio Times*, 30 April 1994; the *Telegraph* magazine, 27 May 1995; The *Mail on Sunday*, *You* magazine, 28 May 1995; *Hello!*, 30 June 1990; David Evans, *Scissors and Paste: A Collage Biography of Dusty Springfield* (1995), p. 4.

3 The *People*, 7 July 1968.

4 The *Telegraph* magazine, 27 May 1995; *Today*, 11 April 1964.

5 The *Sunday Times*, 7 June 1964; *New Musical Express*, 15 July 1966; The *Melody Maker*, 16 July 1966; The *Daily Mail*, 12 June 1990; Evans, *Scissors and Paste*, p. 23; *Woman*, 12 August 1985.

6 *New Musical Express*, 15 July 1966; *Woman*, 12 August 1985; *News of the World*, 25 August 1964; *Woman's World*, May 1978.

7 Dusty Springfield interviews: *Dusty: Full Circle*, BBC television, 1 May 1994; and *Remembering Dusty Springfield*, pt 1, BBC radio, 2 March 2000.

8 Dusty Springfield interviews: *Woman's World*, May 1978; *Dusty: Full Circle*; *Later... with Jools Holland*, BBC television, June 1995.

9 *Woman's World*, May 1978; The *Daily Mail*, 12 June 1990; The *Sun*, 13 June 1990.

10 Dusty Springfield interviews: *Dusty: Full Circle*; and The *Mail on Sunday*, *You* magazine, 28 May 1995.

11 *Woman's World*, May 1978.

12 *Today*, 11 April 1964; *Record Mirror*, 26 September 1970; *Woman's World*, May 1978; *New Musical Express*, 15 July 1966; Sotheby's sale catalogue, *Rock 'n' Roll Memorabilia*, 14–15 September 1999, pp. 52–3.

13 *Woman's World*, May 1978.

14 Dusty Springfield interviews: *Today*, 11 April 1964; *New Musical Express*, 15 July 1966; *The Dame Edna Experience*, London Weekend Television, 1989; Evans, *Scissors and Paste*, p. 10; *Definitely Dusty*, BBC television, 26 December 1999.

15 H. G. Wells, *The History of Mr Polly* (1910), ch. 9.

16 Dusty Springfield quoted in Evans, *Scissors and Paste*, p. 34.

17 Lucy O'Brien, *Dusty*, 3rd edn (2000), p. 19.

18 Dusty Springfield interviews: *News of the World*, 16 August 1964; The *Sunday Express*, 8 March 1964; *Gay Times*, September 1985, reprinted in *A Boy Called Mary: Kris Kirk's Greatest Hits* (1999).

Chapter 2. A Means to an End

1 Dusty Springfield quoted in Lucy O'Brien, *Dusty*, 3rd edn (2000), p. 20.

2 Tom Springfield interview, *Scene*, 21 March 1963; Dusty Springfield quoted in David Evans, *Scissors and Paste: A Collage Biography of Dusty Springfield* (1995), pp. 15–16, 22.

3 Sylvia Jones interview, The *Mirror*, 4 March 1999.

4 Quoted in Evans, *Scissors and Paste*, p. 14.

5 Quoted in O'Brien, *Dusty*, p. 21.

6 Evans, *Scissor and Paste*, p. 18.

7 *Record Mirror*, 26 September 1970.

8 *Gay News*, 24 February 1978.

9 *Record Mirror*, 26 September 1970.

10 Sleeve-notes for *I Only Want To Be With You* (EP, 1964).

11 Quoted in Evans, *Scissors and Paste*, p. 9.

12 The *Observer*, 12 February 1989; *Scene*, 21 March 1963.

13 BBC audition report on the Springfields, 30 September 1960, BBC Written Archives.

14 *Dusty: Full Circle*, BBC television, 1 May 1994.

15 Dusty Springfield interviews: Evans, *Scissors and Paste*, pp. 19–20, 25; *Dusty: Full Circle*; *Record Mirror*, 26 September 1970; The *Observer*, 12 February 1989. Mike Hurst interview included

in *Definitely Dusty*, BBC television, 26 December 1999.

16 Johnny Franz interview, *New Musical Express*, 19 August 1966.

17 O'Brien, *Dusty*, p. 42.

18 Judith Simons, The *Daily Express*, 15 February 1963.

19 The *Daily Express*, 15 February 1963.

20 Dusty Springfield quoted in Evans, *Scissors and Paste*, pp. 26–7.

21 *Dusty: Full Circle*.

22 Dusty Springfield interviews: The *Sun*, 20 January 1978; *Gay Times*, September 1985, reprinted in *A Boy Called Mary: Kris Kirk's Greatest Hits* (1999); The *Observer*, 12 February 1989; *Dusty: Full Circle*; Evans, *Scissors and Paste*, pp. 25–6.

23 Ann Leslie, The *Daily Express*, 25 February 1965.

24 Quoted in Evans, *Scissors and Paste*, p. 10.

25 The *Daily Express*, 3 December 1965; George Eells, *The Life That Late He Led: A Biography of Cole Porter* (1967), p. 112.

26 Quoted in O'Brien, *Dusty*, p. 89.

27 *Record Mirror*, 3 September 1966.

28 The *Daily Express*, 25 October 1963; The *Observer*, 12 February 1989; Evans, *Scissors and Paste*, p. 23.

29 The *Sunday Times*, 17 August 1985; Evans, *Scissors and Paste*, pp. 19–20.

30 The *Sunday Express*, 8 March 1964; Evans, *Scissors and Paste*, pp. 22 and 23.

31 Mike Hurst interview included in *A Girl Called Dusty*, BBC radio, 27 March 1999.

32 The *Sun*, 20 January 1978; The *Sunday Express*, 8 March 1964.

33 Mike Hurst, quoted in O'Brien, *Dusty*, pp. 39–40.

34 Dusty Springfield quoted in Evans, *Scissors and Paste*, p. 28.

35 Dusty Springfield interview included in *Remembering Dusty Springfield*, pt 1, BBC radio, 2 March 2000.

36 Quoted in O'Brien, *Dusty*, p. 47.

37 *Dusty: Full Circle*.

38 The *Evening Standard* (London), 24 September 1963.

39 Dusty Springfield quoted in Evans, *Scissors and Paste*, p.16.

Chapter 3. A Girl Called Dusty

1 Marcelle Bernstein in the *Observer* magazine, 26 January 1969.

2 Derek Wadsworth interview, *Remembering Dusty Springfield*, pt 1, BBC radio, 2 March 2000.

3 Quoted in David Evans, *Scissors and Paste: A Collage Biography of Dusty Springfield* (1995), p. 35.

4 The *Evening Standard* (London), 16 August 1985.

5 Tom Dowd quoted in Lucy O'Brien, *Dusty*, 3rd edn (2000), pp. 122–3.

6 The *Daily Star*, 18 May 1979.

7 The *Observer*, 12 February 1989; Evans, *Scissors and Paste*, pp. 35–6; the *Telegraph* magazine, 27 May 1995; The *Daily Express*, 25 February 1965.

8 Penny Valentine, The *Guardian*, 4 March 1999; Evans, *Scissors and Paste*, p. 48; the Jean Rook interview, The *Daily Express*, 9 August 1985; Dusty Springfield interview included in *Remembering Dusty Springfield*, pt 4, BBC radio, 23 March 2000.

9 Quoted in Evans, *Scissors and Paste*, p. 35.

10 Madeline Bell interview, *Remembering Dusty Springfield*, pt 1.

11 Keith Altham, quoted in Dusty Springfield obituary, The *Independent*, 4 March 1999; Vic Billings, quoted in O'Brien, *Dusty*, p. 89; Neil Tennant, funeral tribute, 12 March 1999, printed in Sotheby's sale catalogue, *Rock 'n' Roll Memorabilia*, 14–15 September 1999, pp. 52–3.

12 Mike Hurst interview, *Channel Four News*, 3 March 1999; Dusty Springfield interview, *Q*, April 1989.

13 Jean Rook interview, The *Daily Express*, 9 August 1985.

14 *Dusty: Full Circle*, BBC television, 1 May 1994; the *Telegraph* magazine, 27 May 1995; The *Observer*, 12 February 1989; the Jean Rook interview, The *Daily Express*, 9 August 1985; The *Sunday Times*, 17 August 1985; *TV Times*, 1967; *Record Mirror*, 3 September 1966; The *Evening Standard* (London), 3 September 1970.

15 Ivor Raymonde, quoted in O'Brien, *Dusty*, p. 94.

16 The *People*, 7 July 1968.

17 *TV Times*, 1967.

18 *Teen Trends*, January 1966; The *Sunday Times*, 7 June 1964; The *Evening Standard* (London), 5 September 1970; *Gay News*, 24 February 1978; Michele Kort, 'The Secret Life of Dusty Springfield', *The Advocate*, 27 April 1999.

19 The *Sunday Mirror*, 4 April 1965; interview quoted in Evans, *Scissors and Paste*, pp. 44–6.

20 Sir John Suckling's 'Ballad upon a Wedding' (1646), of course.

21 The *Evening Standard* (London), 3 September 1970.

22 *Radio Times*, 24 December 1963, p. 33.

23 Elkan Allan, quoted in Hilary Kingsley and Geoff Tibbles, *Box of Delights* (1989), p. 72.

24 Richard Mabey, *The Pop Process* (1969), pp. 106–7.

25 Dusty Springfield, quoted in Evans, *Scissors and Paste*, pp. 51–2.

NOTES

26 Vic Billings, quoted in the *Daily Mail*, 14 January 1964.

27 *Today*, 11 April 1964.

28 The *Sunday Express*, 25 October 1964.

29 Interview, *Today*, 11 April 1964; George Melly, *Revolt into Style: The Pop Arts in Britain* (1970), p. 93.

30 Evans, *Scissors and Paste*, p. 39.

31 Johnny Franz interview, *New Musical Express*, 19 August 1966.

32 Dionne Warwick interview, *Dusty: Full Circle*.

33 Dusty Springfield interview in ibid.; Simon Napier-Bell, 'Perfection in the stairwell', *The Independent on Sunday*, 7 March 1999.

34 Peter Jones, sleeve note to *Golden Hits* (1966).

35 Quoted in Evans, *Scissors and Paste*, p. 39.

36 *Melody Maker*, 16 July 1966.

37 ibid., 12 September 1970.

38 The *Telegraph* magazine, 27 May 1995.

39 The *Daily Mirror*, 19 July 1969; Evans, *Scissors and Paste*, pp. 46–7.

40 ibid., p. 42; Veronica Groocock in *Record Mirror*, 3 September 1966.

41 *Dusty: Full Circle*; Evans, *Scissors and Paste*, pp. 42–3.

42 *Melody Maker*, 16 July 1966.

43 Brooks Arthur, quoted in O'Brien, *Dusty*, p. 54.

44 Jerry Wexler interview, *Definitely Dusty*, BBC television, 26 December 1999

45 Interview included in *Remembering Dusty Springfield*, pt 2, BBC radio, 9 March 2000.

46 *Dusty: Full Circle*; Evans, *Scissors and Paste*, p. 39.

47 Quoted in ibid., pp. 46–7; Fred Perry and Stanley Dorfman quoted in the *Observer* magazine, 26 January 1969.

48 *Seven Days that Rocked the World*, pt 2, BBC radio, 31 May 2000.

49 Vic Billings, quoted in O'Brien, *Dusty*, p. 50; Dusty Springfield, interview included in *Bacharach and David: Hitmakers*, BBC radio, 25 January 1997.

50 The *Daily Sketch*, 16 September 1966.

51 Dusty Springfield, quoted in Evans, *Scissors and Paste*, pp. 53–4.

52 *Disc Weekly*, 19 February 1966.

53 The *Daily Mirror*, 14 September 1966; The *Daily Sketch*, 16 September 1966.

54 *Today*, 11 April 1964.

55 ibid.; Mike Hurst interview, included in *A Girl Called Dusty*, BBC radio, 27 March 1999.

56 *News of the World*, 16 August 1964.

57 ibid., 25 August 1964.

58 Frank Allen, *Travelling Man: On the Road with the Searchers* (1999), p. 57–8.

59 Evans, *Scissors and Paste*, p. 57.

60 Martha Reeves and Mark Bego, *Dancing in the Street: Confessions of a Motown Diva* (1994), pp. 114–16; Martha Reeves interview in *Remembering Dusty Springfield*, pt 2.

61 Allen, *Travelling Man*, p. 53.

62 *Dusty: Full Circle*.

63 Allen, *Travelling Man*, p. 53.

64 Dusty quoted in Evans, *Scissors and Paste*, pp. 58–9; Pat Rhodes quoted in O'Brien, *Dusty*, p. 148.

65 Dusty Springfield quoted in ibid., pp. 58–9, and in O'Brien, *Dusty*, p. 56.

66 *Gay Times* interview with Kris Kirk, September 1985, reprinted in *A Boy Called Mary: Kris Kirk's Greatest Hits* (1999).

67 The *Telegraph* magazine, 27 May 1995.

68 *Gay News*, 24 February 1978.

69 *The Times*, 7 June 1995.

70 Evans, *Scissors and Paste*, p. 60.

71 Interview included in 'Remembering Dusty Springfield', pt 2.

72 Interview included in ibid.

73 Interview included in *Bacharach and David: Hitmakers*.

74 Interviews included in *A Girl Called Dusty* and in Evans, *Scissors and Paste*, p. 26.

75 *Record Mirror*, 9 April 1966; The *Liverpool Echo*, 28 December 1966; Doug Reece in the *Dusty Springfield Bulletin*, no. 40 (2000).

76 Allen, *Travelling Man*, p. 53.

Chapter 4. South Africa

1 *Dusty: Full Circle*, BBC television, 1 May 1995.

2 The *Daily Mirror*, 16 December 1964.

3 The *Daily Mail*, 16 December 1964; The *Daily Express*, 16 December 1964; The *Daily Mail*, 26 April 1965.

4 The *Guardian*, 7 June 1990.

5 Quoted in Lucy O'Brien, *Dusty*, 3rd edn (2000), p. 72.

6 R. Quibell, quoted in *The Times*, 17 December 1964.

7 Cabinet papers, quoted in *The Times*, 1 January 1996.

8 ibid.

9 The *Daily Mail*, 26 April 1965; The *Daily Mirror*, 26 April 1965.

10 The *Guardian*, 7 June 1990.

Chapter 5. Everything's Coming Up Dusty

1 The *Sun*, 29 January 1965; Dusty Springfield interview included in *Remembering Dusty Springfield*, BBC radio, pt 2, 9 March 2000.

2 *Melody Maker*, 16 July 1966; *Record Mirror*, 26 September 1970; Martha Reeves and Mark Bego, *Dancing in the Street: Confessions of a Motown Diva* (1994), pp. 119–20; David Evans, *Scis-*

sors and Paste: A Collage Biography of Dusty Springfield (1995), pp. 65–6.

3 Vicki Wickham interview included in *A Girl Called Dusty*, BBC radio, 27 March 1999; Reeves and Bego, *Dancing in the Street*, pp. 127–9; Mary Wilson, *Dreamgirl & Supreme Faith: My Life as a Supreme*, revised edn (1999), p. 162; Dusty Springfield interview in *Dusty: Full Circle*, BBC television, 1 May 1994.

4 Dusty Springfield interview, *Disc and Music Echo*, 24 September 1966; Madeline Bell interview included in *Remembering Dusty Springfield*, pt 2, BBC radio, 9 March 2000.

5 *Dusty: Full Circle*.

6 *The New Grove Dictionary of Jazz*, 2 vols (1988), Vol. 1, p. 582.

7 John Hendricks interview, included in *There I Go, There I Go: The Story of Vocalese*, BBC radio, 3 and 10 January 1998.

8 Dusty Springfield interviews: *Today*, 11 April 1964; *Radio Times*, 13 August 1966; *Remembering Dusty Springfield*, pt 2, BBC radio, 9 March 2000.

9 The *Sunday Express*, 8 March 1964.

10 *Q*, April 1989.

11 *New Musical Express*, 22 April 1966.

12 Dusty Springfield interview included in *Remembering Dusty Springfield*, pt 2, BBC radio, 9 March 2000; Simon Napier-Bell, *You Don't Have to Say You Love Me*, revised edn (1983), pp. 2–4, and 'Perfection in the stair well', The *Independent on Sunday*, 7 March 1999.

13 *Radio Times*, 13 August 1966.

14 *Disc and Music Echo*, 24 September 1966.

15 *New Musical Express*, 30 September 1966; *Sunday Mirror*, 4 December 1966; *Q*, April 1989; Tom Dowd, quoted in

Lucy O'Brien, *Dusty*, 3rd edn (2000), p. 125.

16 Dusty Springfield interview included in *Bacharach and David: Hitmakers*, BBC radio, 25 January 1997; Burt Bacharach interviews included in *Definitely Dusty*, BBC television, 26 December 1999, and *Dusty: Full Circle*.

17 Quoted in O'Brien, *Dusty*, p. 110.

18 Quoted in *Woman*, 22 July 1978.

19 Clive Westlake interview included in *Remembering Dusty Springfield*, pt 3, BBC radio, 16 March 2000.

20 *New Musical Express*, 13 July 1968.

21 Clive Westlake quoted in O'Brien, *Dusty*, p. 119.

22 Sleeve notes for *Dusty ... Definitely* (1968).

23 The *Observer* magazine, 21 January 1969; Madeline Bell interview included in *Remembering Dusty Springfield*, pt 3, BBC radio, 16 March 2000; Vic Billings interview, The *Evening News* (London), 26 May 1967.

Chapter 6. Memphis

1 Jerry Wexler and David Ritz, *Rhythm and the Blues: A Life in American Music* (1994), p. 223.

2 Jerry Wexler interviews: *Jerry Wexler: Soul Man*, 3-part series, BBC radio, 21 July–4 August 1999; and in Lucy O'Brien, *Dusty*, 3rd edn (2000), p. 123.

3 *New Musical Express*, 22 April 1966.

4 Tom Dowd quoted in David Evans, *Scissors and Paste: A Collage Biography of Dusty Springfield* (1995), p. 88.

5 Dusty Springfield interviews: sleeve notes for *Dusty In Memphis* (1969); *New Musical Express*, 11 January 1969; *Melody Maker*, 21 December 1968.

6 The *Telegraph* magazine, 27 May 1995.

7 Dusty Springfield, quoted in Evans, *Scissors and Paste*, p. 95, and in the *Telegraph* magazine, 27 May 1995.

8 The *Daily Express*, 18 September 1979; *A Girl Called Dusty*, BBC radio, 27 March 1999; *Definitely Dusty*, BBC television, 26 December 1999; *Dusty: Full Circle*, BBC television, 1 May 1994; O'Brien, *Dusty*, p. 125; Evans, *Scissors and Paste*, p. 95.

9 Wexler, *Rhythm and the Blues*, pp. 222–4; and quoted in O'Brien, *Dusty*, p. 124.

10 *Dusty: Full Circle*, BBC; O'Brien, *Dusty*, pp. 127, 129.

11 *Remembering Dusty Springfield*, pt 3, BBC radio, 16 March 2000; Evans, *Scissors and Paste*, p. 97.

12 Dusty Springfield interviews: *Melody Maker*, 21 December 1968; *Rolling Stone*, 13 July 1978; and in *Dusty: Full Circle*. Jerry Wexler: interview included in *Dusty: Full Circle*; and *Rhythm and the Blues*, p. 224.

13 ibid., p. 208; *Melody Maker*, 21 December 1968.

14 O'Brien, *Dusty*, p. 127; Evans, *Scissors and Paste*, p. 96.

15 Arif Mardin interview in *Remembering Dusty Springfield*, pt 3, BBC radio, 16 March 2000; Dusty Springfield quoted in Evans, *Scissors and Paste*, p. 95.

16 Quoted in O'Brien, *Dusty*, p. 129.

17 *Melody Maker*, 21 December 1968.

18 Michele Kort, 'The Secret Life of Dusty Springfield', *The Advocate*, 27 April 1999; Neil Tennant interview included in *Dusty: Full Circle*.

19 Tom Dowd and Arif Mardin quoted in O'Brien, *Dusty*, p. 131.

20 *Melody Maker*, 21 December 1968; *New Musical Express*, 11 January 1969.

Chapter 7. The Marriage Question

1 The *People*, 7 July 1968.

2 *News of the World*, 16 August 1964.

3 *Rave*, November 1965.

4 The *Daily Express*, 9 August 1985.

5 The *Evening Standard* (London), 5 September 1970.

6 *Today*, 11 April 1964.

7 The *Daily Mirror*, 24 February 1964.

8 The *Sunday Express*, 8 March 1964.

9 The *Daily Express*, 25 February 1965.

10 *News of the World*, 30 August 1967.

11 *Melody Maker*, 16 July 1966.

12 The *Sunday Mirror*, 4 April 1965; The *People*, 7 July 1968.

13 The *Observer*, 26 January 1969.

14 *News of the World*, 30 August 1967.

15 Frank Allen, *Travelling Man: On the Road with the Searchers* (1999), pp. 56–7. He includes blurred photographs, taken by Norma Tanega, of himself and Dusty in an awkward embrace, but the main interest of the pictures is perhaps Dusty's hair 'off duty'.

16 Madeline Bell interview, *Definitely Dusty*, 26 December 1999; *News of the World*, 30 August 1967; The *Sun*, 19 February 1988.

17 The *Sun*, 13 June 1990.

18 The *Sunday Express*, 8 March 1964.

19 *Today*, 11 April 1964.

20 Martha Reeves and Mark Bego, *Dancing in the Street: Confessions of a Motown Diva*, 1994, p. 126; Allen, *Travelling Man*, p. 54.

21 The *Observer*, 26 January 1969.

22 Lucy O'Brien, *Dusty*, 3rd edn (2000), pp. 175–6.

23 *News of the World*, 30 August 1967.

24 The *Evening Standard*, 5 September 1970.

25 The *Daily Express*, 9 August 1985.

26 *Woman's World*, May 1978.

27 The *Mail on Sunday*, *You* magazine, 28 May 1995.

28 *Today*, 11 April 1964; The *Evening Standard*, 3 September 1970.

29 *News of the World*, 10 April 1988.

30 The *Daily Star*, 18 May 1979.

Chapter 8. Am I the Same Girl?

1 Dusty Springfield interview for the sleeve notes of the American version of the LP, *A Brand New Me* (1970).

2 The *Evening Standard* (London), 5 September 1970.

3 Steve Barri and Dennis Lambert quoted in Lucy O'Brien, *Dusty*, 3rd edn (2000), pp. 150–1; Dusty Springfield interview, *Rolling Stone*, 13 July 1978.

Chapter 9. The Descent into Hell

1 *Record Mirror*, 3 September 1966.

2 *Woman's World*, May 1978.

3 *Dusty: Full Circle*, BBC television, 1 May 1994; *Woman*, 22 July 1978; The *Observer*, 12 February 1989.

4 Dusty Springfield quoted in David Evans, *Scissors and Paste: A Collage Biography of Dusty Springfield* (1995), p. 47.

5 *Gay Times*, September 1985, reprinted in *A Boy Called Mary: Kris Kirk's Greatest Hits* (1999); The *Evening Standard* (London), 3 September 1970.

6 The *Daily Telegraph*, 1 January 1971.

7 The *Sun*, 2 May 1970; The *Daily Mirror*, January 1970.

8 The *Daily Express*, 9 August 1985.

9 Sleeve-notes, *Ev'rything's Coming Up Dusty* (1965); *Evening News*, 26 May 1967; *Melody Maker*, 21 December 1968; *Record Mirror*, 26 September 1970; *The Times*, 7 June 1995.

10 The *Telegraph* magazine, 17 May 1995; The *Evening Standard* (London), 5 September 1970; *Melody Maker*, 16 July 1966; The *People*, 23 March 1969.

11 *News of the World,* 10 April 1988.

12 Dusty Springfield interviews: The *Sun,* 20 January 1978; The *Sunday Express,* 14 January 1973; *Q,* April 1989; *Rolling Stone,* 13 July 1978. Vicki Wickham interview: *Remembering Dusty Springfield,* pt 3, BBC radio, 16 March 2000.

13 The *Daily Express,* 5 December 1972; The *Daily Mirror,* 19 December 1972; *TV Times,* 16 April 1977.

14 *Rolling Stone,* 13 July 1978.

15 The *Daily Star,* 18 May 1979.

16 *Gay Times,* September 1985, reprinted in *A Boy Called Mary: Kris Kirk's Greatest Hits* (1999).

17 *Woman,* 22 July 1978; *Gay Times,* September 1985.

18 The *Daily Mirror,* 17 March 1989.

19 *Rolling Stone,* 13 July 1978; *News of the World,* 10 April 1988.

20 *Woman,* 22 July 1978; *News of the World,* 19 February 1978.

21 *News of the World,* 10 April 1988; the *Telegraph* magazine, 27 May 1995; The *Mail on Sunday, You* magazine, 28 May 1995; The *Mail on Sunday,* 7 March 1999; Michele Kort, 'The Secret Life of Dusty Springfield', *The Advocate,* 27 April 1999.

22 The *Evening Standard* (London), 3 September 1970.

23 *Woman's World,* May 1978.

24 Dusty Springfield quoted in Lucy O'Brien, *Dusty,* 3rd edn (2000), pp. 155–6.

25 *Rolling Stone,* 13 July 1978; *News of the World,* 10 April 1988; Vicki Wickham interview included in *Definitely Dusty,* BBC television, 26 December 1999.

26 Dusty Springfield interviews: *News of the World,* 19 February 1978; The *Sun,* 19 February 1988 and 12 June 1990; The *Sunday Mirror,* 10 August 1980; *Gay Times,* September 1985; The *Daily Mirror,* 17 March 1989; The *Daily Mail,* 12 June 1990; *Radio Times,* 30 April 1994. Penny Valentine, The *Guardian,* 4 March 1999; *Disc and Music Echo,* 8 October 1966; *Woman,* 22 July 1978.

Chapter 10. Beginning Again

1 *Rolling Stone,* 13 July 1978.

2 *Gay News,* 24 February 1978.

3 The *Daily Express,* 9 August 1985.

4 Interview included in *A Girl Called Dusty,* BBC Radio 2, 27 March 1999.

5 *Woman,* 12 August 1985.

6 *Gay News,* 24 February 1978.

7 *News of the World,* 19 February 1978.

8 The *Telegraph* magazine, 27 May 1995; *Gay Times,* September 1985, reprinted in *A Boy Called Mary: Kris Kirk's Greatest Hits,* 1999.

9 The *Evening Standard* (London), 8 March 1979.

10 The *Sun,* 6 April 1979.

11 *News of the World,* 9 December 1979; Lucy O'Brien, *Dusty,* 3rd edn (2000), pp. 167–8; *Gay News,* 24 February 1978.

12 Dusty Springfield, quoted in David Evans, *Scissors and Paste: A Collage Biography of Dusty Springfield* (1995), p. 119.

13 Dusty Springfield: quoted in O'Brien, *Dusty,* p. 186; interview, *Telegraph* magazine, 27 May 1995.

14 The *Daily Mail,* 29 April 1985; The *Sunday Mirror,* 9 September 1984.

15 *Gay Times,* September 1985.

16 Simon Bell, quoted in O'Brien, *Dusty,* p. 190.

17 The *Sun,* 23 February 1989.

18 Vic Billings, quoted in O'Brien, *Dusty,* p. 189.

19 *Gay Times*, September 1985.

20 The *Sun*, 23 February 1989.

21 The *Sunday Times*, 11 August 1985.

22 *Gay Times*, September 1985.

23 ibid.

24 The *Sun*, 23 February 1989.

25 Peter Stringfellow, Sky News, 3 March 1999.

26 *Radio Times*, 30 April 1994.

Chapter 11. Pet Shop Girl

1 Dusty Springfield interviews: 'Around and Around', VH-1 television, 1995; *Hello!*, 30 June 1990.

2 Peter Stringfellow interview, The *Sun*, 23 February 1989; article by Neil Tennant in the *Sunday Times*, 9 August 1987; Neil Tennant interview, *Essentially: The Pet Shop Boys Story*, BBC radio, 8 April 2000.

3 Neil Tennant, funeral tribute, 12 March 1999, printed in Sotheby's sale catalogue, *Rock 'n' Roll Memorabilia*, 14–15 September 1999, pp. 52–3.

4 Peter Stringfellow interview, The *Sun*, 23 February 1989.

5 The *Daily Express*, 9 August 1985.

6 Neil Tennant, funeral tribute; Mary Riddell, The *Daily Mirror*, March 1989; Alan Jackson, quoted in Lucy O'Brien, *Dusty*, 3rd edn (2000), pp. 190–1.

7 The *Telegraph* magazine, 27 May 1995.

8 Dusty Springfield interview included in *Remembering Dusty Springfield*, pt 4, BBC radio, 23 March 2000.

9 *Hello!*, 30 June 1990.

10 The *Observer*, 12 February 1989.

11 *News of the World*, 10 April 1988; the *Telegraph* magazine, 27 May 1995.

12 Anthony Husher interview, The *Maidenhead Advertiser*, 12 March 1999.

13 Ibid.

14 Neil Tennant interview, *Definitely Dusty*, BBC television, 26 December 1999; O'Brien, *Dusty*, p. 217.

15 Neil Tennant, funeral tribute, and interview for *Definitely Dusty*.

16 Neil Tennant: interview for *Dusty: Full Circle*, BBC television, 1 May 1995; funeral tribute; and interview for *Definitely Dusty*.

17 The *Daily Mail*, 12 June 1990.

18 *Radio Times*, 30 April 1994.

19 *Q*, April 1989.

20 Interview, *The Dame Edna Experience*, London Weekend Television, 1989.

21 Interview, BBC radio, quoted in O'Brien, *Dusty*, p. 213.

22 Sean O'Hagan, 'My date with Dusty', The *Observer*, 7 March 1999.

Chapter 12. Time and the River

1 The *Daily Mail*, 26 November 1991.

2 *Radio Times*, 30 April 1994.

3 Quoted in Lucy O'Brien, *Dusty*, 3rd edn (2000), p. 232.

4 *Radio Times*, 30 April 1994.

5 The *Mail on Sunday*, *You* magazine, 28 May 1995.

6 ibid.

7 Interview, 'This Morning', 1995.

8 *The Times*, 7 June 1995.

9 Sean O'Hagan, 'My date with Dusty', The *Observer*, 7 March 1999.

10 This account of Dusty's last days is based on interviews given by Lee Everett Alkin (The *Mail on Sunday*, 25 April 1999), Simon Bell (The *Express*, 14 June 1999) and Vicki Wickham (The *Guardian*, 30 November 1999).

11 Clive Westlake, interview included in *Remembering Dusty Springfield*, pt 4, BBC radio, 23 March 2000.

'I'm not saying I'm Goody Two Shoes…':
Interview, *Q*, April 1989.

Index

INDEX

O'Brien, Gerard Anthony (OB), *father*,
    1–3, 4–5, 6, 12, 46, 51, 114, 141
O'Brien, Mary, *see* Springfield, Dusty
O'Day, Alan, 121
O'Hagan, Sean, 157, 162
O'Jays, The, 117
On a Clear Day You Can See Forever, 86
Orlando, Tony, 111
Osborne, Tony, 24

Palladium, 20, 28, 61 n
Paramor, Norrie, 45
Parlophone, 148, 154
Paul, Billy, 117
Paul and Paula, 69
Peking Medallion, The (film), 83
Perry, Fred, 50, 88
Pet Shop Boys, The, 34, 43–4, 48, 96,
    104, 140 n, 147–57, 162; 'West End
    Girls', 147; 'What Have I Done To
    Deserve This?', 147–50
Philadelphia, 116–18
Philips, 150
Phillimore, Mr Justice, 73
Piaf, Edith, 41
Pick of the Pops, 37
pigs: as art-lovers, 75
Pitney, Gene, 42, 51, 102
Poole, Brian, 30, 31, 52
Pope, Carol, 143
Porter, Cole, 24 n, 25
Post Office Tower, 52
Potter, Brian, 121–2
Presley, Elvis, 50, 101
Profumo affair (1963), 152
Prowse, Juliet, 45 n
Prudential Insurance, 163
Pulp Fiction (film), 100 n

Radcliffe, Jimmy, 57, 70
radio, 3, 4, 17, 37, 41, 51, 68, 110
Radio Times, 37, 159
Rashkow, Mike, 120
Ravel, Maurice, 99, 103

Rawlings, Victor, 75
Raymonde, Ivor, 35, 44, 155; 'I Only
    Want To Be With You', 29; 'I Wish
    I'd Never Loved You', 58; 'Stay
    Awhile', 41–2; 'Your Hurtin' Kinda
    Love', 66
Ready Steady Go!, 33, 36, 37, 38,
    39–40, 66, 67–8, 74
Reddy, Helen, 119
Reece, Doug, 58
Reeves, Martha, 54, 56 n, 66, 67, 74 n,
    111
Rhodes, Pat, 56
Rich, Buddy, 79–83
Richard, Cliff, 158
Rio de Janeiro, 66
*Roar of the Greasepaint, the Smell of the
    Crowd, The*, 71
Robinson, Smokey, 67
Rodgers, Richard, 25, 42
Rolling Stone, 135
Rolling Stones, The, 37, 50, 61 n
Ronalde, Ronnie, 14
Ronettes, The, 55, 56
Rook, Jean, 114, 149
Ross, Diana, 55, 67, 141 n
Rottingdean, 141
Rough Trade, 143
Royal Albert Hall, 140–1
Royal Marsden Hospital, 160, 164
Rutherford, Margaret, 10 n
Ryan, Paul and Barry, 58

Sager, Carol Bayer, 141
St Anne's Convent, 2, 3, 50
St Benedict's, 2
Sammes, Mike, 45
Sampey, Denise, 37
Samwell, Ian, 42
San Remo Song Festival (1965), 32 n,
    65, 75
Sandpebbles, The, 90
Sarstedt, Peter, 103
Sassoon, Vidal, 33

202

INDEX

203

INDEX

INDEX

INDEX